Roger Debreceny, Carsten Felden, Maci

New Dimensions of Business Reporting and XBRL

WIRTSCHAFTSINFORMATIK

Roger Debreceny, Carsten Felden,
Maciej Piechocki

New Dimensions
of Business Reporting
and XBRL

With a preface by Roger Debreceny, Carsten Felden
and Maciej Piechocki

Deutscher Universitäts-Verlag

Bibliografische Information Der Deutschen Nationalbibliothek
Die Deutsche Nationalbibliothek verzeichnet diese Publikation in der
Deutschen Nationalbibliografie; detaillierte bibliografische Daten sind im Internet über
<http://dnb.d-nb.de> abrufbar.

1. Auflage Juli 2007

Alle Rechte vorbehalten
© Deutscher Universitäts-Verlag | GWV Fachverlage GmbH, Wiesbaden 2007

Lektorat: Frauke Schindler / Anita Wilke

Der Deutsche Universitäts-Verlag ist ein Unternehmen von Springer Science+Business Media.
www.duv.de

Umschlaggestaltung: Regine Zimmer, Dipl.-Designerin, Frankfurt/Main
Gedruckt auf säurefreiem und chlorfrei gebleichtem Papier
Printed in Germany

ISBN 978-3-8350-0835-9

Preface

The concept of highly integrated and IT-supported information supply chains, summarized by the term *Integrated Business Reporting*, has increasingly moved into the foreground of research interest. Current discussions on the improvement of intra-enterprise and extra-enterprise reporting processes cannot be realized without a clear and uniform description of the involved elements. Facing a constantly changing operational and analytical application landscape, individual research projects are not sufficient to build a complete understanding of the research issues within the XBRL community. Based on the idea of supporting the information flows within enterprises and across complex information supply chains the eXtensible Businesses Reporting Language (XBRL) is established as a standard that supports intra- and inter-enterprise reporting as well as to a variety of information consumers. A key objective of the XBRL standard is to increase the efficiency of the usage of information systems at the interface of business management and information technology. Today, the information integration market is fragmented to a considerable degree. Many proprietary solutions are used, from which no solution fulfills the complete requirements of a Web-oriented world. In these circumstances, XBRL works as a multifaceted solution. XBRL can be used to interconnect information systems in order to realize a wide variety of data exchanges.

The aim of this anthology is to analyze the social and technical nature and role of XBRL in information supply chains and capital markets along with analysis of the XBRL standard and taxonomies. The book provides a more critical view of XBRL from a research perspective. Included papers present different projects in the XBRL area as well as indicating future directions for XBRL research. The anthology

- presents the latest research findings from international XBRL researchers;

- familiarizes the reader with the implications of XBRL research;

- presents latest research projects within the XBRL community;

- offers perspectives for researchers, standard setters, computer scientists and market and business participants;

- indicates future directions for the XBRL standard.

Based on this background the current research questions are taken up and discussed from different perspectives in this anthology. Looking from a technical perspective, the research spectrum encompasses the internal perspective on up to the final user layer. Apart from these technical issues there are also key socio-technical aspects, which are vital to our understanding of XBRL adoption and use. In order to present this multilayered view of XBRL, the anthology has been divided into three main sections.

The first section covers broad questions of the role that XBRL plays in the broad information environment, with a focus on economic, adoption and usage concerns.

The second section addresses domain issues, not only in the traditional area of financial reporting but also in broader compliance and business reporting.

Finally, the papers in the third section discuss some of the technical questions associated with XBRL and with the interaction of XBRL and other IT domains.

We trust that the papers in this anthology will appeal to readers in IT functions within organizations, software houses, participants in a variety of information supply chains and, of course, researchers within several disciplines. These papers represent the state of the art in XBRL research. The papers in the anthology demonstrate that XBRL research is vital and active. Yet, there is clearly a need for more research in all aspects of the XBRL endeavour.

We thank the individual authors, who were able to write their papers despite busy calendars. We thank André Graening and Harald Kienegger for their assistance with editorial revisions. We are particularly pleased with the co-operation with the DUV publisher and particularly thank Ute Wrasmann and Anita Wilke.

Finally, we wish productive reading for the readers of this anthology. Please use our e-mail addresses for any communication on the issues raised in the book: roger@debreceny.com, carsten.felden@bwl.tu-freiberg.de and maciej.piechocki@bwl.tu-freiberg.de.

Roger Debreceny, Carsten Felden, Maciej Piechocki

Table of Contents

Introduction

Research into XBRL – Old and New Challenges

Roger Debreceny

University of Hawai`i at Mānoa, USA
roger@debreceny.com

Contents

1   Introduction

The XBRL 1.0 specification, or more accurately XFRML 1.0 specification, was released in 2000. This was only some two years only after the proposals by Charlie Hoffman to the AICPA and the first serious academic discussion of applying XML technologies to business and financial reporting (Debreceny et al. 1998; Hoffman 1999; Lymer et al. 1999). In the intervening period, we have seen a rapidly increasing level of interest in the policy implications of XBRL. A search of XBRL on Google.com returns an extraordinary 1.4m links. Similarly, a search on bibliographic databases such as ABI/Inform discloses more than five hundred papers from the academic and professional literature. In what is a relatively short period of technology adoption, the XBRL world has also seen significant maturing of specifications, architectures, taxonomies and software tools. In an important third dimension of adoption, the XBRL organization itself has matured significantly over this period. XBRL International and its national jurisdictions are comprised of more than four hundred corporations, agencies and not-for-profit organizations. These foundational elements have clearly been vital for the observed adoption of XBRL in important information supply chains. Whilst not at the rate that early proponents might have suggested (e.g. Coffin 2001a, 2001b; Hannon 2000), the use of XBRL within areas such as credit monitoring of financial institutions and in reporting corporate performance to a variety of securities markets does signal that XBRL has become a core enabling technology in business reporting.

There are, however, many challenges facing both XBRL and the XBRL research community. Whilst on the surface, the search evidence provided in the previous paragraph indicates a level of interest and maturity on a par with XML standards such as RDF, XML Query or sectoral XML standards including ebXML and UDDI. When digging a little deeper, however, it becomes clear that the state of XBRL knowledge development is not quite as promising as the citation statistics might suggest. Much, perhaps most, of the literature is professional in nature and in a largely expository mode. There are less than twenty peer-refereed research studies that systematically address XBRL from socio-technological, technical or business or financial reporting perspectives. This is hardly indicative of vital support in the research community for the future development or adoption of XBRL. The papers in this volume provide an indication of the future directions for XBRL research in several important dimensions of XBRL as a technology and XBRL as a socio-technical artifact. I now survey the current state of XBRL research using these studies as a representative sample of the future direction for XBRL. Unfortunately, there is no current survey of research trends or needs. The closest that exists to such a survey is Debreceny et al. (2005). As I proceed to survey the research questions that face the XBRL community, I will draw on the relevant elements of that paper.

The remainder of this paper proceeds as follows: In the next section, I discuss the application of XBRL as a generic solution for information exchange. I first address questions of where XBRL fits within broader societal settings which allows us to better understand directions for XBRL adoption. I then address the application of XBRL in a series of disparate knowledge domains. Some of those domains are aligned with the traditional focus of XBRL in financial reporting. Others, however, move well beyond this domain. The penultimate section addresses research questions of technology. A key direction that comes from the papers in this volume is the way in which XBRL is being seen as a technical foundation for broader information exchange than was envisaged by those that sketched out XBRL as a solution strictly for business reporting, and particularly for financial reporting. In the final section, I address some overall challenges for research in XBRL.

2   XBRL in a Socio-Technical Setting

It is easy to see XBRL as a technology or an elegant (or perhaps not so elegant) solution to, without recognizing that as Locke and Lowe point out, XBRL is part of a broader set of organizational and sociological relationships within both national and international settings. The original design of XBRL established the standard as a generic solution to business reporting needs. Particular knowledge domains are represented in taxonomies, rather than in the specification. This deliberate design flexibility coupled with the multi-lingual foundations of XML allows XBRL to be used in a wide variety of reporting environments around the world. Locke and Lowe employ Actor Network Theory (Bruni and Teli 2007; Doolin and Lowe 2002; Latour 2005; Law and Hassard 1999) to analyze the relationships of XBRL players within a complex influencing and adoption environment.

Locke and Lowe identify the key constituencies within the XBRL community and then their interaction with the XML community and the various constituencies of reporting domains. There is little direct interaction between these latter two constituencies. In some fashion, not yet well researched and understood, the XBRL plays an intermediary role between the XML community and the domain-specific information supply chain actors. The former group has strong technical foundations coupled with a broad understanding of the need for high-semantic web content (Berners-Lee et al. 2001; Berners-Lee 1998). The XML community is unlikely to have a detailed and clear understanding of the needs of particular supply chains. Conversely, the participants within various information supply chains are unlikely to be able to evaluate alternative technical solutions to improve the effectiveness and efficiency of their supply chain. Just how far beyond the historical foundations of financial reporting the XBRL community can push adoption remains to be seen.

The nature of adoption path is also considered by Locke and Lowe. They consider *User*, *Task*, *Technology*, and *External environment* in their model. A particular are of research interest that is also under-researched is the application of XBRL within internal organizational information and reporting environments. The interaction between uses the Global Ledger taxonomy (www.xbrl.org/GLTaxonomy/ Garbellotto 2007; Haseqawa et al. 2004), financial reporting taxonomies and internal reporting environments is ripe for a wide variety of research investigations (see also Debreceny et al. 2005, 200).

Pinsker addresses a somewhat narrower but more manageable question, which is the issue of XBRL and firm continuous disclosure (Benston et al. 2003; Debreceny and Rahman 2005; Lymer et al. 1999; Skinner 2003). Pinsker interestingly proposes application of Computer Mediated Communication Apprehension (CMCA) (Scott and Timmerman 2005) to our understanding of how enterprises might apply XBRL to continuous disclosure. Perhaps less interestingly, Pinsker suggests using the well-established Technology Acceptance Model (TAM) as an appropriate research paradigm for understanding perception of XBRL in adoption decisions. I am not convinced of the effectiveness of TAM or its variants to analyze XBRL adoption but Pinsker is making an important point. Perception is reality when it comes to technology adoption and we need to understand this when we come to research XBRL adoption. Equally, Pinsker's concern with absorptive capacity of entities is also an important notion (Cohen and Levinthal 1990; Lane et al. 2006; Phelps et al. 2007). There has been much discussion of the cost-benefit analysis of XBRL adoption (Debreceny et al. 2005, 197-198). Determining the absorptive capacity of potential adopters will be an interesting research question. Pinsker sets out a number of testable hypotheses and we need research to address these hypotheses.

Clearly economic factors are an important consideration in any understanding of XBRL as a socio-technical artifact. Wagenhofer provides an overview of the economic interplay between organizations and users of performance data and the role that information technologies including HTML and XBRL play in the intermediation between these parties. Importantly, Wagenhofer points to the key role played by regulators and by the auditing process in improving information quality. Wagenhofer reminds us that it is all very well to discuss the technical aspects of the socio-technical paradigm, but we ignore the role of those that add value to the information and transmission at our peril.

Locke and Lowe point to the difficulty of conducting research in the interaction of actors within the XBRL ecosphere and the various uses of XBRL. Given the importance of XBRL and the extent of interest in the technology, it is easy for researchers to provide a solid justification for their research endeavors. There are many ways to overcome the barriers to research on XBRL. Even though we are nearly a decade into XBRL development and adoption, it is still a relatively early stage in the history of XBRL. Having survived the initial stages of the adoption lifecycle, XBRL moves into a more mature and in many ways more interesting phase of development. Many different research techniques will be required to address questions of XBRL's socio-technical settings. Case studies (Chang and Jarvenpaa 2005), Delphi studies (Baldwin et al. 2005), surveys and experimental studies are all appropriate research methodologies for this stage of XBRL development.

3   XBRL Knowledge Domains

Applying XBRL to a variety of knowledge domains is, as might be expected, the focus of a number of studies in this book. Moving XBRL taxonomy development and XBRL adoption beyond the realm of business reporting to other areas of reporting assessing XBRL against other metadata standards such as RDF and OWL (see www.w3.org/2001/sw/; Kitcharoensakkul and Wuwongse 2001; Lee and Goodwin 2006). The business case for XBRL is not as clear the further one moves from business reporting in general and financial reporting in particular. Piechocki et al. have undertaken a systematic analysis of the application of the *European Union 2002/91/EG guideline on the Energy Performance of Buildings*. Interestingly, Piechocki and his colleagues have systematically applied basic principles for information exchange applied within the European Union. In addition, they employ DIN ISO 9126, which is an international standard that defines software quality criteria. Piechocki et al. find that XBRL meets both the EU and 9126 standards. Piechocki et al. do not, however, apply other metadata standards such as RDF, using the same criteria. This is a new and important area of XBRL research. Other case studies will be necessary and comparisons with other metadata standards might be applied in such case studies. An outcome of such research may be a methodical approach to determining which metadata standard has comparative advantages in differing information supply chains.

If we draw back within the more comfortable boundaries of the financial reporting domain, there are many open research questions. Locke and Lowe raise interesting questions on the relationship between XBRL and accounting standard setters (see also Debreceny et al. 2005, 200). My working hypothesis is that there is only the slightest of links between accounting standard setting and standard setters. For example, the Chair of the IASB addressed the 14th XBRL international conference in Philadelphia. In his address, Sir David Tweedie spent most of his time on developments with IFRS and convergence between US GAAP and IFRS. He made much of the potential of XBRL to aid use of IFRS: "We at the IASB and the IASC Foundation (our oversight organisation) view XBRL as an important tool that will enable these users to take full advantage of the increased comparability and transparency offered by IFRSs" (Twee-die 2006). Not a word, however, on how XBRL might influence the setting of account-ing standards. Yet, clearly, there is much that XBRL can do to allow financial report-ing to move beyond the iron grip of paper-based publication paradigms (Ijiri and Kelly 1980; Johnson 1970; Sorter 1969). Research on this question is effectively a null set and there is much yet to be done - we do not even have a catalog of how XBRL could be applied to allow interactive reporting of assumptions underlying financial state-ments. Teixeira also addresses this issue, albeit somewhat more tangentially, and is clearly not hopeful of ready solutions that would allow multi-GAAP reporting. Wa-genhofer also speculates on how accounting standards setting would change if events were atomically tagged with XBRL metadata.

If we retreat further into the XBRL *comfort zone* of financial reporting, we come to the important question of inter-taxonomy comparability. Arguably the most important comparison are the similarities and differences in measurement and disclosure prin-ciples under US Generally Accepted Accounting Principles (GAAP) and International Financial Reporting Standards (IFRS) (Nobes 2006; Tarca 2004). After reviewing state of convergence projects between these two bodies of knowledge, noting the forthcoming developments with the US GAAP taxonomy, Sir David observed in his 2006 speech: "It is my belief that we would be missing an opportunity if we failed to account for convergence considerations when the US GAAP XBRL taxonomy is being developed. To the extent that US GAAP and IFRSs are converging, so should the XBRL taxonomies. We would not want different tags for a particular item, if they are the same under both accounting standards, to provide different results" (Tweedie

2006). These issues are addressed from a policy and research level by Teixeira and at an operational level by Swanson et al. (see also Debreceny et al. 2005, 193, 199). Teixeira reminds us that not only are there important measurement differences between US GAAP and IFRS but disparities in disclosure. Some of these disparities are tractable, but most are not. The need for research on inter-GAAP taxonomy interoperability is urgent – and long overdue.

Staying within the financial reporting domain, a first attempt at understanding the differences between the US GAAP and IFRS taxonomies, using a major international corporation has been undertaken by Swanson et al.. Swanson and his colleagues analyze both measurement and disclosure issues between US GAAP and IFRS. They then assess the ability of the US GAAP and IFRS taxonomies to represent the reporting for the same corporation – BHP Billiton. Unfortunately, Swanson et al. find many issues, particularly with the income statement. Some of these issues are probably intractable because of fundamental disclosure differences. Some, however, arise because of differences in taxonomy design which is tractable within the broader XBRL community.

4   XBRL and Related Technologies

Whilst research and writing on XBRL has long discussed adoption and the socio-technical nature of the standard, interrelationships with other relevant technology streams is relatively new. The contributions of Chamoni, Gluchowski and Pastwa and Felden each, in their very different ways, demonstrate how XBRL can potentially be applied in areas far beyond the original design objectives for the standard.

Much of the interest with XBRL within organizations has focused on employing XBRL GL in a primarily transaction-oriented focus. Klement shows exactly how such an integrated system that, additionally, can be linked to external reporting using XBRL financial reporting taxonomies. He shows that well designed XBRL systems can allow drill down from final reports to atomic transactions. Chamoni takes us down a quite different path. Chamoni analyzes the interrelationship between XBRL and business intelligence (BI). XBRL was not designed explicitly as a BI technology. It was designed as a metadata representation language. Yet as Chamoni notes, XBRL may provide a foundation for BI at a much higher level of abstraction than might have first been envisaged. Chamoni describes an interesting maturity model for BI. In this model, Chamoni portrays XBRL playing a native role in areas such as text mining and web reporting. While an important first step, the study by Chamoni provides only a tantalizing preview of future XBRL-based BI implementations. There is a clear need for case studies and research pilots that would test the propositions made by Chamoni.

Exploring a similar theme, Felden explores the use of XBRL in a multi-dimensional knowledge environment. Surprisingly, given the foundations of XBRL in accounting and financial reporting, which at least implicitly deals with multidimensional information (Ijiri 1982, 1987; Ijiri and Kelly 1980; Mattesich 1964), the XBRL specification dealt with multidimensional information in a somewhat naïve fashion. The recent *add on* XBRL Dimensional Taxonomies (XDT) goes some way to overcome the weaknesses of the XBRL specification. Following an analysis of reporting in the energy sector, Felden finds that XBRL and XDT has the potential to perform highly sophisticated multidimensional tasks such as directly facilitating OLAP solutions. Again, however, the future described by Felden gives rise to a desire for more realized case studies and practical work benches.

As an XML standard, XBRL is explicitly designed to meet only specific needs. There is, for example, no concern with security in XBRL given a host of XML security solutions. Similarly, there is effectively no direct support for transport layer in XBRL. Gluchowski and Pastwa provide a process model for the transport of XBRL metadata, within the complex information environment that characterizes the supervision of financial institutions within the realm of Basel II. Gluchowski and Pastwa describe a potential - but not realized - *Referential Architecture* for linking transactional systems in the clients of financial institutions via financial institutions and up to regulatory agencies. To be repetitive, it will be interesting to see these architectures tested first in the research laboratory and then in practical case studies. If we take the adoption of XBRL in financial reporting as an exemplar, we can see that the workbenches created by, for example, Charlie Hoffman in the late 1990s or by PricewaterhouseCoopers for Nasdaq, were highly influential.

Finally, we come to the question of where XBRL fits within the broader XML standards environment. Schmitt takes us on a very important path. Is XML a necessary foundation for XBRL, but only a foundation? Or, alternatively, can the XML technical community draw upon other XML standards to undertake tasks for which there is no readily available XBRL solution. Schmitt undertakes a qualitative assessment of various XML standards including XSLT, XPath and XQuery. Fortunately for the XBRL community, the author finds that a significant number of XML standards have the potential for direct interaction with XBRL. Much yet remains to be done to test directly these conclusions. For example, Schmitt finds that SQL/XML has the potential to operate on XBRL data for purposes of mapping, transformation and reporting (www.sqlx.org; Funderburk et al. 2002). Schmitt notes that the next stage in his research program is to create full-text retrieval techniques that bind together XBRL and other XML standards. This work is important and urgent.

The work by Chamoni; Gluchowski and Pastwa; Klement and Schmitt and Felden would seem to provide many post-graduate students in computer science and information systems with a host of research opportunities.

5   Conclusion

The papers in this volume provide tangible evidence of the current and future state of XBRL research. The fact that this study is being published in that oldest of knowledge mediums, the paper-based book produced with moveable type, shows that tested technologies are not easily replaced by new technologies. XBRL does, however, seem to have met a survivorship test. In discussions and presentations on XBRL I have often made the prediction that XBRL data will be transmitted across networks long after I have shuffled off this mortal coile, to quote Shakespeare in Hamlet. Of course, I will not be able to directly test this hypothesis and will leave that to other parties. Yet, despite the clear and important long-term adoption of XBRL, there is much yet to do in the XBRL research field. I trust that the intellectual, societal and technical foundations of XBRL will have largely been resolved before that aforementioned untimely event. The shape of that research agenda is relatively well understood and a number of different research strands are well explicated in this volume. Meeting that research agenda is quite a different challenge, however. In this paper, I have repeatedly called for more case studies, more theoretical contributions, more test beds and more real world implementations. Many of those research tasks will require interdisciplinary approaches. Journal editors will equally need to be innovative in the way that they approach research into XBRL, which is at this stage still highly speculative and tentative. The XBRL research community has, however, the potential to add to the overall objectives of the XBRL endeavor – an endeavor that has the potential to add significantly to societal integration.

References

Baldwin, A. A.; Brown, C. E.; Trinkle, B. S. (2005): XBRL: An Impacts Framework and Research Challenge, Journal of Emerging Technologies in Aaccounting 3, pp. 97-116.

Benston, G., Bromwich, M., Litan, R. E., Wagenhofer, A. (2003): Following the Money: Corporate Disclosure in an Age of Globalization, Washington, DC: AEI-Brookings Joint Center for Regulatory Studies.

Berners-Lee, T.; Hendler, T.; Lassila, O. (2001): The Semantic Web. Scientific American 284 (5), pp. 34-43.

Berners-Lee, T. (1998): Semantic Web Road map, World Wide Web Consortium, http://www.w3.org/DesignIssues/ Semantic.html, last downloaded 2002-07-15.

Bruni, A.; Teli M. (2007): Reassembling the social - An introduction to actor network theory, Management Learning 38 (1), pp. 121-125.

Chang, C.; Jarvenpaa, S. (2005): Pace of Information Systems Standards Development and Implementation: The Case of XBRL, Electronic Markets 15 (4), pp. 365-376.

Coffin, Z. (2001a): The Advent of Real-Time Accounting, Practical Accountant 34 (8), pp. 48-48.

Coffin, Z. (2001b): The Top 10 Effects of XBRL, Strategic Finance 82 (12), p. 64.

Cohen, W. M.; Levinthal, D. A. (1990): Absorptive capacity: a new perspective on learning and innovation, Administrative Science Quarterly, pp. 128-152.

Debreceny, R.; Gray G.; Barry, T. (1998): Accounting Information in a Networked World - Resource Discovery, Processing and Analysis, paper read at American Accounting Association Annual Meeting, at New Orleans.

Debreceny, R.; Rahman A. (2005): Firm-specific determinants of continuous corporate disclosures, The International Journal of Accounting 40 (3), pp. 249-278.

Debreceny, R. S.; Chandra, A.; Cheh, J. J.; Guithues-Amrhein, D.; Hannon, N. J.; Hutchison, P. D.; Janvrin, D.; Jones, R. A.; Lamberton, B.; Lymer, A.; Mascha, M.; Nehmer, R.; Roohani, S.; Srivastava, R. P.; Trabelsi, S.; Tribunella, T.; Trites, G.; Vasarhelyi, M. A. (2005): Financial Reporting in XBRL on the SEC's EDGAR System: A Critique and Evaluation, Journal of Information Systems 19 (2), pp.191-210.

Doolin, B., Lowe, A. (2002): To reveal is to critique: actor-network theory and critical information systems research, Journal of Information Technology 17 (2), pp. 69-78.

Funderburk, J. E., Malaika, S., Reinwald, B. (2002): XML programming with SQL/XML and XQuery, IBM Systems Journal 41 (4), p. 642.

Garbellotto, G. (2007): The Global Ledger for Financial Services, Strategic Finance 88 (10), pp. 59-61.

Hannon, N. (2000): The Brave New World of XBRL, Strategic Finance 82 (6), p. 73.

Haseqawa, M.; Sakata, T.; Sambuichi, N.; Hannon, N. J. (2004): Breathing New Life Into Old Systems, Strategic Finance 85 (9), pp. 46-51.

Hoffman, C. (1999): The XML Files, Journal of Accountancy 187 (5), pp. 71-77.

Ijiri, Y. (1982): Triple-Entry Bookkeeping and Income Momentum, Sarasota, Fla: American Accounting Association.

Ijiri, Y. (1987): Three postulates of momentum accounting. Accounting Horizons 1 (1), pp. 25-34.

Ijiri, Y.; Kelly, E. (1980): Multidimensional accounting and distributed databases: their implications for organizations and society, Accounting, Organizations and Society 5 (1), pp. 115-123.

Johnson, O. (1970): Toward an "Events" Theory of Accounting, Accounting Review 45 (4), pp. 641-653.

Kitcharoensakkul, S.; Wuwongse, V. (2001): Towards a Unified Version Model Using The Resource Description Framework (RDF), International Journal of Software Engineering & Knowledge Engineering 11 (6); p. 675.

Lane, P. J.; Koka, B. R.; Pathak, S. (2006): The Reification of Absorptive Capacity: A Critical Review and Rejuvenation of the Construct, Academy of Management Review 31 (4), pp. 833-863.

Latour, B. (2005): Reassembling the Social: An Introduction to Actor-Network-Theory, Oxford: Oxford University Press.

Law, J.; Hassard, J. (1999): Actor network theory and after, Oxford, Malden, MA, Blackwell.

Lee, J.; Goodwin, R. (2006): Ontology management for large-scale enterprise systems, Electronic Commerce Research & Applications 5 (1), pp. 2-15.

Lymer, A.; Debreceny, R.; Gray, G.; Rahman, A. (1999): Business Reporting on the Internet, London, International Accounting Standards Committee.

Mattesich, R. (1964): Accounting and Analytical Methods, Homewood, Ill, Richard D Irwin.

Nobes, C. (2006): The survival of international differences under IFRS: towards a research agenda, Accounting & Business Research 36 (3), pp. 233-245.

Phelps, R.; Adams, R.; Bessant, J. (2007): Life cycles of growing organizations: A review with implications for knowledge and learning, International Journal of Management Reviews 9 (1), pp. 1-30.

Scott, C. R.; Timmerman, C. E. (2005): Relating Computer, Communication, and Computer-Mediated Communication Apprehensions to New Communication Technology Use in the Workplace, Communication Research 32 (6), pp. 683-725.

Skinner, D. J. (2003): Should firms disclose everything to everybody? A discussion of "Open vs. closed conference calls: the determinants and effects of broadening access to disclosure", Journal of Accounting and Economics 34 (2), pp. 181–187.

Sorter, G. (1969): An "Events" Approach to Basic Accounting Theory, Accounting Review 44 (1), pp. 12-19.

Tarca, A. (2004): International Convergence of Accounting Practices: Choosing between IAS and US GAAP, Journal of International Financial Management & Accounting 15 (1), pp. 60-91.

Tweedie, D. (2006): Keynote Speech, Paper read at 14th XBRL International Conference, at Philadelphia.

General Implications

Researching XBRL as a Socio-technical Object

Joanne Locke, Alan Lowe

Waikato University,
New Zealand Aston University,
Birmingham Waikato University New Zealand,
New Zealand

jlocke@mngt.waikato.ac.nz
alowe1@waikato.ac.nz

Contents

1 Introduction

The Extensible Business Reporting Language (XBRL) is a grammar based on XML that is defined and described in the XBRL 2.1 specification. Instance documents are created by combining XBRL taxonomies and linkbases with data (*facts*) for a particular context. An alternative view is, XBRL is a mechanism for communicating information for decision-making between interested parties based on a generally accepted way of representing and digitally transmitting symbols of actions and events. XBRL may be both of these and many other things depending on how we frame our methodological understanding for the purposes of research. In this section we present an approach that conceives XBRL as a socio-technical object in the tradition of post-social perspectives (Knorr Cetina 1997; Latour 1996, 1999).

XBRL may be seen as a technological artefact looking to act as a solution to a problem. It is afforded equal status as an actor in a network of relations that come together in the construction of a complex socio-technical object. From this perspective XBRL is much more than a metadata standard designed to enable advances in business reporting. XBRL becomes the outcome and at the same time the facilitator of complex linkages creating a network of connections among institutions, individuals and other technologies associated with compiling and delivering business reports and submissions to government agencies and regulators. It is the effects of these socio-technical arrangements that our research seeks to explain. XBRL and its impact within accounting and business reporting and more broadly its impact on business and social arrangements are rich topics for research from the postsocial perspective. In this section we explore the potential for research by examining some applications of this research programme to XBRL.

Much of the literature to date on XBRL has followed the course of business fads (Abrahamson 1996; Scarbrough, Swan 2001). It has been building a significant volume of articles, but much of the material published has followed a predictable pattern of professional publications that focus on the promotional while tending to pay much less attention to the problems associated with the technology[1]. There are very few academic research articles published on XBRL so far[2]. This reflects the lack of knowledge about XBRL amongst accounting and Information Technology (IT) academics and the difficulty of examining aspects of a technology that is unsettled.

---

[1] A representative sample form over the period of XBRL's development include: Boyd, Teixeira (2004a); Coleman (2002); Cover (2000); Hucklesby, Macdonald (2000, 2004); Strand et al. (2001); Teixeira (2005); Zarowin, Harding (2000).
[2] See for example: Debreceny and Gray (2001); Bovee et al. (2002); Hodge et al. (2004).

XBRL may be seen to occupy a somewhat tenuous position at present. From a re-search perspective the relative lack of implementations precludes the application of a number of research approaches such as surveying users or undertaking case studies. This situation is expected by XBRL proponents to change over the next few years. We believe that a postsocial and socio-technical perspective will open up a programme of research that will be of benefit to understanding XBRL as a technical object embedded in relationships with other objects and social settings (Bloomfield, Vurdubakis 1997; Law 1996, 2002; Lowe 2004; Knorr Cetina 1997; Knorr Cetina, Bruegger 2002; see also Giddens 1990, 1994).

The interaction or potential interaction of the technology with users and the features and characteristics of the social settings which surround the development of the tech-nology become critical to understanding why it develops as it does. Taken together these approaches seek to enable research that tries to examine shortfalls in the manner in which the technology is developed or deployed and how we might better predict its trajectory as a successful innovation (Appadurai 1986; Kopytoff 1986; Mueller and Carter 2005).

This approach offers the potential for valuable research into where and why XBRL is as it appears to be and insights into how and why it may mature into an accepted inter-national business reporting digital communication standard or potentially "miss the mark". It directs our attention to the complex relationships and forms that objects in society may take and allows scope for our studies to focus in on specific times and places or to encompass XBRL's global nature.

The scope for research is extensive. Our aim in this section is to focus attention on the socio-technical aspects of XBRL in a way that we hope highlights XBRL's develop-ment and diffusion into the business community. We see this as being affected by as-pects of how the technology is presented to its potential users who are many and va-ried. This is not just a matter of superficial notions of how best the technology might be sold to interested parties – it is a more fundamental examination of such things as: the breadth of expertise involved in development; aspects of governance; tracing the biography of the technology and concerns about the ability of the technology to enrol allies and supporters.

The section seeks to provide a broad introduction to the postsocial and socio-technical approaches to researching XBRL. In the next section the theoretical perspective is out-lined and a summary of influences from the literature provided. Section 3 relates this material more specifically to XBRL and uses a diagram as a construct for a general illustration of how we see the postsocial perspective may be applied. The following section describes three specific XBRL research projects as exemplars. Some concluding comments that include a description of the challenges faced in undertaking research of this type complete the chapter.

2   Socio-technical Objects and their Impact on Social Relations

This section of the paper presents a brief outline of the broad theoretic framework that we employ. *Postsocial* refers to hypothesised changes in the composition of society and social arrangements (Knorr Cetina 1999; Latour 1996, 1999). Authors argue from this perspective that social relations can no longer be seen as structured solely as a consequence of human interactions but that it is increasingly the case that our lives and culture are influenced by our reliance on technology and our relationships with technological objects (Latour 1987; Law 1999, 2002). Socio-technical perspectives, in part, draw from the ideas contributed by postsocial theorists on the increasingly important place of technology in structuring society (Knorr Cetina 1997, 1999; Lash 2001; see also Giddens 1990, 1994). Socio-technical object are understood to include both the *hardware* of technology, such as mobile phones and laptop computers, and *virtual* objects such as computer software, accounting packages and ERP systems, email and other types of ICT technologies. These objects are socio-technical in at least two respects: they only work in settings that are constituted by humans; and they are of course also the product of human creativity. XBRL is such a technology, a socio-technical object which is intended to enable improved business communication. At the same time it will produce many side-effects by affecting how individuals and institutions who come in contact with the technology work. Some of these side-effects will be unanticipated but may nevertheless be of significance (Ciborra et al. 2001).

We conceive XBRL to be a socio-technical object which will both impact and be impacted by social arrangements as it develops. Our view from a socio-technical perspective is that the development of XBRL the technology and of organizational networks of which it is a part will evolve in an unpredictable and organic way. It follows that the development of such technologies is a complex process which engages aspects of the technical, social and political in a heterogeneous collection of objects and actors (Knorr Cetina 1999, 2001; Latour 1993, 1999; Law 1986, 1999, 2002).

Table 1 provides a summary of the main conceptual underpinnings of our research perspective. We draw from a range of literature that has in common its emphasis on the role of the object in constituting society as we experience it, an acceptance of the heterogeneous nature of social arrangements and a constructionist understanding of society, facts and technology. The consequence of this combination of perspectives is that it makes little sense to study the technology in isolation from its social context. In order to understand how XBRL has and will develop and the effects it may have on business reporting and accounting practices we need to examine the broader social and objectual relations within which it is set. This means that our research should consider aspects of the nature of the technology and in relation to any competing technologies that might be available or perhaps become available. But that in addition to this we need also to examine the broader social and organizational arrangements that are involved in fabricating XBRL.

Table 1: Theoretical Framework for Research Using a Postsocial Perspective, (adapt. Lowe 2004)

Level of theorization	Theoretic Research Framework
Social theory/ concepts	Postsocial relations/technological forms of life A move toward post-social relations, reflecting an ontology based upon a depth of understanding of social relations (Knorr Cetina 1999; Lash 2001). Some of the aspects identified in this literature include: an increased reliance on relations with objects (both of a solid technological character and an ephemeral knowledge based nature; the increased incidence and experiencing of generic spaces; a faster pace of life (at least in the developed world) and the pervasive influence of ICT (information and communications technologies).
Implications and effects at the social and cultural level	A knowledge based society One interpretation of a knowledge society is that it is composed of social arrangements which are based on knowledge. Social culture and work relations are increasingly affected by technologies and the growth of expert knowledges (Beck 1992; Giddens 1990; Knorr Cetina 1999).
Research styles/ programmes Broadly constructionist – relying on empirical enquiry. Theoretical framework provided by the concepts described above.	Actor Network Theory (ANT) Research in the Sociology of Science and Science Studies has provided perspectives on the diverse ontology and epistemology of different disciplines (Callon 1986; Barnes, Shapin 1979; Knorr Cetina 1997; Latour 1987). Such studies examine the way in which expert work is performed at the micro level through anthropological and ethnographic methods. A broad theoretical school can be identified as ANT (actor network theory); see Callon 1980; Law 1992, 2002; Latour 1987, 1999). These studies commenced in the hard sciences but have made a considerable impact in sociology and organisation studies (Blackler 1993; Bloomfield 1995; Knorr Cetina, Bruegger 2002; Law 1996). This research is characterised by its *empirically realist* style (Lee, Hassard 1999; see also Calas, Smircich 1999; Law 2002; de Laet, Mol 2000). The importance placed on network relations and the need to trace the networks by following the actors (Latour 1987), the role of knowledge objects and object relations in enriching social and work cultures (Knorr Cetina 1997, 1999).

It is necessary to say a little more about the literature which we believe helps to define the philosophical position that we adopt for our research. There are some influential writers who have argued that our society is increasingly affected by the impact of specialist knowledge and of the growth of expert and professional groupings within society. Some writers argue that we live in a *knowledge society* (Bell 1973; Drucker 1993; Giddens 1990), while others refer to alternative concepts such as the *information society* (e.g., Lyotard 1984); or *risk society* (Beck 1992). Knorr Cetina (1999) focuses particular attention on epistemic cultures – which she sees as being built up around groups of scientific communities. These writers provide subtly different interpretations of how these ideas might impact on social arrangements. They share a common view that the growth of expert knowledge systems has implications for the society in which we live. In particular they regard changes in science and technology as affecting society through interrelated processes which produces complex feedback effects. These effects are partly from the social impact of the implementation of the new technology but are also consequent on the development and growth of groups of experts or knowledge workers within society. These groups form their own epistemic cultures which affect social interactions. ANT regards technology and society or social arrangements as being co-constructed (Latour 1991).

The emphasis of Actor Network Theory (ANT) is on the networks of relations that allow objects to act in a similar way to human actors. The central concepts of the theory concern that manner in which action is typically, if not always, produced by humans and objects in concert. But that even further to this we need to take account of the incorporation of intentions and the residue of past actions into technological objects. This aggregation of human knowledge into technological objects certainly has the effect of producing objects which impact on human behavior. Modern human activity is everywhere constrained and circumscribed by technology. Some might say it is supporting and enabling. The important thing is that there is broad acceptance of the reliance of society on technology objects. Technology here is defined broadly to include virtual objects such as computer software and ideas as well as technological artifacts.

Studies that explore socio-technical networks or arrangements can apply a range of methods. Research based on post-social perspectives is focussed on following the actors at different levels of granularity, until the network can be described, at least to the satisfaction of the researchers. ANT and other post-social perspectives have in some instances used ethnographic or intensive case study approaches (Callon 1986; Knorr Cetina 1999; Knorr Cetina, Bruegger 2002; Latour 1996) in other contexts archival material has been used as the basis for historical reconstructions (Latour 1988; Law 1986; Jones, Dugdale 2002). These authors have all used elements of ANT or closely related socio-technical perspectives to seek explanations of the role of technology in organizations and society. Interpretive case research in accounting and organization theory has increasingly been motivated by approaches and ideas from the social studies of science literature (Bloomfield, Best 1992; Calas, Smircich 1999; Bloomfield et al. 1992; Bloomfield, Vurdubakis 1997; Briers, Chua 2001; Dechow, Mouritsen 2005; Doolin 1999; Engeström, Blackler 2005; Ezzamel 1994; Lowe 2001, 2004; Preston, Cooper, Coombs 1992; Quattrone, Hopper 2005).

This section provided a very brief introduction to research that falls into the broad category of postsocial research. Key elements of the socio-technical construction of hard and virtual objects and references to seminal articles in the area provide an entry point for further in depth reading in the area. The next section shows how these broad ideas relate to XBRL.

3   XBRL as an Infrastructure Standard

In this section we establish broad definitions of the ideas that we want to work with to examine the underpinning of XBRL development. Our main concern is to describe how we see XBRL belonging to a socio-technical system. Our analysis brings in other concepts, some of which are in more common use, but which we conceptualize from our research perspective. These include classification systems, standards and infrastructure.

The classification systems and associated software that constitute information standards and information infrastructures may be seen as technology objects (Bowker, Star 2000; Hanseth, Monteiro 1997). These writers have in common the use of a socio-technical perspective on the analysis of the impact of these technological objects on society. Bowker and Star argue that we severely underestimate the impact of systems on organizations, individual and social arrangements. While Hanseth and Monteiro argues that:

... the processes producing the standards which make up the technical back-bone of an information infrastructure ... are neither ready-made nor neutral. The ... socio-technical complexity of establishing an information infrastructure [has] so far ... been severely underestimated by those involved (Ibid).

Bowker and Star (2000) talk of standards and systems of classification that often combine together or are interrelated in such a way as to provide multiple:

... layers of technology [that] accrue and expand over space and time. Systems of classification (and of standardization) form a juncture of social organization, moral order and layers of technical integration. Each subsystem inherits, increasingly as it scales up, the inertia of the installed base of systems that have gone before... Infrastructures are never transparent for everyone, and their workability as they scale up becomes increasingly complex (Ibid).

We argue that XBRL is a standard and classification system that provides an infrastructure for interoperability. In order to understand its likely impact and trajectory of requires that we try to examine aspects of its progress and the processes of its development. Treating XBRL as a socio-technical object focuses attention on the socio-technical elements of the network to which XBRL belongs. This requires us to use research approaches that seek to track the processes, structures and perhaps individuals that influence the development of XBRL over time and through space. We need to take care to examine the other classification systems and infrastructures with which XBRL interacts and from which it draws and we need to do all this without losing sight of the need to seek to reveal those aspects of the development that seem opaque. It is often these aspects that are the most taken for granted. Ideas and concepts have become an accepted part of XBRL – they have been black-boxed within the XBRL technology (Latour 1999). An example of a technical aspect of XBRL that is now taken for granted is the ability to classify monetary elements as debits or credits. Aspects of XBRL that seek to reflect the accounting model make it more distant from simpler XML structures (Hamscher 2002a; Waldt 2004[3]). We can re-open the black box and question some of the fundamental assumptions that are now part of the technology – what alternatives are lost, what is gained? By whom and how were these technical issues identified, resolved and decisions made?

Though XBRL can be seen as a small part of the technology of business reporting it has been held out as a solution to some of the most intractable problems of communicating meaningful information to stakeholders and regulators of commercial and other organizations (Boyd, Teixeira 2004b; Cuneo 2002; Garthwaite 2000; Hucklesby, Macdonald 2000; McNamar 2003). If this is correct, in the context of other classificatory systems and information technologies with which it interacts, it may be influential in affecting the direction in which these other technologies and business reporting develops. XBRL together with other information technologies such as the Internet (and its associated standards such as HTML and XML) and a host of regulatory and accounting structures will form part of a much larger infrastructure. It is this role as part of a much larger set of technical and business concerns that leads to the very strong

---

[3] Note in particular the exchange between readers at the end of the article.

claims that proponents of XBRL make. To what extent XBRL meets the claims made for it will be determined largely by its assimilation into this socio-technical network of information and regulatory infrastructure systems and organizations. The acceptability of the standards which XBRL comes to comprise and the software packages through which it is delivered will be only part of the XBRL development and implementation story. How the XBRL standard has and will be fabricated is a more complex story of mundane classifications and complex social interaction. This complex set of relations between objects, institutions, and individuals may be scanned to achieve a broad perspective or brought into closer focus. To illustrate the possibilities, one simple extraction from this rich set of potential networks is shown in Figure 1.

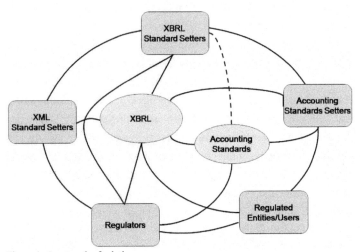

Figure 1: A network of relations

The rest of the discussion in this section will use this diagram as a focus for exploring how research into XBRL may be shaped using a postsocial perspective. Three aspects are explored; tracing networks, the granularity of the focus; and particular research issues reflected in the diagram that will be explored further in the next section.

3.1   Tracing Networks

The first thing to note about Figure 1 is that it presents relationships between *technology objects* (XBRL and accounting standards) and organisations/institutions as *established*. From a postsocial perspective, particularly applying ANT, research seeks to trace networks of relationships by following the actors – both humans and virtual objects. *Obvious* institutional relationships are not taken for granted but like all other aspects of the network the researcher traces the actors and the objects to see what relationships and effects emerge.

Figure 1 is being presented here as a tool for making our discussion more concrete. The diagram is a simplified representation that helps show the scope of some of the interactions we seek to examine in our research. It could be said to emerge from research we have undertaken, but that we don't have space here to report in full. It does need to be made explicit, however, that the application of the methods we are discussing in this paper does not start with the imposition of a predetermined network based on prior knowledge. Any network of relations is only established during the research process by discovering what linkages are seen to affect outcomes.

A brief outline of how we started work on tracing the relations reflected in the diagram is that we focussed on the object ... reading literature about it, attending conferences and seeking to work with it 'hands-on'. As our understanding developed we identified categories of individuals who were closely intertwined with the technology; some directly with technical aspects, some were important in the social recognition and adoption of XBRL as a data standard, and many had multiple roles.

Some of the relationships represented in Figure 1 may be more contentious than others. The link between the XBRL standard setters (XII) and XBRL is unlikely to be surprising. Other linkages are less obvious and raise issues that could be the subject of further research. An example is between XBRL standard setters and accounting standards setters. Are individuals with a primary concern with XBRL in a position to influence the development of accounting standards? If so, is their influence on the standard setting body passive or active?

A related issue is the direction of the relationship between accounting standards and XBRL. It may not be currently contentious to argue that the XBRL technology should be influenced by accounting standards, but what about the other direction? Should accounting standards and the principles they represent be subject to the influence of the new possibilities that technologies such as XBRL make available (Jensen, Xiao 2001; Ashbaugh et al. 1999; Wallman 1997)? Should the fact that XBRL would be much more effective in facilitating comparability if there was only one set of accounting standards applied internationally be a driver for accounting standards convergence? We can explore how these possibilities are played out by observing actors in associated networks, tracing their relationships and influences.

3.2   Granularity

The description of relationships and issues above glosses some aspects of the socio-technical environment by focussing on particular issues. So for example at a finer level of granularity, we could argue about the extent to which XBRL is influenced by accounting standards, because in fact there are (at least) two XBRLs – FR and GL.4 XBRL-GL is not designed to focus on external reporting but occupies the space between tagging transactions and external reporting (Hamscher 2002b; Lutes, Cohen 2006). Its design is driven by different considerations, in a similar fashion to the difference between external financial reporting and management accounting. Peeling back the layers on the XBRL object represented in the diagram reveals the possibilities for exploring the networks surrounding the two different XBRLs, how their allies form relationships to promote their views, the tensions and strengths this may create, the reason for generally representing XBRL as one technology, the opportunities that this obscures and the trajectories for these technologies that are so closely bound, and yet are developing, at least to some extent, separately.

Other layers of the elements represented in the diagram may be peeled back (or drilled down) to explore greater detail in the network. For example the relationships within the XBRL standard setters' entity: between the central consortium body (XII), its subcommittees and the jurisdictions. What are the patterns of relationships? How do people in these entities interact with the technology objects that are aligned to support and develop XBRL itself? Looking at the diagram the possibilities seem to stretch out endlessly and we wonder how far down the rabbit-hole do we want to go? And yet Figure 1 is itself just a slice out of the bigger set of relations that constitutes the infrastructure for communicating business information. The Internet itself, the potentially competing XML standards (e.g. eb-XML), the potentially complementary XML standards (e.g. eb-XML[5]), governments and international conglomerates with vested interests are just a few of the actors not represented in our extraction from the greater set of possible relations. How will we know how far the network extends (Miller 1997) or what other technologies and institutions are affected? How will we predict the outcomes and impacts for participants in the network – including XBRL itself?

---

[4]   It is generally accepted that FR stands for Financial Reporting. This form of XBRL has also been referred to as GP (general purpose). GL originally was understood to be an abbreviation for general ledger (Anonymous 2001) but more recently its allies and supporters feel that it is better represented as *Global Ledger* (personal communication from Eric Cohen, 2006).

[5]   Eb-XML is a data standard that potentially overlaps XBRL. XII has announced a programme of co-operation with eb-XML developers (Interoperability pledge http://www.xbrl.org/Governing Documents/Interoperability-Pledge.htm).

These are substantial questions and ones to which we can only ever find partial answers. A research programme inspired by ANT would be intent on providing convincing explanations of how things have come to be settled as they are. The research seeks to explain how and why the technology appears as it does to us now. Not to portray what it now is and does but to understand how the multitude of interests and influences has been accommodated and to reveal the compromises that have been made and why. The contribution of the research is to our understanding of the technology and its imperfections and accommodations. No explanation can ever be argued to be complete since the researcher cannot follow all the actors and cannot observe all the machinations as they occur. The construction of a network of relations and the explanations it provides is therefore always partial. Nonetheless the insights it may offer are important and it is particularly well suited to emerging technology objects, like XBRL.

3.3 Research Issues

In the previous two sections we have described several different perspectives that a postsocial approach affords research on XBRL. In this section the particular issues that we will explore in more depth are located with reference to Figure 1.

The first issue we explore is the use of techniques by proponents of the technology to enrol allies who will support the XBRL technology. XBRL is a network standard which must be adopted by a critical mass of users to be viable. This is part of the essence of this object, its nature and part of its biography. Another of XBRL's characteristics is that while it is part of the world of business and accounting at the same time it belongs to the world of IT and XML. In Figure 1 these elements are represented; people associated with XML, people associated with accounting and the two technology objects. We explore the use of 'boundary objects' to facilitate the creation of relations between groups who may otherwise lack incentives to co-ordinate their activities and support the technology development.

The second of the issues we explore uses a model of open source software development. This movement has disrupted many long-held beliefs about how best to organise large, complex tasks and the need to vest ownership with innovators and creators in order to motivate the production of new technologies (Lerner, Tirole 2001; Weber 2004). The open source model allows us to shift our focus to the XBRL standard setters and explore how the management of processes around XBRL's development compares with open source approaches. It simultaneously opens up our perspective to the possibility of many people from heterogeneous backgrounds and interests who may be willing to participate in the XBRL project, just as so many give their time freely to other technology development projects around the world (Lerner, Tirole 2001; Shah 2003). The massive reach of the World Wide Web and open source methods for the virtual organisation of contributions to a project, opens out the rather limited view we present in Figure 1 to help us to imagine the boundlessness of possible networks and connections.

The third issue shifts attention to financial market regulators and regulated entities as those currently implicated in the diffusion of XBRL. We explore the impact of elements of the nature of XBRL that may impact on regulated entities as they respond to encouragement from regulators to submit tagged reports. The tenor of the early responses to implementation and whether or not these entities fully embrace the incipient functionality of XBRL is traced to implications for its wider diffusion.

4   Illustrating Postsocial Research on XBRL

Our purpose in this section is to provide more detailed explanation of the philosophical and methodological view we have applied to understanding both XBRL and other socio-technical systems (Locke, Lowe 2005; Lowe, Locke 2005). We describe below the broad context of three research projects we are pursuing, as introduced in relation to Figure 1 above. We intend to build upon the setting we have introduced to provide specific paths into relevant literatures and methods to potentially stimulate complementary research.

4.1   XBRL as a Boundary Object

In this project we want to deploy a conceptual framework that will enable us to construct an empirical assessment of the XBRL technology and community. Here we hope to reveal some of the mechanisms that have influenced outsiders to take part in the development of XBRL. The key concept concerns the use of boundary objects that encourage individuals and groups with disparate views and cultures to contribute something to the XBRL project. The concept of boundary objects is drawn from writers in accounting (Briers, Chua 2001; Dechow,Mouritsen 2005), information systems (Hanseth, Monteiro 1997) and more broadly (Bowker, Starr 2000; Fujimura 1992; Guston 1999; Star, Griesemer 1989).

The nature of XBRL means that it is essential to get different groups of professionals to co-operate together to create the technology and its ecosystem. XBRL needs accounting professionals and computer/IT professionals to combine their skills in order for the technology to work well for less highly trained users. These two groups of professionals need to be able to communicate at a level that allows the creation using XML technology of schema, taxonomies, presentation and calculation linkbases etc. that conform to requirements both in XML and in accounting terms. This requires a significant level of communication across different groups of knowledge workers. These groups typically have been said to possess alternative views of knowledge and form their own *epistemic cultures* (Knorr Cetina 1999). Bridging the divide between epistemic cultures, different professional mores and values, and different national cultures is the role of boundary objects.

The concept of *boundary objects* has a significant history in the sociology and social study of science literature. Star and Griesemer (1989) adopt the concept to enable them to make sense of the more general process of translation[6] (Callon 1986; Latour 1987). Star and Griesemer propose a more structured framework by deploying boundary objects as *receptacles* into which they are able to categorise different objects and practices that are:

...plastic enough to adapt to local needs ... yet robust enough to maintain a common identity ... weakly structured in common use, and become strongly structured in individual site use. These objects may be abstract or concrete. They have different meanings in different social worlds but their structure is common enough to make them ... recognisable. (Ibid, p.393, emphasis added)

Boundary objects which are able to display these attributes contribute to the translation and interessement[7] (Callon 1986; Latour 1987) of actors with differing interests and from different social 'worlds'. Star and Griesemer state "that the trick of translation required two things: ... developing a clear set of [standardizing] methods to 'discipline' the information obtained ... and [the] generat[ion] ... of boundary objects [to] maximise ... autonomy and the communication between the ... worlds (p. 404, emphasis added)." According to Star and Griesemer the boundary objects they identify and describe operate to preserve autonomy and most importantly from our perspective to enable good communication across social boundaries. These boundaries may be thought of a consequence of differences in culture, professional allegiance, politics or

---

[6]   Translation has a particular meaning in the context of the literature we draw from. Latour uses the term translation to refer to the construction or 'fabrication' of objects. These objects are most easily perceived as hard technological objects - the result of combining human ideas and physical objects. But this process also refers to less solid technological objects such as inscriptions, computer software, accounting techniques and rules.

[7]   Interessement is a term used to capture the process of persuading actors with similar interests to become allies.

religion, education etc. Boundary objects are used to enable co-operation and co-ordination of effort across the different groups.

Research using this perspective would seek to identify boundary objects and investigate their role in the development of the XBRL community and technology. It would build theory and explanation of the development of XBRL and the XBRL community to examine boundary objects that have played a part in the *diffusion* of XBRL. Questions could include: how has the XBRL community developed over time? How has this development been achieved? To what extent is it the result of apparently deliberate policy versus chance? What devices and/or technologies have been implicated in the *spread* of XBRL?

Star and Griesemer (1989) identify four types of boundary objects. They present four analytical distinctions that are not mutually exclusive but are intended to assist "researchers to define [the] conceptual and technical work space" (Fujimura 1992, note 10). The four types are; repositories, ideal types, coincident boundaries and standardized forms. In order to focus the discussion, only ideal types and standardized forms will be described and illustrated in the context of an exploration of XBRL.

Ideal types include the use of diagrams and representations that help to communicate. An atlas, an accounting report, or the use of grading scales for assessment, are examples. These are transportable and easily communicated. They can be adapted to new circumstances or new contexts – by adapting the rules of representation they use to a new setting. Ideal types arise from abstraction. Star and Griesemer (1989) argue that they "result in the deletion of local contingencies from the common object and have the advantage of adaptability" (Ibid). In extending this concept to a study of XBRL we might consider the role of the various objects that are associated with the XBRL community: diagrams that recur in publications, or on websites; taxonomies or applications software. The use of simplified diagrammatic representations to translate complex ideas and communicate them to potential allies is widely acknowledged as influential in both the academic and business literature (Latour 1999; Lowe 2004, 2007; Preston, Young 2000; Preston et al. 1996).

Standardized forms are boundary objects devised as methods of common communication across dispersed work groups. Star and Griesemer (1989) describe some of the devices which made it possible to get different groups to contribute information to a natural science project in California. The groups included museum curators, scientists, amateur collectors and animal trappers. In this case, a form was designed and distributed to amateur collectors to fill out when they obtained an animal. The form enabled the collection of standardized information that could then be analysed by the scientists. This is one example of the way one group is encouraged to contribute to a project that is not their main interest. They are enrolled as allies and help to provide useful information to make the project more successful. Standardized forms do not have to be *forms* as such. This category of boundary objects includes things such as forms of social interaction that are standardized in order to enable people from different *social worlds* to interact. Meetings run using committee rules and conferences are examples of standardized forms of social interaction that may be strictly structured to allow the dissemination and/or collection of information from disparate groups.

The XBRL technology needs the input of different groups to be effective. We would argue that this need to enrol different groups of interested parties is one reason why the XBRL Consortium runs bi-annual conferences. These gatherings are one way to communicate with potential user groups and hopefully enrol them into the project to establish a business reporting standard. There are a number of very different groups who need to be encouraged to contribute to the XBRL project. They include: organizations that will use the technology for reporting - both public and private sector; regulators and other government institutions who will be the recipients of some of these reports and software vendors who's expertise will be required to make the XBRL technology accessible to users. The software vendors also have a potentially critical role to play in the distribution of the technology to users.

The role of XBRL working groups are of interest as another standardized form of interaction in which it is possible to engage with individuals representing different types of organizations who may provide knowledge, skills and expertise from different groups of professionals. Currently the XBRL Consortium has six working groups.[8] The Jurisdev group has the shortest purpose description out of the six[9], but is particularly interesting from our perspective because of its focus on seeding XBRL in countries around the world through the establishment of 'jurisdictions.' The form of jurisdictions and the way in which they are structured to require support from at least ten companies and a professional accounting body (Hannon 2004) are identified by XII as creating collaboration that is "the most effective way of promoting XBRL" (http://www.xbrl.org/FormingJurisdictions/). These standardized forms of organising across different stakeholders in the development of XBRL are unique in their particu-

---

[8] Accounting, Domain, Jurisdev, Assurance, GL and Specification (www.xbrl.org/working groups.aspx).

[9] "The Jurisdiction Development Working Group exists to "encourage and support the creation of new XBRL jurisdictions" (www.xbrl.org/workinggroups.aspx).

lar application but commonly understood social structures within which to facilitate contributions and gain allegiance or commitment to the technology.

So far in this section we have explored how two types of boundary objects may be deployed in order to promote contributions to the XBRL project. There is another perspective we can take. XBRL itself may be cast as a boundary object. It is a technology that has as its purpose the communication of representations about entities to disparate groups. The social groups that are the focus of the technology are broadly the same groups who have found other ways to communicate in the past (e.g. EDI, accounting packages, ERPs, Excel, PDF[10]). But the claims for XBRL are that it will be able to achieve a much greater level of effectiveness and inclusiveness as a communication device.

An example of XBRL acting as a boundary object is its use by *Companies House* (a UK based regulator). In their project, an *intelligent document* was created using PDF and XBRL as devices to enable data, tagged in XBRL, to be transferred between regulated companies and Companies House over the Internet (XBRL UK e-filing of Company Tax and Accounts Conference 2006; Chase 2006). The intelligent form provides helpful descriptions of what is to be entered into boxes in the form, is structured to permit and make difficult correct and incorrect pathways through the form and has built-in checks so that amounts must be in expected directions (positive or negative) and sub-totals and totals balance correctly. It is carefully designed to meet requirements for legal sign-off and the XBRL tags enable automated validation at the regulator end. This is a sophisticated combination of technologies that facilitates the communication of what may seem to accountants to be simple company information, but which to other people in society engaged in running small companies, may be difficult to get right. The success of the initial optional uptake of this technology is reflected in very low in error rates on submissions:

The rejection rate for XBRL accounts, based on our experience so far, has been less than one per cent. This service is providing early adopters with a faster, more convenient way for companies to comply with their statutory obligations under the Companies Act (Jones, J.: Business Transformation Programme Manager for Companies House, http://www.decisionsoft.com/PR-20060420-CH.html).

This illustrates the way in which technologies such as XBRL can be combined to achieve standardized communication across different individuals and institutional

---

[10] These acronyms are widely used. They stand for Electronic Data Interchange (EDI), Enterprise Resource Planning systems (ERPs), and Portable Document Format (PDF).

groups. The technology referred to here works by channelling the submitter organization through the design of the intelligent document. The outcome is a successful communication across two very different groups: submitting companies and the regulator, over the Internet. In this environment XBRL is, in conjunction with other technologies, the boundary object that is enabling the communication to take place.

4.2   An Open Source Model and XBRL

In this section we describe a theoretic investigation of the effect of governance structure and constituency on the development of XBRL. We use constructs taken from the literature on the development of open source software. Open source projects are varied in nature but are said to have a number of features that are very different to software development within the typical commercial setting. There are a number of significant differences that can be identified in the nature of governance structures and constituency. These participatory arrangements are argued to have had very significant influences on the success of some of the major open source developments.

The success of open source has challenged accepted notions of organizing and the need for direct monetary reward for creativity (Weber 2004). Its key facilitator is the virtual space and time created by the Internet. Asynchronous contributions from contributors from all over the world may be collected and seen by all, exchanged and discussed at very little marginal cost to the individual participant. Why skilled programmers contribute their time for free is explored in a number of studies (Lerner, Triole 2001; Shah 2003) but it is at least in part because they enjoy the challenge and the virtual society they experience on-line. Open source communities are prime examples of postsocial relationships and the mechanisms they use to facilitate contributions from disparate people may be seen as boundary objects. The open source approach to project development is therefore an inherently interesting perspective from which to explore XBRL as an 'open source' data standard.

The analysis of the phenomenon of open source software development has been pursued from a number of perspectives: as a social phenomenon (de Joode 2004; Lehmann 2004; Ljungberg 2000; Tuomi 2001); novel governance arrangements (de Joode 2004; Ljungberg 2000; Schweik, Semenov 2003; von Hippel, von Krogh 2003) and in terms of technology acceptance (Lerner, Tirole 2002; Moore 2002).

Bonaccorsi and Rossi (2003) provide a model to test the conditions under which open source software will reach a critical mass of adoptions. Successful open source developments share a number of distinctive elements: in terms of design and development processes and exhibit distinctive governance structures. The Bonaccorsi and Rossi model of open source projects provides a framework against which it is possible compare similar elements of the governance and development of XBRL and the XBRL Consortium. It would make sense to focus research on those elements of the process which are most relevant in explaining the development of XBRL. This could include the following:

- project governance,

- motivation of participants in the project,

- key elements of the diffusion process,

- mobilizing human, physical, and technological resources.

An analysis of these factors requires a research methodology that includes a complex set of elements, including technology, institutions and people. An approach based on ANT provides the researcher with a valuable perspective from which to consider the interactions of a heterogeneous combination of human actors and technological objects. A feature of successful open source projects is that individuals who belong to very disparate groups in society belong and become enthusiastic about adopting the technology. They bring to the project access to a range of matériel and contacts with individuals not currently involved in the project who may be enlisted as allies as the software takes shape. The question arises as the XBRL project diverges from the constructs of open source projects – what possibilities are lost? What is gained? How is the trajectory of the development of XBRL altered by these choices?

To explore these questions requires the development of research approaches that reflect this complex interaction of human and nonhuman elements. Rather than focusing just on the technology we see a need to examine the technical features of XBRL but also to examine the key aspects of its location in a network of institutional arrangements. XBRL will only succeed if it mobilizes sufficient users who believe it to be of value in business reporting and information transmission purposes or will serve regulatory requirements. These effects can be properly considered only using a research perspective which accords sufficient attention to the mixing of human and non-human elements.

The open source model of software development provides some interesting contrasts to the XBRL project. The XBRL International Consortium aims to provide a freely available data standard for the exchange of financial reports which has much in common with the typical open source philosophy. It is evident, however, that the approach of the Consortium has differed in a number of ways to the typical open source project. The simplest example is the committee based governance system that relies on face to face meetings and uses conferences as a key means of recruiting participants. It makes sense to subject these differences to study in an effort to reveal what effect they may have on the successful development of the XBRL project. Applying understandings of the processes and structures used in open source developments offers the opportunity to discover more appropriate approaches for XBRL. These alternative ways of doing things may well lead to a different trajectory for the technology, its implementation and governance.

The three features of the open source model we identified above could be developed into a research programme which would seek to examine some of the following issues:

- Governance – the governance procedures of open source projects tend to be rel-atively unconstrained and authority is based on accepted meritocracy. Hierar-chies and formal management positions are not the foundation of governance. The XBRL consortium is much more like a commercial venture in terms of its governance arrangements with evidence of hierarchy in management structures and of controls on how the technology is developed and who by. XBRL devel-opment seems to be characterised by a relatively homogeneous community when compared to open source projects.

- Diffusion of the XBRL technology – in order to become the dominant standard for electronic business reporting adoption of XBRL will need to achieve a criti-cal mass of user organisations and individuals. The pattern of diffusion of XBRL has also evolved very differently to that of a typical open source project. The recent adoption of XBRL particularly in the European Community has been strongly driven by regulatory authorities. This is effectively a supply or *push style* of adoption. In contrast successful open source projects tend to be distin-guished by a demand driven process in which users or adopters grow organical-ly in response to perceptions of the intrinsic value of the technology.

- Motivation – a feature of open source development is the lack of financial in-centives. Open source projects are said to make use of a so called *hybrid* busi-ness model however in which free software is bundled with specialist applica-tions or support services. There could be some interesting similarities and per-haps differences that may be identified here between open source projects and the arrangements which seem to apply to XBRL. This is certainly an area where research comparing XBRL and open source practices could be beneficial.

- Mobilization of resources – the XBRL Consortium uses a combination of techniques to garner resources for the project. A distinguishing feature between the consortium's approach and the open source model is that membership of the consortium is based on the payment of fees. Jurisdictions contribute fees to the consortium. The consortium provides a promotion and development resource in return. However, the fees alone would not be enough. They could never be set at a level that was sufficient to support XBRL's development, because the members are not going to end up with ownership of the product and so cannot earn a direct return on money they invest. The shortfall is contributed by volunteers who give their time for free and individuals who are permitted to work on the project in work time. The work is not opened up to wholesale volunteer contribution however. The volunteers may self-select but they have to become part of a closed group development process.

These four areas offer considerable scope to researchers who are interested in the processes and structures that are implicated in the development of the XBRL technology over time. The open source model provides a conceptual framework from which we might examine XBRL and the structures and processes put in place by the XBRL Consortium. It was argued earlier in this section that the ability of XBRL to become the dominant standard for electronic business reporting requires a complex fabrication of heterogeneous elements – consisting of XBRL and other related technology, institutions of various types and humans - developers, regulators and adopter/users.

Research into XBRL could be seen as trying to trace how these complex amalgamations of elements are brought together in some cases deliberately and in other cases as a result of unplanned coincidences and effects. XBRL would then best be theorised as both an effect and a cause of the changes taking place in the digital reporting environment. The regulators provide an important ally that may have multiple effects. On the one hand the heavy involvement of these actors will affect the development of the technology – in some cases these effects may seem minor and of a relatively trivial nature. Other effects may be substantial and could impact the nature of the functionality of the technology in more permanent ways. Relatively inflexible and formal governance structures may also impact on the manner in which the technology develops.

These aspects of governance and control together with the comparatively restricted and homogeneous nature of the XBRL community are likely to have substantial impacts on the technology. A research programme using an ANT perspective would combine the ideas from the open source model while seeking to identify how the human and non-human elements we have described combine to affect the XBRL technology. ANT motivated research would seek to trace the manner in which these heterogeneous elements are woven into complex networks of interrelations. The research would provide an understanding of how these networks determine the outcome of the controversies that take place as a new technology is constructed; the compromises that are reached and how and by whom these determinations are influenced.

4.3 A Socio-technical Perspective on Implementation

The focus adopted in this project switches to the adopting entities (regulated entities/users in Figure 1). We concentrate our attention on how XBRL can become infused throughout adopting organizations as part of an implementation process, highlighting the socio-technical relations that are involved.

Table 2: Technology Implementation Stages, (adapted from Cooper, Zmud 1990)

Stage	Description
Initiation	Identification of organizational/IT opportunities or problems and potential solution. The pressure to change arises out of organizational demand (pull) or IT innovation or both.
Adoption	IT innovation is agreed upon and resources committed to permit implementation through a process of negotiation.
Adaptation	The IT application is developed, installed and maintained. It is incorporated into the systems and processes of the organization. Training and support are provided to make the system available for use.
Acceptance	Members of the organization commit to the new application and use it.
Routinization	The application becomes part of the normal governance structures of the organization and is regarded as 'normal'.
Infusion	The use of the technology is expanded to an integrated, comprehensive application of its functionality. The full extent of its potential impact (benefits) for the organization is implemented.

Features of XBRL, both technical and social in nature, that are likely to influence its attractiveness to organizations that adopt it as a result of regulator imperatives are explored. We have selected a model of technology implementation (see Table 2) (Cooper, Zmud 1990; Kwon, Zmud 1987; Tornatzky, Klein 1982; Tornatzky, Fleischer 1990; Sullivan 1985). In adapting the model we implicitly allow the technology to impact on the setting as well as vice-versa – this is a key concept of the socio-technical perspective. We theorize the effect of the stages of the implementation model in combination with environmental (contextual) factors on the successful infusion of XBRL in reporting organizations. Infusion is described in Table 2 and relates to the extent to which the features and functionality of the technology are incorporated into the user organization. Four contextual factors have been identified from the technology implementation literature. There is a degree of overlap across the categories but it is convenient to describe them separately here. The four factors are:

- User – the users are those who are involved in the implementation and use of the innovation. In relation to our research on XBRL implementation in reporting entities we might focus on two professional groupings – IT programmers and accountants or finance officers.

- Task – task uncertainty may have a significant impacting on implementation. Other task related factors are; task variety, complexity and autonomy of the individual responsible for the task.

- Technology – complexity of the technology is the key - "the degree to which an innovation is perceived as relatively difficult to understand and use" (Tornatzky, Klein 1982). It is likely that higher levels of complexity have a negative impact on the implementation of a new technology (Kwon, Zmud 1987). Compatibility of the technology with the organization's values or practices (Tornatzky, Klein 1982) may be mitigating factors.

- External environment – in general the environment is conceptualized as a resource or a source of information (Kwon, Zmud 1987). This idea captures interorganizational dependence and the extent to which ideas or resources are exchanged with other organizations (Ibid). XML applications are fundamentally based on the increasing need for organizations to be interconnected and interoperable in a networked businesses environment. There are other environmental factors which may have both positive and negative effects on the implementing organization (Kwon, Zmud 1987).

For this research we have constructed a model of technology innovation which combines the implementation stages from Table 2 with these four contextual factors. This provides a framework for analysis which enables issues of the technology along with aspects of the social and institutional context to be considered. In the following paragraphs we will briefly illustrate a few insights that will clarify the way in which sociotechnical factors may act in combination to influence the implementation of XBRL technology.

External environment - in relation to the external environment a number of elements may be important. We suggest that the position taken by institutional regulators to the XBRL technology will be an important consideration for reporting entities. Uncertainties about the stability, of the systems and architecture that regulators may require entities to adopt, is likely to affect the commitment to and implementation of XBRL by reporting entities. If there are concerns about major changes to the XBRL specification or the level of commitment to XBRL by regulators, this is likely to act to reduce the willingness of regulated entities to invest in the changes needed to adopt XBRL-based systems.

Other uncertainties in the external environmental may be beneficial for XBRL at least in the short term. The introduction of IFRS, the impact of Sarbanes-Oxley and capital market concerns after recent corporate collapses are all events that have caused significant uncertainty (Dodd, Sheehan 2004; Gealy 2004; Giner, Rees 2005; Benson et al. 2003). A number of writers have argued that XBRL could help in resolving some of these uncertainties (Boyd, Teixeira 2004b; Buys 2004; Cuneo 2002; Hannon 2004; Hodge et al. 2004; McNamar; 2003; Teixeira 2005; www.xbrl.org/Regulators MoreInfo/).

Technology - in relation to task and technology compatibility there are again elements of both the technical and social that are likely to impact on implementation. The question is: how extensively will XBRL technology be implemented within the reporting organizations? It is widely claimed that XBRL is useful not just in the final step of electronic reporting to external parties, but that it will also be useful in internal reporting. Given this view XBRL could facilitate a variety of internal reporting outcomes. This scenario would offer clear efficiencies for the many entities that operate with disparate systems internally, but there may be resistance to the spread of XBRL internally. The sources of the resistance may come from existing tensions between XML approaches to data storage and management and more common relational database and EDI approaches (Sliwa 2000; Sliwa, King 2000). Depending on the internal IT personnel's views on this issue, they may see XBRL tagging as redundant in a relational database and a hindrance to its smooth running.

The progression from emphasising adoption for external reporting to internal operations raises issues for entities outside of the adopting organisations. We do not have space here for an extended discussion, but one of the imminent issues will be briefly described. As XBRL's journal taxonomy (XBRL-GL) is implemented the XBRL project is potentially exposed to competition with other standards for the recording and transfer of business transaction data. The *domain space* between journals and transactions is quite small (Ramin, 2005). Existing standards for transactions include eb-XML, ACORD, OFX, HR_XML and IFX (Hamscher 2002b). Proponents of the various standards are often at pains to distinguish their specialist contribution and claim

that there is no competition (Hamscher 2002a; Lutes, Cohen 2006). However, a proli-
feration of standards ultimately undermines the fundamental purpose of XML – to
create a consistent basis for the exchange of data to enhance inter-operability (see
www.oasis.org). The imperative of the standardisation task is to reduce the number of
standards[11]. However, XBRL has been approved by OASIS as a data standard for taxa-
tion purposes allowing it to provide specialist coverage of a unique domain that draws
from both journal level data and external reporting data. This may give it a stronger
foothold as a core standard for internal and external business reporting. Nonetheless
other transaction level standards such as eb-XML have also achieved a wide level of
diffusion and acceptance (Geyer 2004; Knox et al. 2004).

This is an area of considerable complexity where outcomes are not just a matter of
who has the superior technology (David 1985; Moore 2002). Social and institutional
factors come to play a part in terms of the effects of the attitudes of both reporting
entities and regulatory agencies to change and innovation. If they are already using an
existing technology and it is significantly diffused in the external environment it may
be very difficult to get traction for a new technology even if it is superior in some way.

5   Conclusions

We have argued that XBRL is best conceived as a socio-technical object. It cannot be
separated from its context and is designed to serve a highly integrated role in the construction and communication of business information. Any information communication technology plays an important role in the construction of meaning and cannot be
treated as a means to transmit pure, un-interpreted facts. This is clearly apparent in
accounting reporting in general and certainly must apply to the XBRL technology that
seeks to apply semantic value to accounting data. It is this interpretation that underlies
our view of XBRL and business reporting in general. XBRL as it is envisaged will
exist in a virtual world where accounting and business information will be routinely
transmitted and transformed by a range of information users. The technology will enable the construction of virtual accounting representation in remote locations as information is readily available on websites of a number of agencies and user organisations
(Cuneo 2002; Hucklesby, Macdonald 2000).

---

[11] The XBRL consortium agreed informally in 2001 to an interoperability pledge with UN/CEFACT,
OASIS, OMG and HR-XML which states in part that they will avoid "duplication of efforts and
overlapping development" (Interoperability pledge, www.xbrl.org/Governing Documents
/Interoperability-Pledge.htm, downloaded 19/08/2005)

We have provided a broad introduction to how a postsocial perspective may be applied to research on XBRL. In particular the methods applied in ANT are described and explored. Figure 1 is used as a device to create a window on the possibilities for research by demonstrating the potential scope as the granularity of focus is refined or broadened. We have also described three particular research programmes that use the switching of levels of granularity for analysis, and demonstrate different foci in the network of possibilities.

Our introduction would not be complete, however, if we did not recognise the challenges and limitations of the research approach we are advocating. ANT researchers must make choices about the granularity of their study and the extent of the network they follow (Bruni 2005; Monteiro 2001). Designing a research strategy that enables the researcher to follow the actors (Quattrone, Hopper 2005) and the traces that will reveal the network of relations is problematic for a number of reasons both practical and conceptual (Law 1999, 2002; Miller 1997). Miller notes the difficulty of knowing where the network ends or which network nodes are the critical ones. These are largely irresolvable uncertainties. It is up to the researcher[s] to make a judgement on these issues.

Other problems in following the actors are physical and economic. It is not feasible within the constraints of a normal research team to follow all the traces left by the actors constructing XBRL. Even to attend the conferences is a major issue of travel and cost and of course the conferences are only one venue of XBRL activity. There are a host of committee meetings that are attended by XBRL people and of course other meetings and teleconferences that impact on decisions that may later turn out to be significant or not. Then there are all the regulators and other institutions and organizations that have a part to play. Even if it were possible to track all participants, there would be limitations arise from whether or not the researcher is able to obtain permission to observe. Our experience with participants in the XBRL project is that they are very open to research interest in their project. There must of course be limits, and like all field researchers we have been asked to keep matters confidential and we have been excluded from access to meetings or conversations which would be affected by our presence. It is impossible to avoid this situation in many research settings.

There are other research options that might fill in some of the missing links, such as using documentary analysis and following electronic traces (Quattrone and Hopper 2005). Such sources could be used but they could also introduce further threats to the data and analysis we might construct. ANT research has been successfully constructed from archival material (Jones, Dugdale 2002; Latour 1988; Law 1986), but, some authors have expressed concerned with the importance of tracking developments as they happen. Latour (Latour 1987) argues that we need to try to engage in research before the technology in which we are interested becomes fixed, known and unproblematic. The object of beginning the research process at this early stage in the deployment of XBRL is so that we have the opportunity to observe and document the process through which the system takes shape. The research aim is to focus on the crucial decisions which fix one part of the technology or another. This line of theorising has led accounting researchers to write of the fabrication of accounting systems being processual and unpredictable (Preston et al. 1992; Bloomfield et al. 1992). The researcher needs to be able to observe the system implementation or technology:

"...before the controversies involved in its fabrication are closed, before the complexities of its inner workings are taken for granted and before the patterns of organizational power and influence, instrumental in the formation of [the technology] ... are forgotten or rationalized." (Preston et al. 1992)

We do not see these as insurmountable issues – they are effectively the kind of decisions that researchers make all the time – just not always consciously. Where the research ends and how it is framed by research questions or hypotheses provide exactly this function – they truncate the research subject in order to make the research fit into a viable project. The design of individual research projects produced by these decisions is often quite arbitrary. The combination of impossible and possible, opportunities and coincidences frame the development of research, just as they have a role to play in the development of all technologies and knowledge. The task of the researcher is to take the possibilities and opportunities and carefully craft an insight that promotes understanding. In this chapter we have contributed something by sharing our experience with applying a postsocial perspective on XBRL.

References

Abrahamson, E. (1996): Management fashion. Academy of Management Review 21, pp. 254-285.

Anonymous (2001): XBRL.org Releases 'XBRL for General Ledger' and W3C XML Schema Version of Financial Statements Specification, http://xml.coverpages.org /ni2001-06-21-b.html, downloaded in July 2005.

Appadurai, A. (1986): Introduction: Commodities and the Politics of Value, in: Appadurai, A. (ed) The Social Life of Things: Commodities in Cultural Perspective. Cambridge University Press, Cambridge, pp.3-63.

Ashbaugh, H.; Johnstone, K.M.; Warfield, T.D. (1999): Corporate reporting on the Internet, Accounting Horizons 13, pp.241-257.

Barnes, B.; Shapin, S. (1979): Natural Order: Historical studies in scientific culture., Sage.

Beck, U. (1992): Risk Society: Towards a New Modernity, Sage, London.

Bell, D. (1973): The Coming of Post-Industrial Society: A Venture in Social Forecasting, Basic Books, New York.

Benson, G., Bromwich, M.; Litan, R.E.; Wagenhofer, A. (2003): Following the Money: The Enron failure and the state of corporate disclosure, AEI-Brookings Joint Center for Regulatory Studies.

Blackler, F. (1993): Knowledge and the theory of organizations: organizations as activity systems and the reframing of management, Journal of Management Studies 30, pp. 864-884.

Bloomfield, B.P.; Coombs, R.; Cooper, D.J.; Rea, D. (1992): Machines and Manoeuvres: Responsibility Accounting and the Construction of Hospital Information Systems, Accounting, Management and Information Technologies 2, pp. 197-219.

Bloomfield, B.P.; Best, A. (1992): Management consultants: systems development, power and the translation of problems, Sociological Review 40, pp. 533-560.

Bloomfield, B.P. (1995): Power, machines and social relations: delegating to information technology in the national health service, Organization 2, pp. 489-518.

Bloomfield, B.P.; Vurdubakis, T. (1997): Paper Traces: Inscribing Organisations and Information Technology In: Bloomfield, B.P. (ed) Information technology and Organisations; Strategies, Networks and Integration, Oxford University Press, Oxford.

Bonaccorsi, A. Rossi, C. (2003): Why open source software can succeed, Research Policy 32, pp. 1243-1258.

Bovee, M.; Ettredge, M.L.; Srivastava, R.P.; Vasarhelyi, M.A. (2002): Does the Year 2000 XBRL Taxonomy Accommodate Current Business Financial-Reporting Practice?, Journal of Information Systems 16, pp. 165-182.

Bowker, G.C.; Star, S.L. (2000): Sorting things out: classification and its consequences, MIT Press, Cambridge (MA).

Boyd, G. Teixeira, A. (2004a): What in the world is XBRL?, Chartered Accountants Journal 83, pp. 4-6.

Boyd, G. Teixeira, A. (2004b): XBRL and IFRS: working together, Chartered Accountants Journal of New Zealand 83, pp.46.

Briers, M.; Chua, W. F. (2001): The role of actor-networks and boundary objects in management accounting change: A field study of an implementation of activity-based costing, Accounting, Organizations and Society 26, pp. 237-269.

Bruni, A. (2005): Shadowing Software and Clinical Records: On the Ethnography of Non-Humans and Heterogeneous Contexts, Organization 12, pp. 357-378.

Buys, P.W. (2004): XBRL solutions for IFRS conversions, Accountancy (SA), pp. 10-11.

Calas, M.B.; Smircich, L. (1999): Past postmodernism? Reflections and tentative directions, Academy of Management Review 24, pp. 649-671.

Callon, M. (1980): Struggles and Negotiations to Define What is Problematic and What is Not the Sociologic of Translation, in: Knorr Cetina, K.D.; Krohn, R.; Whitley R. (edd), The Process of Scientific Investigation, Reidel D., Dordrecht.

Callon, M. (1986): Some elements of a sociology of translation: domestication of the scallops and the fishermen of St Brieuc Bay, in: Law, J. (ed): Power, Action and Belief: A New Sociology of Knowledge?, Routledge and Kegan Paul, London, pp. 196-233.

Chase, E. (2006): PDF and XBRL Case Studies in Intelligent Financial Reporting, http://www.xbrl.org/us/us/SanJose200601/Chase.pdf#search=%22corefiling%20comp anies%20house%20XBRL%22, downloaded in October 2006.

Ciborra, C.U.; Braa, K.; Cordella, A.; Dahlbom, B.; Failla, A.; Hanseth, O.; Hepsø, V.; Ljungberg, J.; Monteiro, E.; Simon, K.A. (2001): From control to drift: The dynamics of corporate information infrastructures, Oxford University Press, Oxford.

Coleman, R. (2002): The universal language: XBRL is gradually coming into its own as a key tool in financial reporting, CMA Management 45.

Cooper, R.B.; Zmud, R.W. (1990): Information technology implementation research: A technological diffusion approach, Management Science 36, pp. 123-139.

Cover, R. (2000): AICPA leads global XBRL initiative, http://xml.coverpages. org/XBRL-Ann.html, downloaded in January, 2005.

Cuneo, E.C. (2002): XBRL: Still A Ways Away From Saving The Day; But the standard is seen as an important part of restoring consumer and investor confidence in Big Business, Information Week 1.

David, P.A. (1985): Clio and the economics of QWERTY, American Economic Review 75, pp. 332-337.

de Joode, R.van W. (2004): Innovation in Open Source Communities Through Processes of Variation and Selection, Knowledge, Technology & Policy 16, pp. 30-45.

de Laet, M.; Mol, A. (2000): The Zimbabwe bush pump, Social Studies of Science 3, pp. 225-263.

Debreceny, R.; Gray, G. L. (2001): The production and use of semantically rich accounting reports on the Internet: XML and XBRL, International Journal of Accounting Information Systems 2, pp. 47-74.

Dechow, N.; Mouritsen, J. (2005): Enterprise resource planning systems, management control and the quest for integration, Accounting, Organizations and Society 30, pp. 691-733.

Dodd, C.; Sheehan, V. (2004): On your mark, get set..., Charter 75, pp. 66-67.

Doolin, B. (1999): Sociotechnical networks and information management in health care, Accounting, Management and Information Technologies 9, pp. 95-114.

Drucker, P.F. (1993): Post-Capitalist Society, HarperCollins, New York.

Engeström, Y. Blackler, F. (2005): On the Life of the Object, Organization 12, pp. 307-330.

Ezzamel, M. (1994): Organizational Change and Accounting: Understanding the Budgeting System in its Organizational Context, Organization Studies 15, pp. 213-240.

Fujimura, J. (1992); Crafting science: Standardized packages, boundary objects, and "translation", in: Pickering, A. (ed): Science as Culture and Practice, University of Chicago Press, Chicago, pp. 168-211.

Garthwaite, C. (2000): The language of risk: Why the future of risk reporting is spelled XBRL, Balance Sheet 8, pp. 18-20.

Gealy, S. (2004). IFRS: more than simple conversion, this is transformation. Accounting and Business, pp. 28-29.

Geyer, C. (2004): ISO Approves ebXML OASIS Standards, http://www.oasis-open.org/news/oasis_news_03_29_04.php, downloaded in January 2005.

Giddens, A. (1990): The Consequences of Modernity, Stanford University Press, Stanford (CA).

Giddens, A. (1994): Living in a Post-Traditional Society, In: Beck, U.; Giddens, A.; Lash, S. (Eds): Reflexive Modernization, Stanford University Press, Stanford, (CA).

Giner, B.; Rees, W. (2005): Introduction to special section on IFRS adoption, European Accounting Review 14, pp. 95-99.

Guston, D.H. (1999): Stabilizing the boundary between USA politics and science: The role of the Office of Technology Transfer as a boundary organization, Social Studies of Science 29, pp. 87-111.

Hamscher, W. (2002a): XBRL and its relationship to XML Web Services, ebXML and other infrastructures for e-Business, http://www.xbrl.org/technical/guidance/Hamscher-XBRL-Web-Services-2002-05-25.pdf, downladed in April 2007.

Hamscher, W. (2002b): XBRL and its adjacent XML languages: An overview, http://www.standardadvantage.com/Docs/XBRL-Adjacent-Specs-2002-05-27.

Hannon, N. (2004): XBRL grows fast in Europe, Strategic Finance 86, pp. 55-56.

Hanseth, O.; Monteiro, E. (1997): Inscribing behaviour in information infrastructure standards, Accounting, Management and Information Technologies 7, pp. 183-211.

Hodge, F.D., Kennedy, J.J.; Maines, L.A. (2004): Does Search-Facilitating Technology Improve the Transparency of Financial Reporting?, The Accounting Review 79, pp. 687-703.

Hucklesby, M.; Macdonald, J. (2000): XBRL = Better, faster, cheaper, Chartered Accountants Journal of New Zealand 79, pp. 34-36.

Hucklesby, M.; Macdonald, J. (2004): The three tenets of XBRL-adoption, adoption, adoption!, Chartered Accountants Journal of New Zealand 83, pp. 46-47.

Jensen, R. E; Xiao, J. Z. (2001): Customized financial reporting, networked databases, and distributed file sharing, Accounting Horizons 15, pp. 209-212.

Jones, T. C.; Dugdale, D. (2002): The ABC bandwagon and the juggernaut of modernity, Accounting, Organizations and Society 27, pp. 121-163.

Knorr Cetina, K. D. (1997): Sociality with objects: Social relations in postsocial knowledge societies, Theory, Culture & Society 14, pp. 1-30.

Knorr Cetina, K. D. (1999): Epistemic Cultures, Harvard University Press, Cambridge (MA).

Knorr Cetina, K. D. (2001): Postsocial Relations: Theorizing Sociality in a Postsocial Environment, in: Ritzer, G.; Smart, B. (Eds): Handbook of Social Theory, Sage, London, pp. 520-537.

Knorr Cetina, K. D.; Bruegger, U. (2002): Traders' engagement with markets: A postsocial relationship, Relationship, Theory, Culture and Society 19, pp. 161-185.

Knox, R.; Abrams, C.; Andrews, W.; Friedman, T.; Harris, K.; Linden, A. (2004): Hype cycle for XML technologies, Gartner Research.

Kopytoff, I. (1986): The Cultural Biography of Things: Commoditization as Process, in: Appadurai, A. (Ed): The Social Life of Things: Commodities in Cultural Perspective. Cambridge University Press, Cambridge, pp. 64-94.

Kwon, T.H.; Zmud, R. W. (1987): Unifying the Fragmented Models of Information Systems Implementation, in: Boland, R. J.; Hirschheim, R. A. (Eds): Critical Issues in Information Systems Research, John Wiley, New York.

Lash, S. (2001): Technological Forms of Life, Theory, Culture and Society 18, pp. 105-120.

Latour, B. (1987): Science in action: How to follow scientists and engineers through society, Harvard University Press, Cambridge (MA).

Latour, B. (1988): The Pasteurization of France, Harvard University Press, Cambridge (MA).

Latour, B. (1991): Technology is society made durable, in: Law, J. (Ed): A sociology of monsters. Essays on power, technology and domination, Routledge, London, pp. 103-131.

Latour, B. (1993): We Have Never Been Modern, Harvester Wheatsheaf, Hemel Hempstead.

Latour, B. (1996): Aramis: Or the love of technology, Harvester Wheatsheaf, Brighton.

Latour, B. (1999): Pandora's Hope. Essays in the Reality of Science Studies, Harvard University Press, Cambridge (MA).

Law, J. (1986): On the Methods of Long Distance Control: Vessels, Navigation and the Portuguese Route to India, in: Law, J. (ed): Power, Action and Belief: A New Sociology of Knowledge?, Routledge and Kegan Paul, London, pp. 234-263.

Law, J. (1992): Notes on the theory of the actor-network: ordering, strategy, and heterogeneity, Systems Practice 5, pp. 379-393.

Law, J. (1996): Organizing accountabilities: ontology and the mode of accounting, in: Munroe R, Mouritsen J (Eds): Accountability: Power, Ethos and the Technologies of Managing, International Thompson Business Press, London.

Law, J. (1999): After ANT: Complexity, Naming and Topology, in: Law, J.; Hassard J. S. (Eds): Actor Network Theory: and After, Blackwell, Oxford, pp. 1-14.

Law, J. (2002): Objects and spaces. Theory, Culture and Society 19, pp. 91-105.

Lee, N.; Hassard, J. S. (1999): Organization Unbound: Actor-Network Theory, Research Strategy and Institutional Flexibility. Organization 6, pp. 391-404.

Lehmann, F. (2004): FLOSS developers as a social formation, First Monday 9.

Lerner, J.; Tirole, J. (2001): The open source movement: Key research questions, European Economic Review 45, pp. 819.

Lerner, J.; Tirole, J. (2002): Some Simple Economics of Open Source, The Journal of Industrial Economics, 50 (2), pp. 197-234.

Ljungberg, J. (2000): Open source movements as a model for organising, European Journal of Information Systems 9, pp. 208-216.

Locke, J.; Lowe, A. (2005): ERP implementation and trust relations in post-bureaucratic organisations: A case investigation European Accounting Association Congress, Goetburg, Sweden.

Lowe, A. (2001): Casemix accounting systems and medical coding: Organisational actors balanced on "leaky black boxes", Journal of Organizational Change Management 14, pp. 79-100.

Lowe, A. D. (2004): Postsocial Relations: Toward a Performative View of Accounting Knowledge, Accounting, Auditing and Accountability Journal 17, pp. 604-628.

Lowe, A.; Locke, J. (2005): The Biography of an ERP: Fabrication of 'Best Practices' in a Virtual Object Critical Perspectives on Accounting Conference.

Lowe, A. (2007): Accounting as Representation: Some Evidence on the Disputation of Boundaries Between Production and Accounting, Critical Perspectives on Accounting in press.

Lutes, T.; Cohen, E. E. (2006): XBRL in Tax and Government, http://www.xbrl .org/GLKeyFeatures/GL_WebSeminar_LutesCohen_051215.pdf, downloaded in October 2006.

Lyotard, J. F. (1984): The Postmodern Condition, University of Minnesota Press, Minneapolis (MN).

McNamar, R. T. (2003): New technology can help avoid a second Enron. Regulation 26, pp. 62-67.

Miller, P. (1997): The multiplying machine, Accounting Organizations and Society 22, pp. 355-364.

Monteiro, E. (2001): Actor network theory and information infrastructure, in: Ciborra, C. U.; Braa, K.; Cordella, A.; Dahlbom, B.; Failla, A.; Hanseth, O.; Hepsø, V. et al. (eds): From control to drift: The dynamics of corporate information infrastructures, Oxford University Press, Oxford, pp. 71-83.

Moore, G. A. (2002): Crossing the chasm: Marketing and selling high-tech products to mainstream customers, HarperCollins, New York.

Mueller, F.; Carter, C. (2005): The Scripting of Total Quality Management within its Organizational Biography, Organization Studies 26, pp. 221-247.

Preston, A. M.; Cooper, D. J.; Coombs, R. W. (1992): Fabricating Budgets: A Study of the Production of Management Budgeting in the National Health Service, Accounting, Organizations and Society 17, pp. 561-593.

Preston, A. M.; Wright, C.; Young, J. J. (1996): IMag[in]ing annual reports, Accounting, Organizations and Society 21, pp. 113-137.

Preston, A. M.; Young, J.J. (2000): Constructing the global corporation and corporate constructions of the global: a picture essay, Accounting, Organizations and Society 25, pp. 427-449.

Quattrone, P.; Hopper, T.; (2005): A 'time-space odyssey': management control systems in two multinational organisations, Accounting, Organizations and Society 30, pp. 735-764.

Ramin, D. (2005): How eBusiness Standardization can help XBRL, 11th XBRL International Conference. Boston.

Scarbrough, H.; Swan, J. (2001): Explaining the Diffusion of Knowledge Management: The Role of Fashion, British Journal of Management 12, pp. 3-12.

Schweik, C. M.; Semenov, A. (2003): The institutional design of open source programming: Issues for addressing complex public policy and management problems, First Monday 8.

Shah, S. (2003): The nature of participation and co-ordination in open and gated source software development communities HBS - MIT Sloan Free/Open Source Software Conference: New Models of Software Development; June 19-20, Boston and Cambridge (MA).

Sliwa, C. (2000): Bloated file size an issue for XML, Computerworld.

Sliwa, C.; King, J. (2000): B-to-B hard to spell with XML: E-commerce growth may stall before disparate efforts yield concrete standards, Computerworld.

Star, S. L.; Griesemer, J. R. (1989): Institutional ecology, 'translations and boundary objects: amateurs and professionals in Berkeley's museum of vertebrate zoology. Social Studies of Science 19, pp. 387-420.

Strand, C. A.; McGuire, B. L.; Watson, L. A.; Hoffman, C. (2001): The XBRL potential, Strategic Finance 82, pp. 58-63.

Sullivan, C. (1985): Systems planning in the information age. Sloan Management Review, pp. 3-12.

Teixeira, A. (2005): What XBRL means for IFRS, Chartered Accountants Journal 84, pp. 53-54.

Tornatzky, L. G.; Klein, L. (1982): Innovation characteristics and innovation implementation, IEEE Transactions on Engineering Management 29.

Tornatzky, L. G.; Fleischer, M. (1990): The Processes of Technological Innovation: Issues in Organization and Management, Lexington Books, Massachusetts.

Tuomi, I. (2001): Internet, innovation, and open source: Actors in the network, First Monday 6.

von Hippel, E.; von Krogh, G. (2003): Open source software and the "private-collective" innovation model: Issues for organization science. Organization Science 14, pp. 209-223.

Waldt, D. (2004): XBRL: The Language of Finance and Accounting, http://www.xml.
com/pub/a/2004/03/10/xbrl.html, downloaded in June, 2006.

Wallman, S. M. H. (1997): The future of accounting and financial reporting, Part IV:
"Access accounting", Accounting Horizons 11, pp. 103-116.

Weber, S. (2004): The success of open source, Harvard University Press, Cambridge
(Ma).

Zarowin, S.; Harding, W. E. (2000): Finally, Business Talks the Same Language,
Journal of Accountancy Online Issues.

The Implications of XBRL for Financial Reporting

Alan Teixeira

International Accounting Standards Board
United Kingdom

ateixeira@iasb.org.uk

Contents

1 Introduction and Motivation

In 2000 XBRL became part of accounting terminology. An ambitious project to generate a public domain XBRL resource has attracted the support of the accounting standard setters in all leading jurisdictions as well the support of regulators, leading software houses and professionals.[1] Much has been promised and there is an ongoing debate on just how it will change financial reporting. In the XBRL discussions to date
little reference has been made to the literature on information dissemination, particularly as it relates to efficient markets, earnings management and the voluntary disclosure of financial information. In this respect the debate is incomplete and somewhat
naive. If what we know about the incentives managers face is factored into the debate
some of the claims about XBRL appear exaggerated.

The purpose of this paper is to identify the financial reporting implications of XBRL
and, in doing so, identify research opportunities. This requires specification of the purpose, characteristics, limitations and power of XBRL in the context of capital markets
research. The commentary develops as follows. Section 2 describes XBRL. Section 3
discusses Taxonomy design issues. Section 4 describes its potential implications and
the related research opportunities. Section 5 provides a summary.

2 XML and XBRL

2.1 What is XBRL?

To be able to exchange data electronically it is necessary for two parties exchanging
the data to agree on how to tag it (format) and what those tags mean (names). Once
they agree on the protocol they can generate electronic documents that use that common language and conduct business-to-business transactions. An increasingly common
method of exchanging data is through XML – eXtensible Mark-up Language.

XML is very flexible and, because the tagged data are in simple text based ASCII format, can be read into virtually any program without special interfaces. XML can be
thought of as a mediation language (or layer). It mediates between different systems
and functions. The use of mediation layers is not new. Similar approaches exist in the
telecommunication industry where, rather than creating separate interfaces between
each system, a mediation level is established as an industry standard.

---

[1] See Hannon (2001) for a description of the project.

As noted, a critical part of XML based data exchange is agreeing on the tagging protocol. Part of the XBRL initiative is the establishment of a public domain financial reporting classification system (taxonomy) which any can use as the basis for data exchange.[2] A taxonomy is analogous to a dictionary. Rather than having several different terms for the same thing such as *Receivables*, *Debtors*, *Trade Debtors* or *Accounts Receivable* the taxonomy specifies a standard term. This means a user can, using XBRL-enabled software, find that component without having to know the entity-specific term used. In principle, each type of instance document requires a taxonomy. For example a 10K filing under US GAAP would accord with an appropriate taxonomy. As a result, because GAAP is jurisdiction-specific it is considered necessary to have a taxonomy for each set of rules.[3]

XBRL is, however, much more than XML because it uses XLink (XML Linking Language) to link the XML elements together. Accounting, after all, has many well known presentation and calculation relationships and these relationships can be embedded in XBRL using XLink.

To give an analogy, the English language comprises many words. But it is the rules and conventions that define how these words are ordered and related that give the words meaning. The grammatical syntax and common use conventions allow us to use the words to deliver simple or complex messages.[4] XML tagged data can be thought of as being equivalent to the words and XBRL as the rules and conventions that give meaning to the data. The rules that define XBRL are the difference between data and information. For example, XBRL specifies the rules to allow a user to determine how certain numbers add, whether the numbers are budgeted, actual or forecast, the period or point in time financial data relates to and the authority underpinning a certain piece of information.

The electronic package containing data tagged using XBRL protocol is called an XBRL Instance. The files are in simple text based ASCII format, with the XBRL tags used to identify and describe its content. The document that contains the tagging specification for each instance document will have an associated taxonomy, which is necessary to be able to read an instance.

---

[2]   A taxonomy is XML-XBRL independent. It is the generic name for a classification system.
[3]   It is technically possible to generate a Taxonomy that meets more than one purpose, with the resultant instance documents being subsets.
[4]   To illustrate, the question *How are you?* could illicit the responses *Really good* or *Good really*. They have different meaning despite having the same two words.

3   Taxonomy Design

One of the perceived advantages of XBRL is that it helps with the development of an agreed tagging system that will facilitate data sharing. That is, data elements can be compared – such as sales to revenue – across entities or jurisdictions. At a basic level, however, Taxonomy design can impact element comparability.

3.1   The IFRS-GP and US GAAP Taxonomies

There are two dominant GAAP taxonomies currently developed or under development. They are an IFRS-GP taxonomy being overseen by the IASCF and a US GAAP taxonomy being developed principally by XBRL US. These taxonomies are contrasted in this paper since they reflect the dominant GAAP globally.

At the risk of oversimplification, the IFRS-GP and US GAAP taxonomies attempt to specify the elements required to be disclosed by their respective financial reporting standards. For example, IFRS requires the disclosure of *Cash and cash equivalents*. This item is specified as an element in the IFRS-GP taxonomy.

All taxonomy designers must make decisions about how to build their classification system. The scientific world has many stories to tell about the lack of agreement between classification systems. In a similar manner, the developers of the IFRS-GP and US GAAP taxonomies have had to make design decisions. One of the key objectives of any taxonomy is to develop it in a way that people will want to use it. To be able to use the IFRS-GP or US GAAP taxonomy users must be able to find the items they are seeking to classify (tag) consistently and easily. Two of the most common problems encountered by the designers are the presentation structure and completeness. A financial reporting taxonomy could be designed to follow the structure of financial reporting standards or financial statements, for example. Both the IFRS-GP and US GAAP taxonomies are presented using a financial statement structure.[5] This reflects the objective of creating a practical and comprehensive taxonomy. In many ways the taxonomies are similar to the model financial statements published by accountancy firms.

A consequence of this design decision is that, to be comprehensive, the taxonomy designers have needed to add many elements that are not specified by IFRS or US GAAP. These include sub-totals, for example, but also include elements that reflect the most commonly observed types of elements within required disclosures. For example, IFRS and US GAAP do not specify the classes of property, plant and equip-

---

[5]   It is possible to present a taxonomy in multiple ways. With XBRL the use of XLink makes multiple viewing much easier.

ment that must be disclosed - only that certain information about each class must be presented. Both taxonomies provide common types of classifications, such as motor vehicles and machinery. In a similar manner, the designers have constructed tables and disclosures reflecting how preparers have been observed to present information about financial instrument related risks, for example. And further, items commonly observed as being disclosed on the face of the primary financial statements are, generally, presented in the taxonomy as being part of the primary financials even if there is no specific requirement in an IFRS or US GAAP to disclose that information on the face.

In short the taxonomy designers are attempting to meet competing objectives. They are attempting to capture IFRS and US GAAP requirements as well as make the taxonomies easy to use through structure and comprehensiveness. The difficulty with the latter is that the designers cannot avoid interpreting their respective standards and implying that the taxonomy reflects an appropriate representation of the requirements of the standards. This is not problematic, of course, unless the taxonomy designers hold their taxonomies out to capture IFRS or US GAAP.

3.2   Comparability of the IFRS-GP and US GAAP Taxonomies

There is clearly a move to converge global GAAP. It is important to ask, therefore, if the IFRS-GP and US GAAP taxonomies will facilitate comparison of data across jurisdictions. There are two reasons why they might not – differences in GAAP and differences in taxonomy design.

3.2.1 GAAP

There are many differences in the way elements are measured as a result of differences in IFRS and US GAAP. These will, by construction, be reflected in the relevant taxonomies. For example IFRS allows PPE to be revalued, whereas US GAAP does not. These differences can make direct mechanical comparison of certain elements inappropriate. The differences between IFRS and US GAAP are well documented, although the economic impacts of the differences are not as well understood.

IFRS and US GAAP sometimes require elements to be disclosed in different places. For example, US GAAP treats interest payments as an operating cash flow in the Statement of Cash Flows. IFRS allows this to be classified as either an operating or financing cash flow.

XBRL facilitates the comparison of these elements. That is:

[US GAAP] Interest payments

 = [IFRS] Interest Payments (Operating)

 = [IFRS] Interest Payments (Financing).

Hence, individual elements can be mapped directly, even though they may appear in different places. However, different placement can cause the aggregations they form to differ. In this example, the *Cash from Operations* will depend on where the interest payments are placed. The existence of differences in placement of individual elements makes the comparison of the summary aggregations potentially problematic.

3.2.2 Taxonomy Design Differences

There are, for example, differences in the level of detail between taxonomies that reflect taxonomy design decisions rather than differences between IFRS and US GAAP. The US GAAP Taxonomy has more detail and, as a consequence, many elements cannot be mapped directly to the IFRS-GP taxonomy simply because there is no equivalent.

The level of detail also impacts the *Other* element, designed to capture items not otherwise specified. For example, the US GAAP taxonomy specifies *Computer Lists, Media Content* and *Customer Lists* in its list of intangibles. These are not specified in the IFRS-GP taxonomy. As a result, the taxonomy element *Other Intangibles* will differ between US GAAP and IFRS-GP taxonomies, because *Computer Lists, Media Content* and *Customer Lists* will be included in this element under the IFRS-GP definition but not the US GAAP definition.

3.2.3 Aggregation

The IAS and US Taxonomies do not always aggregate elements in the same manner. For example, the US Taxonomy has an aggregation element in non-current assets called *Investments*. There is no equivalent element in the IAS Taxonomy. It appears to be similar to investments in subsidiaries, associates and joint ventures (specified as three elements in IAS).

XBRL can facilitate cross-jurisdictional comparison of financial data. Because the jurisdictional taxonomies are designed to integrate, it should be technically possible to identify equivalencies. However, there are different levels of comparability because of differences in jurisdictional GAAP and the way the Taxonomies have been designed.

4   Implications of XBRL

4.1   Accounting Standard Setting

Although there is limited evidence in print, commentators at XBRL conferences have suggested that XBRL will have a significant impact on accounting standard setting and will eliminate GAAP differences. XBRL does not eliminate differences in GAAP interpretation. Estimates, such as the rate of depreciation and expected useful life of an asset and judgements such as whether a particular item of expenditure should be capitalised or expensed are not eliminated by XBRL. The accounting choices currently available to users can only be eliminated by regulators, not the introduction of a mediation tool. XBRL is indifferent to how a number is calculated. To claim that interpretive differences are eliminated ignores the evidence that managers have incentives to manage earnings, for many reasons. The empirical evidence supports the existence of such activity.[6] As long as some choice or flexibility exists in accounting these differences will remain.

XBRL does not prevent entities from using their own language to describe a particular component of the financial statements. XBRL allows descriptors to be incorporated in the tagging process. The differences we currently observe in terminology are therefore likely to remain, although the concept of standardisation encouraged by XBRL may transfer to the financials.

Claims have also been made that different jurisdictional definitions of GAAP will disappear with XBRL (e.g. Coffin 2001). In defence of Coffin, his assertion seems to be that XBRL will mean analysts will no longer have to reconcile differences because entities will be able to render financial statements using different XBRL taxonomies from the same data. He does not claim that we will have one GAAP. What he describes is technically feasible. As long as the data captured in an entity's information system are sufficient to apply the requirements of a specified GAAP the data can be shaped in any way.

As a simple example, interest relating to borrowings on the construction of an asset might be required to be capitalised in one jurisdiction and expensed in another. An appropriately specified database can capture sufficient information about the transaction that will allow the data to be shaped in both ways in subsequent reports. Hence, multi-GAAP reporting from one source is possible. XBRL facilitates this process. However, standard setting bodies are the only parties able to eliminate the actual dif-

---

[6]   See Jones (1991) for example.

ferences. And, apart from traditional GAAP reconciliations, there is no evidence that entities will provide users with the detail they require to reshape the data.

4.2   The Financial Reporting Supply Chain

4.2.1 Continuous Reporting

Some commentators, Coffin (2001) and Hucklesby (2000) for example, have suggested that XBRL will lead to continuous, perhaps daily, financial reporting. This view ignores the wealth of evidence on the role of regulation and the incentives managers have to keep markets informed through voluntary disclosures.[7] There is no evidence to suggest that regulators will, or should, impose more frequent financial reporting than currently exists. All XBRL allows is the fast transfer of this data should the regulators move in this direction.

This still leaves the potential that entities will move towards continuous reporting. The literature on the voluntary disclosure of financial information is mature enough to suggest that this is unlikely to happen. Companies already have the capacity to release information far more frequently than they do but it is reasonable to suggest that the proprietary cost of doing so exceeds the perceived benefit. There is also the question of what is meant by continuous reporting. Regular reporting of fundamentals such as sales or passenger loadings can be classed as continuous financial reporting. It is also less prone to measurement error than attempting to report an aggregate such as profit over a narrow window.

It is possible that XBRL will alter the cost-benefit equilibrium, by reducing costs, and it is this change is more likely to have an impact on the level of continuous reporting.

4.2.2 Web Reporting

The level and quality of Web based financial reporting has been described as disappointing by some commentators. Examples range from HTML coded pages, PDF files of printed reports to Excel spreadsheet data. Reporting via the web is often viewed as an additional cost to companies, supplementing their traditional reports rather than replacing them.

XBRL has the potential to increase the level and quality of web based reporting because of the standardisation of tagging. There are potential research projects examining the effectiveness of different communication methods. For example, there is evidence that footnote disclosures are treated differently to the primary financial state-

---

[7]   See Healy and Palepu (1993) and Skinner (1994) for example.

ments. Whether this is true in a web environment, particularly where readers are able to manage some of the presentation structure, is a potential area of interest. And at a basic level, the impact of XBRL on the level of Web based reporting is also of interest.

Hodge et al. (2004) provide the first evidence that an enabling technology such as XBRL can impact the decision making processes of users. It appears to reduce search costs. This is an area of research potential and international interest (see also Debreceny 2005).

4.2.3 Audit Process

Increased reliance on continuous auditing is a natural consequence of moving all the components of the annual report into databases from which XBRL instance documents may be rendered. The mapping of the ledger to the XBRL taxonomy and the mapping of the taxonomy to a web site would require verification. And the audit process might focus on managing database changes, so that any amendments to accounting policies or notes are identified and verified. The process by which reconciliations and supporting notes are compiled would also need to be verified.[8]

Web reporting will undoubtedly become more prevalent, even without XBRL. There are at least two components to attestation on a Web financial report that affect the audit process. The first is web-reporting authentication involving the security of the site itself. The second is a communication issue associated with moving between audited and non-audited sections of the site. Auditors need to develop principles that ensure users are aware of whether the material they are viewing has been audited or not. Researchers have opportunities to examine the audit process generally and the effectiveness of different communication methods.

4.2.4 Electronic Rendering of Financial Statements

If agreement can be reached on this tagging system, and it is clearly more complex than invoice exchange, the possibility exists for companies to be able to file financial statements electronically with regulators, such as EDGAR, stock exchanges, tax authorities and banks (as part of reporting under debt contracts). This happens now, but each application has its own set of rules. XBRL could well subsume these.

The possibilities extend beyond regulatory filing. Each electronic document generated (the instance document) can be used for other purposes. For example, it can be the data from which information is rendered onto the Web or directly to print software. Soft-

---

[8]   See Woodroof and Searcy (2001) for a more detailed discussion.

ware is also being developed to take instance documents and conduct financial statement analysis. There have been claims that electronic rendering will reduce bank loan processing times, improve loan decision making, improve financial statement analysis (and investment decision making) and improve bankruptcy prediction. These are interesting claims that beg analysis.

4.2.5 System to System - Consolidations

Some entities have many different accounting or information systems. Consolidating or sharing this information between systems can require manual intervention. In some cases software vendors develop exchange interfaces that allow their product to import or export to another specified product. XBRL can alleviate the need for multiple interfaces by creating a mediation layer. As long as *Navision* and *Peoplesoft*, for example, can create and read an XBRL instance document these two systems could exchange financial statement data seamlessly.

There will be consequences on the financial reporting supply chain that invite analysis, but researchers will need to move relatively quickly and be patient. Quickly, because an analysis of the impact of XBRL on the supply chain will require documentation of existing supply chains. Patient, because it will take time for XBRL to alter the supply chain.

4.3 Dissemination and Market Efficiency

XBRL has potential implications for market efficiency. Stice (1991) investigated whether stock prices react to the public filing of an SEC 10K form, with quarterly earnings, or the publication of the same information in the WSJ (Wall Street Journal). In most cases the filing and announcement dates were the same, but in some instances the WSJ publication lagged by four days or more. Stice found that stock prices reacted to the WSJ publication. The period Stice examined was characterised by manual processing of 10K forms. Even though the filings were *in the public domain* it appears the costs of monitoring for cases of a WSJ announcement lag exceeded any benefit. Hence, stock prices, at best, reflected the earnings announcement information in the WSJ but not necessarily the information in the SEC filings. It is unlikely that these results would persist today, given the electronic submission of filings. Simply, the electronic exchange of information reduces transaction costs. The Stice study illustrates that any process that relies on the manual (or even semi-automatic) transformation of data has the potential to either delay the release of potentially price sensitive information into the public domain or add interpretive noise to the data.

Any jurisdiction with a dissemination process that involves manual translation of data, summarisation or non-simultaneous distribution could benefit from XBRL. Examining the impact of XBRL in eliminating dissemination inequities is a potential research issue.

4.4   Research Databases

XBRL has the capacity to improve the quality of the data used for archival empirical accounting research. Lev (1989) challenged returns-earnings researchers to shift the focus to research on the quality of earnings, where accounting rules and measurements would be considered explicitly. He suggested a shift to research on the quality of earnings, where accounting rules and measurements would be considered explicitly. Such research, he notes, "… has the potential both to further our understanding of the role of financial information in asset valuation and to contribute meaningfully to accounting policymaking" (Lev 1989, p. 175-176). Brennan (1991) and Beaver (1999) also comment on accounting policy matters. Brennan, for example, notes:

"In addition to simple errors of measurement, the definition of earnings used in these studies would seem to be of importance. Yet the careful consideration given by practising accountants to the manner in which earnings are reported, and to which items are included in earnings, stands in marked contrast to the casual attitude of most researchers toward the definition of the variable under investigation" (Brennan 1991, p. 73).

Differences in measurement transformations result from choices made by rule makers and by managers (when rule makers give them choice). Whatever measurement rules are used they have balance sheet and earnings implications. Accounting researchers who use accounting earnings in earnings-returns studies are assuming that all components are valued the same and that measurement and aggregation differences between firms are unimportant. These are brave assumptions. Beaver (1999) suggests that an extension of the ability of simple accounting summary measures to explain current prices is to "incorporate more accounting into the analysis" (Beaver 1999, p. 41).

COMPUSTAT and other similar databases do not provide easy access to the accounting policy specifications adopted by entities (including depreciation rates for example), which are the conditioning variables on which the earnings, assets and liabilities are measured. XBRL offers the potential to provide enriched data sets by coding these policies. However, this will require a change in the current XBRL Taxonomy specification.

To illustrate, current taxonomies treat accounting policy elements as simple text fields. A more powerful approach is to separate the policy into components using what we know about accounting rules. Accounting methods could be specified using boolean values and quantitative components expressed separately. To illustrate, for each class of assets within *Property, Plant and Equipment* the taxonomy could specify boolean value (true/false) for depreciation methods identified as *straight line, reducing balance* and *other*, (with a field ensuring the reporting entity specifies the actual method used). The asset lives, actual rates of depreciation and residual values could then be specified as a range of numeric values, such as *5* and *10* years specifying the lower and upper life expectancies within a class.

This approach is a departure from most taxonomies produced to date, but it would add considerable power to the analytical potential of instance documents both to analysts and researchers. It would allow researchers and analysts to adjust earnings and readily identify accounting policy differences.

The most common source of accounting data in empirical accounting research is currently COMPUSTAT, from *Standard and Poor's*. The company states, with some pride, that they remove variability and bias from the data to normalize it.[9] This can be problematic, particularly when the data are used in studies of manager reporting behaviour. The legitimacy of inferences drawn about earnings management from data that have been adjusted and managed by COMPUSTAT must be questionable. Teixeira (2001b) has found, for example, that information conveyed by managers in financial statements and earnings announcements is significantly more informative than the same information standardized using adjustments analogous to those used by COMPUSTAT. That is, the discretion exercised by managers was itself informative. Removing manager bias reduced earnings informativeness. Whether the COMPUSTAT procedures bias the analysis reported in the literature is an open question.

5   Conclusions

The implications of XBRL are conjecture. To begin, XBRL is not widely used by entities. Until that happens research opportunities are likely to be relatively limited. It is analogous to assessing the impact of the switch from manual to computerised record keeping in accounting. However, for those interested in the impact of XBRL on the

---

[9] Standard and Poor's Website http://www.compustat.com/www/db/standardize.html

supply chain it will be important that pre-XBRL procedures are documented before XBRL becomes more widely used.

In this chapter, I have suggested that many of the claims made by observers about the implications of XBRL are likely to be exaggerated. Nevertheless, XBRL has the potential to have a significant impact on the external financial reporting function through its impact on the costs and effectiveness of the dissemination process. There are many interesting questions that beg enquiry. And among the bigger beneficiaries are researchers who will potentially have richer and less biased databases available to assist them in answering these questions.

References

Beaver, W. H.; (1999): Comments on - An empirical assessment of the residual income valuation model, Journal of Accounting & Economics, 26 (1-3), pp. 35-42.

Brennan, M.; (1991): A perspective on accounting and stock prices, Accounting Review, 66 (1), pp. 67-79.

Coffin, Z. (2001): The top 10 effects of XBRL, Management Accounting, 82 (12), pp. 64-67.

Debreceny, R. S.; Chandra, A., Cheh, J. J.; Guithues-Amrhein, D.; Hannon, N. J.; Hutchison, P. D.; Janvrin, D.; Jones, R. A.; Lamberton, B.; Lymer, A.; Mascha, M.; Nehmer, R.; Roohani, S.; Srivastava, R. P.; Trabelsi, S.; Tribunella, T.; Trites, G.; Vasarhelyi, M. A. (2005): Financial Reporting in XBRL on the SEC's EDGAR System: A Critique and Evaluation, Journal of Information Systems, 19 (2), pp. 191-210.

Hannon, N. (2001): XBRL: what it is and what it isn't, Management Accounting, 82 (9), pp. 69-70.

Healy, P. M. Palepu, K. G., (1993): The effect of firms' financial disclosure strategies on stock prices, Accounting Horizons, 7 (1), p. 1-11.

Hodge, F. D.; Kennedy, J. J.; Maines, L. A.; (2004): Recognition versus Disclosure in Financial Statements: Does Searchable Technology Improve Transparency?, Accounting Review, 79 (3), pp. 687-703.

Hucklesby, M. and Macdonald, J. (2000): XBRL = Better, faster, cheaper, Chartered Accountants Journal of New Zealand, 79 (8), pp. 34-36.

Jones, J. J. (1991): Earnings management during import relief investigation, Journal of Accounting Research, 29 (2), pp. 193-228.

Lev, B. (1989): On the usefulness of earnings: lessons and directions from two decades of empirical research, Journal of Accounting Research, 27, pp. 153-192.

Skinner, D. (1994): Why firms voluntarily disclose bad news, Journal of Accounting Research, 32 (1), pp. 38-60.

Stice, E. K. (1991): The market reaction to 10-K and 10-Q filings and to subsequent The Wall Street Journal earnings announcements, Accounting Review, 66 (1), pp. 42-55.

Teixeira, A. (2001): GAAP, Manager Discretion and Earnings Quality, The University of Auckland Business School.

Woodroof, J.; Searcy, D. (2001), Continuous audit; Model development and implementation within a debt covenant compliance domain, International Journal of Accounting Information Systems, 2 (3), pp. 169-191.

A Theoretical Framework for Examining the Corporate Adoption Decision Involving XBRL as a Continuous Disclosure Reporting Technology

Robert Pinsker

Old Dominion University,
USA

rpinsker@odu.edu

Contents

1 Introduction[1]

For some time regulators across the globe have been advocating a more modern financial reporting process that would provide additional information (i.e., mainly nonfinancial) in a timelier manner (the AICPA's Jenkins Committee (1994), Financial Accounting Standards Board (FASB; 2000)). Recent regulation, such as Sarbanes-Oxley
section 409 (henceforth, 409; 2002) in the United States and the Corporation Act in
Australia, are requiring public firms to report material information more quickly than
ever before.[2] Since the information being reported to the regulators is also publicly
available, firms need to consider the adoption and consequent use of a technology that
is 1) capable of continuous disclosure (CD); 2) can work with existing Enterprise Resource Planning (ERP) systems to internally gather and then externally report required
information quickly and reliably; and 3) comply with appropriate regulation.[3,4]

XBRL (eXtensible Business Reporting Language) is a relatively new technology that
makes facilitates CD. It has been called a "fundamental transformation in the way
business reporting information will be exchanged" by the Chair of the AICPA (Editorial Staff 2004). XBRL *tags* data and allows it to be disseminated internally or externally regardless of software or hardware (Deshmukh 2004). However, given the traditionally substantial time and monetary costs involved with new information technology (IT) adoption (e.g., electronic data interchange (EDI), database management systems, etc.), many firms have typically taken a *wait-and-see* approach, depending on if
the specific IT is mandated or not. Regulatory mandate of firms to use a specific IT
has been rare, especially in the U.S. Thus, there remains a large amount of uncertainty
whether firms would adopt a CD technology, such as XBRL, that could quickly and
reliably disseminate all required information. Firms may choose to continue using in-

---

[1] I would like to thank Vicky Arnold, Kalle Lyytinen, Shaomin Li, the Old Dominion University
workshop participants, the 2004 Information Systems section midyear meeting participants of the
American Accounting Association, and two anonymous reviewers from the Sixth International Research Symposium on Accounting Information Systems for their helpful comments and suggestions.

[2] For example, if material (i.e., would affect the decision of a *reasonable* user), 409 requires reporting of earnings information, changes in management, and bankruptcies within four days of occurrence. The prior regulation required 15 days to disclose. Sections 674 and 675 of the Corporation
Act require continuous disclosure of similar information; meaning the information is to be reported
the same day as occurrence.

[3] For purposes of the current paper, a CD technology is defined as one that is capable of complying
with the particular jurisdictional disclosure requirements. Given inherent differences across country
requirements, it is not possible to generalize a definition.

[4] The term "firm" in the current paper refers to public corporations, since they typically affect a larger number of market stakeholders than private companies.

formation being derived from disparate sources and *static* presentation technologies (e.g., HTML (Hypertext Markup Language) and PDF (Portable Document File)), while hoping to be able to meet regulatory requirements.[5]

The ultimate goal of technology innovation research is to provide guidance to managers on the questions of whether, when, and how to innovate with IT (Swanson, Ramiller 2004). The purpose of the current paper is to present a theoretical framework, which explores the uncertainty surrounding the firm CD technology adoption decision and, thus, attempt to answer the *whether* question.[6] The purpose is consistent with prior IT innovation research concerned with understanding the factors that facilitate or inhibit the adoption of emerging technologies (see Fichman 2004). XBRL, which has the support of over 300 governmental and private entities, is referred to as the CD technology example throughout the paper for purposes of visualizing a live example.[7]

Four interdisciplinary adoption theories (computer mediated communication apprehension (CMCA), technology acceptance model (TAM), absorptive capacity and neighborhood effect) are considered in the current paper's framework. Contrary to several prior IT adoption frameworks, the current paper's framework recognizes the existence of both individual and organizational decision-making, the possibility of multiple theories as explanation for adoption, and does not limit the applicability of absorptive capacity to only high technology firms (George et al. 2001). According to Huber (1990), integrating theories from the organizational (absorptive capacity), communication (CMCA), and information systems' (TAM) domains can help researchers in each domain become more aware of the existence, content, and relevance of research in the other fields (e.g., agriculture (neighborhood effect)). Additionally, the paper responds to Fichman's (1992) call for multi-level adoption research (i.e., adoption at the individual and organizational levels) by using a management theory that appears to be most applicable (i.e., Li et al.'s (2004) theory). The diverse nature of the theoretical framework provided should stimulate empirical research to contribute to the general knowledge of corporate IT adoption decisions. Such knowledge would

---

[5] Pre 409 and XBRL reporting required information within the required time was difficult for companies. Carter and Soo (1999) reported a significant amount of compliance violations for Form 8-K filers with respect to reporting timelines. Thus, this problem may be exacerbated if a CD technology (e.g., XBRL) is not adopted, given the apparent global shift to faster reporting.

[6] Please see Li and Pinsker (2005) for the "when" and Guithues Amrhein et al. (2006) for the "how."

[7] The focus of this paper is on management's XBRL (as a CD technology) adoption decision (consistent with the initiation stage of Rogers' (1983) model) for external reporting. Adoption benefits to investors, as well as to management in the form of internal reporting are outside of the intended purpose of the paper.

be useful not only to IT personnel, but also to accountants called upon to help corporate clients with the CD technology adoption decision.

Since many countries do not currently require CD or use of a technology capable of it, the framework presented is ex ante in nature. However, ex ante research provides an exciting opportunity for the early advancement of knowledge in a given area (in this case, management decision making). Additionally, given the recent increase in governmentally-required continuous disclosure (e.g., in Australia, the United Kingdom, and Japan (Hucklesby 2003; The CPA Letter 2002) and major accounting scandals (e.g., Enron and WorldCom), the need for management to consider a specific CD technology for disclosure is growing.[8] CD technology adoption differs from other IT adoption/innovation research in two ways: 1) the CD technology adoption decision is international in scale; and 2) CD involves externally communicating to those outside of the supply chain (e.g., investors).

The paper proceeds with a brief description of XBRL, followed by an explanation for the application of multi-level theories. Then, presentation of the competing theories and descriptions of the applicable research proposition are provided. The paper concludes with a summary and ideas for future research.

2 XBRL: A Leading Technology Capable of CD

2.1 Description

"XBRL is a data description language that enables the exchange of understandable, uniform business information. It is based on XML (Extensible Markup Language) and permits the automatic exchange and reliable extraction of financial information across all software formats and technologies, including the Internet," (xbrl.org white paper 2002, 5). Information *tagged* in XBRL can include critical nonfinancial performance measure data. This type of data is typically difficult to aggregate and disseminate quickly using other technologies.

2.2 Potential Reasons for Adoption

Through its use of XML Web Services (i.e., Web-based applications that share data by *talking* to other Web applications) and a standard Web protocol (like Simple Object Access Protocol (SOAP)), information tagged in XBRL is freely communicated across technology media (such as the Internet). In combination with the XBRL General

---

[8] Internationally, this is evidenced by those involved with International Financial Reporting Standards (IFRS) working closely with those involved in XBRL's taxonomies (Li, Pinsker 2005).

Ledger taxonomy, XBRL usage allows for automation and integration of the manual data entry, gathering, and reporting processes. In sum, using XBRL, a company can capture, tag, process, and report information over the Internet reliably in minutes making CD a reality (Guithues Amrhein et al. 2006).

Many significant benefits are expected to accrue to XBRL users as a result. A recent XBRL white paper (2002) listed benefits of XBRL, some of which apply to corporate adopters. Those benefits include minimized cost by allowing more automatic composition and processing of reports to different clients and more confidence in data presented through limiting the risk of erroneous data entry (i.e., the data is only entered once). Pinsker and Li (2006) find corroborating evidence to the benefits listed by interviewing companies across the globe that have fully implemented XBRL into their accounting information systems.

Regulatory bodies in countries such as Australia (through the *Continuous Disclosure initiative*), the UK (through the *Inland Revenue Service*), and the U.S. (through the *SEC's XBRL pilot program*), are interested in more frequent disclosure to themselves and investors. The reusability of XBRL data benefit could result in significant cost savings related to reducing the number of redundant documents. Specifically, businesses in the U.S. alone produce approximately 100 billion documents per year. Many of the documents are produced in various formats, inaccessible to some, requiring the generation of new documents with the same data. Such redundant work is costly to organizations. Deshmukh (2004) estimates almost 20% of U.S. GNP is spent on generating new information, even though 90% of this information already exists in other documents.

There are alternative technologies to XBRL that could facilitate CD. For example, straight XML use could achieve similar results as XBRL use (since XBRL is based on XML). Also, various ERP software combined with a presentation technology (e.g., PDF) could create a fairly quick reporting environment, although perhaps not meeting the applicable regulatory definition of *continuous*, since the data captured by the ERP software would need to be transferred into a PDF format. Therefore, even though XBRL is a leading technology whose use is capable of producing CD, it is not the only option available to firms looking simply to comply with current reporting regulation.

3   Use of Individual and Organizational Theories

In many circumstances, firm subunits are responsible for selecting a proposal for action when faced with making various decisions (Huber 1990). Aside from the many individuals who might participate in this process, there is typically one individual or one group of individuals who is formally accountable for the decision. Accordingly, decision-making may be centered on the formal leader or distributed to various members of the specific firm unit (Duncan 1974).

In terms of IT, Fichman's (1992) theoretical model helped explain the results from various organizational decisions made in past IT adoption and diffusion studies. The model, based on an expansion of classical diffusion theory, used four cells and classified the studies according to the locus of adoption (i.e., individual or firm) and class of technology (i.e., the levels of knowledge burden and user interdependencies). According to the model, U.S. firm adoption studies look at adoption in large aggregates, such as companies and agencies. The typical dependent variable is a binary adoption/non-adoption scenario. Thus, using Fichman's model, the corporate adoption decision of a CD technology (e.g., XBRL) would appear to be a firm-level study.

However, the typical firm structure of smaller U.S. firms is characterized by more centralized, autonomous decision-making (Fichman 1992). Further, since the CD technology adoption issue is on a global scale, a more macro approach to adoption should complement micro-level firm theories. Korpela (1996) challenged the *cultural approach* by stating it is the political economy, and not cultural attributes, that is the main determinant of IT adoption. This view is consistent with Robey's (1977, 1979) environmental/systems perspective of IT adoption.

Li et al. (2004) proposed a theoretical model to further explain IT adoption in various countries. Their model focuses on the nature and dynamics of corporate officer relations and their role as a governance mechanism in two types of governance systems: rule-based and relation-based. When a society is governed by a general rule of law (i.e., laws and regulations are transparent, fair, and universally applied), it is classified as a rule-based country. Rule-based countries work well when there are efficient information infostructures that provide accurate micro-level information on business and economic activities. An important element of the infostructure is the accounting system, of which, financial reporting is critical (for public firms). Common characteristics of rule-based countries include a high level of public trust, codification of key information, and decentralized decision-making. Firms in the U. S., UK, and other western countries would be considered to be in rule-based countries.

Contrary to rule-based countries, relation-based countries exist in societies where public rules are unfair, opaque, with a general lack of rule of law and firms tend to rely on personal relations to govern their interests (Li et al. 2004). A central feature of relation-based countries is that information is largely local and private, due to the reliance of relations instead of a verifiable, public marketplace. Given the private aspect of information, relation-based countries tend to exhibit a more centralized organizational structure with the head holding absolute authority. In many cases, the head of the firm often controls all key information and makes all the important decisions, including IT-related ones (Li 2005). Eastern countries, such as China and Taiwan, as well as all developing countries are relation-based examples.

In summary, corporate location and consequent governance systems are critical factors in addressing the decision to adopt a CD technology. According to Li et al. (2004), and supported by Weidenbaum (1996), the decision to adopt can be decentralized and decided by many corporate participants, or centralized and decided by only top management. Additionally, Fichman (1992) concluded either an individual within a firm or the firm as a whole makes the initial adoption decision for similar technologies. Given the diversity in decision-making, Fichman called for future research to employ a mixed (i.e., both individual and firm) level research design. The current paper answers this call by including two adoption theories for both levels, including two theories discussed in Fichman's analysis: the Technology Acceptance Model (TAM) for the individual level and absorptive capacity for the firm level. The next section describes the four competing theories that may be used as a framework for future research examining the CD technology adoption decision-making process.

4   Adoption Theories and Propositions

4.1   Logic Behind Specific Theories Chosen

The four competing theories to be described next were chosen in aggregate for three reasons. First, the essence of all four theories has application to the IT adoption decision-making process; whereas, some IT-specific theories and frameworks (e.g., diffusion of innovation; Gallivan's (2001) framework) apply more to IT post-adoption, implementation or diffusion processes. Second, the theories have either been included in Fichman's IT adoption (1992) model (e.g., TAM, absorptive capacity) or apply to Li et al.'s (2004) IT model (e.g., Computer Mediated Communication Apprehension, neighborhood effect). Finally, according to Huber (1990), integrating theories from the organizational (absorptive capacity), communication (CMCA), and information systems' (TAM) domains can help researchers in each domain become more aware of the existence, content, and relevance of research in the other fields (e.g., agriculture (neighborhood effect)). In combination, both Fichman and Li et al's models serve as the underlying foundation for the current paper's research framework. The theories are presented in terms of their locus of decision-making, with individual theories before firm-level theories.

5   Individual Decision Making - Computer Mediated Communication Apprehension (CMCA)

Business reporting is a communication between the reporting firm and the information stakeholders (e.g. regulators, stockholders). Newer communication technologies provide more avenues for communicating (Perse, Courtright 1993), which impact traditional media use (Williams et al. 1985). Williams et al. suggested research should investigate the use of interactive media as a "convenient substitute" for traditional forms of communication. One example of interactive media is the Internet. The Internet is becoming an increasingly popular reporting medium due to its low cost and reliability (FASB 2000).

Recent computer mediated communication (CMC) research has identified Uses and Gratifications (U&G) as the most appropriate theoretical framework for its hypothesis testing (Flaherty et al. 1998). U&G is based on five underlying assumptions: communication behavior is goal-directed, purposive, and motivated; people are active in selecting and using communication vehicles to satisfy needs; people are able to identify their own communication motives and gratifications; the media compete with other forms of communication for attention, selection, and use; and people are influenced by various social and psychological factors when selecting among communication alternatives. U&G is suitable for both mediated and interpersonal research (Rubin, Rubin 1985) and is applicable for studying new communication technologies (Rubin, Bantz 1987).

The majority of the prior CMC research has focused on organizational settings, interactions (Rice 1993; Steinfield 1986), or political computer bulletin boards (Garramone et al. 1986). Other researchers have chosen to focus on the uses of communication channels through various message channels (Perse, Courtright 1993) and computer mediated communication (Walther, Burgoon 1992), among other channels. In sum, these studies provide evidence for the impact of changing technologies on interpersonal communication and imply that communication technologies (like the Internet) may be functional alternatives to face-to-face interactions (Flaherty et al. 1998). However, less is known whether communication technologies like the Internet are viable, functional alternatives to paper-based communication (i.e., annual reports) or if the combination of increased speed of reporting in conjunction with changing a communication medium is perceived by regulators and investors as being a more valuable form of communication.[9] An avenue of future CMCA research, beyond CD technology adoption examined in the current paper, would be to examine these questions surrounding Internet communication.

Adopting a CD technology such as XBRL should force management to interact with regulators (and, therefore, investors) much more often (see SEC's XBRL pilot project in the U.S.). The benefit for regulators and investors would be quicker access to firm information. As a result, communication via a CD technology could result in more requests for firm information. The firm would be reaching regulators and investors more quickly, many times in a global sense, using a CD technology, as compared to paper-based reporting.

Reaching regulators and investors more quickly may cause managers to view interactive communications (Internet reporting using a XBRL) with apprehension or anxiety. Internet-based reporting will require a faster processing and dissemination of information. Thus, it is foreseeable that the likelihood of the information containing errors or otherwise incorrect information is increased, raising the opportunities for litigation (a potentially large financial burden on the firm).

Presuming a non-mandatory situation involving a CD technology adoption, firm executives using a XBRL would have greater exposure to a global marketplace (regulatory and capital market). Thus, the raw facts (i.e., whatever the firm is required to and voluntarily discloses) will be out there for everyone to see with firm being somewhat protected from misinterpretation (Wilson 2003). However, should the information disclosed be inaccurate, the firm would have greater risk exposures in the form of litigation if it is relied upon by information stakeholders (i.e., the relevance-reliability trade-off; Hunton et al. 2003).

In countries not mandating some form of continuous disclosure, the incumbent, interim and annual reporting process affords managers more time and flexibility in regards to processing and disseminating information than would a process requiring use of a CD technology. Thus, managers could potentially feel apprehension about switching to a technology that affords them a significantly quicker reporting process. However, managers' perceptions of the benefits of XBRL adoption (previously discussed) may outweigh the costs apprehension would provide (especially if the level of apprehension

---

[9] Regulation, such as 409, and Regulation Fair Disclosure (2000) almost requires electronic communication due to its short timeline for compliance.

is relatively low). Therefore, if the individual who is responsible for the CD technology adoption decision is able to envision a favorable cost/benefit scenario switching from a non-CD capable technology to XBRL, that individual should have low apprehension levels and choose to adopt. Clarke (1991) developed a scale measuring apprehension applicable to this context. It would represent a good measure for testing the proposition below.

Consistent with the current discussion and the fifth U&G assumption (i.e., people are influenced by various social and psychological factors when selecting among communication alternatives), the following proposition is offered:

Proposition 1:   **XBRL adoption will result if the adoption decision-maker has a low level of CMCA.**

5.1   Individual Decision Making - The Technology Acceptance Model (TAM)

A major focus of Information Systems (IS) innovation research has been how potential users' perceptions of an information technology (IT) influence its adoption (Al-Gahtani 2001). User acceptance has often been seen as a critical factor determining the success or failure of IS projects, such as adopting an IT (Attewell, Rule 1984; Davis 1993). Igbaria et al. (1997) reported that system usage has been the primary indicator of IT acceptance in technology diffusion research; however, there are potentially several indicators of IT acceptance in pre-adoption scenarios.

A practical theory that posits IT acceptance contingent upon the perceived user usefulness and perceived ease of use indicators is the TAM. "TAM is an adaptation of the theory of reasoned action (TRA) from psychology specifically tailored for modeling user acceptance of information technology," (Al-Gahtani 2001, 40). The TAM differs from the TRA in two ways. First, the TAM does not include subjective norms because of their uncertain theoretical and psychometric statuses (Davis et al. 1989). Second, the TAM posits only two beliefs – perceived usefulness and perceived ease of use – in predicting an individual's attitude towards adopting an IT as opposed to an expectancy formulation of beliefs used in the TRA.

One measure of the TAM, *perceived usefulness*, is defined as: "the degree to which a person believes that using a particular system would enhance his/her job performance," (Davis 1989, 320). Adams et al. (1992), Davis (1989), and Davis et al. (1989) all reported that user acceptance of an IT is driven to a large extent by perceived usefulness. Further, Davis (1993) argued that perceived usefulness is the most influential determinant of IT acceptance.

The TAM's *attitude toward adoption* contains many different definitions. In the context of the TAM (adapted from Davis 1993), attitude toward adoption can be defined as the degree of perceived effect that an individual associates with adopting a current IT in his/her job. Attitudes guide perceptions, information processing, and behavior. Both attitudes and perceived usefulness have empirically demonstrated significant positive direct effects on IT acceptance (Davis 1989; Al-Gahtani 2001). However, perceived usefulness (in terms of the perceived benefits of adoption), and a manager's attitudes toward the technology, can represent powerful barriers to adoption if either or both are negative.

The TAM is flexible when considering the stage of IT adoption. For adoption research, the TAM actually attempts to capture the individual's intent to accept the IT, rather than IT acceptance through system usage (Agarwal 2000). As will be explained at the end of the current paper, this feature favors using TAM over diffusion of innovation theories in terms of measuring adoption decision-making.

A key purpose of the TAM is to provide a theoretical basis for tracing the impact of external factors on internal beliefs and attitudes (Al-Gahtani 2001). The TAM accomplishes its purpose by identifying a small number of fundamental variables from prior research dealing with the cognitive and affective determinants of IT acceptance. In terms of pre-adoption attitudes toward IT acceptance, an expanded TAM incorporates Karahanna et al.'s (1999) findings that individual attitudes are based on a multifaceted belief structure that includes perceived usefulness and perceived ease of use. It is this expanded TAM presented in figure 1 that would be most beneficial for empirical testing under the current paper's framework.

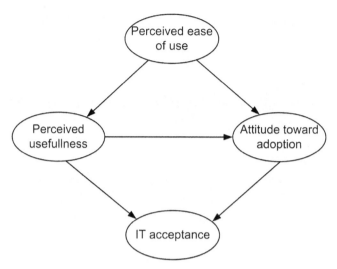

Figure 1: The Expanded (for Attitudes) Technology Acceptance Model (Adapted from Karahanna et al. 1999, Al-Gahtani 2001 and Davis 1989)

Therefore, if the manager responsible for the CD technology adoption decision perceives the benefits to outweigh the barriers and costs, that individual will perceive XBRL to be useful and increase the allocation of the managerial, financial, and technological resources necessary to implement the technology (i.e., choose to adopt; Benbasat et al. 1993). The author is unaware of any mixed findings (i.e., perceived usefulness and attitude have opposite results). Thus, the following propositions are offered:

Proposition 2a: **XBRL adoption will result if the adoption decision-maker has high levels of perceived usefulness toward the technology.**

Proposition 2b: **XBRL adoption will result if the adoption decision-maker has a favorable attitude toward the XBRL and technology in general.**

As previously noted, perceived ease of use has also been used as a variable under the TAM. However, it has been shown to typically possess an indirect/antecedent effect on IT acceptance (Davis 1989, 1993) when used in a combined statistical analysis with perceived usefulness. Due to the lesser potential impact of the variable, the current paper makes no proposition concerning perceived ease of use. Researchers testing the above propositions should use Davis's (1989) scales for perceived usefulness and Karahanna et al.'s (1999) scales for attitude.

5.2   Firm-Level Decision Making - Absorptive Capacity

The ability to evaluate and utilize outside knowledge is critical to a firm's innovativeness (Cohen, Levinthal 1990). This ability is largely based on prior related knowledge. The knowledge may include technological developments in a given field, such as using a CD technology for regulatory reporting (Fichman, Kemerer 1997). Thus, the concept of absorptive capacity refers to a firm's ability to recognize the value of new information, assimilate it, and apply it to commercial ends based on the collective prior knowledge of its employees (Malhotra et al. 2005). Simply stated, a firm's absorptive capacity is its ability to acquire and absorb new knowledge (Link and Siegel 2002).

Absorptive capacity not only considers the acquisition of new knowledge and technologies, but also the potential for exploitation. Thus, absorptive capacity does not only depend on the firm's interface with the external environment, but the transfers of knowledge and relationships within as well (Cohen, Levinthal 1990). The communications among the various organizational units become critical, with some parties assuming *gatekeeper* roles in order to monitor and translate the new information in an understandable fashion. In terms of CD technology adoption, once the decision to adopt has been made, executives could be considered the gatekeepers of the technology, monitoring its use among the various firm units ensuring communication and assimilation of knowledge across functional boundaries.

The risk of an organization not investing to increase its absorptive capacity in a quick moving technological environment is it may never assimilate and exploit new information (Cohen, Levinthal 1990). This is called *lockout* and according to Cohen, Levinthal can occur for two reasons. First, when a firm decides not to develop its absorptive capacity in technology initially, it may not be aware of the significance of signals that could ordinarily cause it to revise its expectations and develop. The effect causes unappreciated new opportunities for development that are not taken advantage of.

Second, the lack of early investment in absorptive capacity makes it more costly to develop in subsequent periods (i.e., early adopter advantage). As Zahra and George's (2002) model indicates, the level of early investment (and consequent advantage) may be due to a firm's realized, rather than potential absorptive capacity. If cost cutting is part of the firm's strategy, more costly technological investments can be seen as unattractive to executives and, thus, not adopted (despite the pressure to conform; consistent with high potential, but low realization). Therefore, not investing in absorptive capacity early on in the IT development stage could result in a firm never investing in that IT and, thus, hurting its knowledge growth and preventing other adoption benefits. For example, not adopting XBRL could result in unrealized process savings through improved reporting efficiencies, which could have spilled over to a reduced cost of capital.

Cohen, Levinthal (1990) argued that a firm's aspiration level in a technologically progressive environment (like regulatory reporting is becoming, if it is not already there) is determined by its past performance and its absorptive capacity. Therefore, the higher a given aspiration level (e.g., the increasingly popular zero defects and continuous improvement corporate landscapes) and firm expertise (and associated absorptive capacity), the more sensitive it is likely to be to emerging technological opportunities. Firms with higher levels of absorptive capacity will be more proactive in regards to exploiting opportunities present in its technical environment, while firms that have lesser levels of absorptive capacity will tend to be more reactive and not exploiting its opportunities (Cohen, Levinthal 1990).

Despite a firm's aspirations, its absorptive capacity may be hindered because of its resource availability. This concept is called *organizational readiness*. Iacovou et al. (1995, 467) define organizational readiness as "the availability of the needed organizational resources." It can be broken down into two parts: 1) the level of financial resources and 2) the technological resources of the firm. The level of financial resources involving CD technology adoptions includes: training, installation costs of relevant software, implementation of any subsequent improvements, and ongoing expenses during usage. Except for possibly training (due to the responsibility related to reporting to many different stakeholders), using XBRL as an example, adoption of a CD technology should appear as favorable to firms, because of its freely available status and relatively low cost of software. Technological resources are concerned with the level of sophistication of IT usage and IT management in a firm. Both need to be considered ex ante in the CD technology adoption decision.

A unique characteristic of CD technology adoption (again using XBRL as the example) is that it is not limited to certain industries. As George et al. (2001) indicate, all prior absorptive capacity research has been conducted within the high technology industry. Firms in this industry are typical early adopters and the technologies researched have not been mandated. As previously discussed in the Introduction section of the current paper, although mandated use of XBRL (or any other CD technology) is rare for any country, recent regulation is requiring many firms to report information to regulators quicker than ever before. It only follows that firms, irrespective of industry, would require a technology to make compliance possible. Further, high levels of absorptive capacity promote innovative firm behavior as a way to identify and exploit new technologies (van den Bosch et al. 1999), although this behavior has not been studied outside of the high technology industry.

In sum, Iacovou et al. (1995) suggest that organizational readiness (and its components) may be needed for IT integration. However, before integration, a firm should assess these factors in determining its level of absorptive capacity. Otherwise, the costs involved could cause severe inefficiencies or in the extreme cases, lack of ability to use should the firm go ahead and make the decision to adopt.

Based on the previous discussion, firms with higher aspirations result in higher levels of absorptive capacity and are more likely to be sensitive to emerging technologies. Consequently, firms that have excellent capabilities to acquire and exploit new knowledge would be expected to have superior innovation and pursue XBRL adoption.[10] Otherwise, they risk lockout effects, which would greatly reduce the likelihood of adoption.

Unlike the previous two propositions, a firm's absorptive capacity can be measured in two equally appropriate ways. Thus, the proposition that follows could either be empirically tested using market data with Zahra and George's (2002) model or experimentally using Link and Siegel's (2002) measures. The following proposition is offered:

Proposition 3:   **Absorptive capacity levels will be positively related to the decision to adopt XBRL.**

5.3   Firm-Level Decision Making - The Neighborhood Effect

Grounded in the learning literature, the neighborhood effect specifies that firms do not make their technology adoption decisions in isolation, but rather under a certain social and physical context (Zhang et al. 2002). Some contexts include regulatory mandate, changes in law, or political and social pressures. Each individual firm's adoption level contributes to the total available of the new technology in a region with an equal weight, which in turn generates the same neighborhood effects for each firm.[11]

---

[10] The current paper assumes that most firms are large enough not to be hindered by a lack of readiness and presumes a predominate corporate environment of setting high-level goals (aspirations).

[11] The neighborhood effect is tied closely to accounting through linking technology adoption to proposed standards. Specifically, some Statements of Financial Accounting Standards require organizations to adopt a change prior to regulatory requirement.

The information systems' literature has discussed topics related to the neighborhood effect. Specifically, Attewell (1992) claimed that firms that are closely connected to existing adopters/users of an innovation learn about it and adopt it early on, while firms on the periphery are slower to adopt. Markus (1987) showed for interactive communications media (e.g., XBRL), adoption becomes progressively more attractive the more it has been adopted by others.

In terms of effect size, Zhang et al. (2002) provided evidence that early successful adopters have a larger effect on neighboring adopters than do early unsuccessful adopters and that education of the technology is a critical factor for facilitating adoption. The results of a recent PricewaterhouseCoopers survey (2002) and the lack of participants in the SEC's XBRL voluntary filing program indicate that perhaps more XBRL education is necessary for adoption decision-makers for that specific CD technology. Thus, firms not currently involved in CD technology adoptions may be waiting to see if the firms in their industry and governmental regulatory agencies that are adopting CD technologies (e.g., XBRL) are successful in their endeavors. Unsuccessful adoptions may cause those who are waiting to reject the idea of CD technology adoption for their own firms.

Given the uncertainty surrounding CD technology adoption, it is conceivable that widespread adoption of CD technologies could take place in a domino effect fashion. Specifically, adoption would occur initially with governmental regulatory authorities, then large firms already involved within the XBRL Consortium (using XBRL as the example), and finally, the rest of the public firms. Early XBRL adoption evidence has met the first part of this prediction (e.g., the FDIC, Federal Reserve Board, and Office of the Comptroller, among other projects, in the U.S. (Blackwell 2003), Direct 2 APRA (the Australian Prudential Regulatory Authority) in Australia, etc.).

In terms of large firms adopting or planning on adopting a CD technology, Microsoft, Reuters, and Morgan Stanley/Dean Witter have already begun presenting their financial statements in XBRL on their Web sites. All firms currently involved in adoption strategies are members of XBRL International. Thus, the *rest* of the firms appear to be taking a *wait-and-see* approach to any form of CD technology adoption.

Even though there are over 20 software vendors now offering products able to use XBRL, the products are *first generation* and, thus, subject to previously unidentified problems. Given the status of the world economies and attention to accounting reporting issues in leading financial nations such as the United States, it is understandable that many firms may not want to risk bugs in the new software, which might lead to litigation. In addition to purchased software issues, for those attempting to create their own software, it is foreseeable that CD technology (e.g., XBRL) adoption also relies on people that know how to implement it, a sound specification with appropriate industry taxonomies, and best practices criteria. Thus, firms might simply be waiting for someone else to *put their toes in the water first* before committing resources toward adoption.

Alternatively, management may view CD technology adoption as advantageous, because it could potentially maintain or obtain perceived technological leadership in the market. Such has been the case in previous IT studies (e.g., Peters 2000; Trombly 2000; Carter, Williams 1959; Cash, Konsynski 1985). Further, pressure to adopt may not come from regulatory bodies, but from competitors. Although perhaps not direct pressure, competition for capital may ensue if investors perceive sufficient benefits to CD and the necessary technology adoption. Thus, it is compelling to discover which approach will *win out* in terms of CD technology adoption: the *wait-and-see, if others are successful we will adopt* (if not mandated) perspective, the perceived technological leadership perspective, or the external pressure perspective.

In sum, the general IT literature has presented perceived technological market leadership and external pressures to adopt as factors that could affect the XBRL adoption decision. However, the results have been primarily obtained post hoc, without theoretical justification. Thus, the current paper projects the neighborhood effect would be more likely to be the dominant adoption factor of the three discussed, if the adopting firms are properly educated. Consistent with the above discussion and recognizing that a true *wait-and-see* perspective would be difficult (at best) to statistically test, the following propositions are set forth:

Proposition 4a: **XBRL adoption will result if the firm decision-makers are highly educated about a XBRL technology.**

Proposition 4b: **Perceived technological market leadership will not affect XBRL adoption.**

Proposition 4c: **XBRL adoption will not be affected by competitive or investor external pressures.**

Propositions 4b and 4c are stated in the null for ease of statistical testing and, if rejected, to provide support for proposition 4a (since they represent valid, alternative perspectives).[12]

6   Conclusions

Recent accounting scandals and the recognition of an inadequate business reporting process have prompted regulators across the globe to unveil new reporting requirements (although, many are not specifically associated with particular technologies). Consistent across these requirements is the focus on reporting processes (e.g., reporting firm information to investors more quickly) and performance measures (both financial and nonfinancial). CD technology may be key to complying with the new requirements. CD technology usage (as evidenced with the current anecdotal XBRL findings and Li and Pinsker's (2005) small sample of completed XBRL adoptions) is expected to produce unprecedented gains in efficiency, interoperability, and timeliness to the adopting firm and greater information accessibility for outside investors.

Despite the potential benefits, uncertainty of adoption remains in the corporate world. Traditionally, many firms outside of the high technology industry, choose a *wait-and see* attitude to gather evidence as to the effectiveness of early adopters and relevant software. Further, adoption of a CD technology would force management to rely on first generation technology with less time to check the accuracy of the information provided, exposing itself to potentially severe litigation threats and increased anxiety. However, if managers could maintain a relatively small amount of apprehension or attempt to maintain a high level or increase its level of absorptive capacity, the current paper proposes that the firm would pursue XBRL adoption.

---

[12] I recognize a limitation to using the neighborhood effect theory is its newness and consequent lack of empirical testing in IT adoption studies (relative to the other theories presented). Thus, its particular application to XBRL adoption is supported primarily with practical evidence to support the related research propositions. This is consistent with the ex ante nature of the current paper.

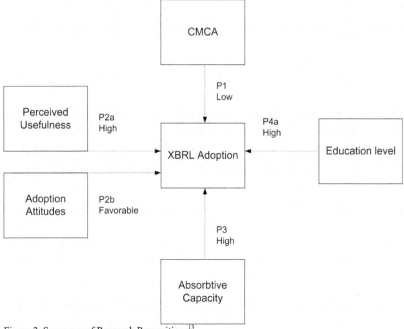

Figure 2: Summary of Research Propositions[13]

The current paper has provided a framework consisting of seven testable propositions grounded in relevant theories and theoretical foundations (i.e., Fichman (1992) and Li et al. (2004)) in order to study the above possibilities (see figure 2 for summary). The diverse nature of the theoretical framework provided should stimulate empirical research to contribute to the general knowledge of corporate IT adoption decisions. Such knowledge would be useful not only to IT personnel, but also to accountants called upon to help corporate clients with the CD technology adoption decision (e.g., if the client is considering volunteering for the SEC's XBRL voluntary filing program).

6.1   Future Research

Future empirical research should distinguish which proposition drives the XBRL adoption decision-making process. Empirical support for applicable propositions could help accounting professionals and management better understand the factors involved in the CD technology adoption process. Accounting consultants involved in assisting in the adoption process would then have an improved understanding from the client's pers-

---

[13]   Propositions 4b and 4c are stated in the null and suggest that perceived market leadership and external pressures do not affect the XBRL adoption decision. Thus, they are not depicted in the figure above.

pective. Armed with the new understanding, they should be able to plan more appropriately for initial meetings with potential adopter clients.

Researchers may want to take the CD technology adoption analysis in a new direction or even expand the possibilities to cover areas not discussed in the current paper. For example, all research propositions presumed the environment of the potential adopter did not involve regulatory mandated use. Future research may want to examine the differences in individual or firm-level CD technology adoption decision making in a regulated versus non-regulated environment. Additionally, XBRL was the specific CD technology example cited in the paper. XBRL is not the only existing technology capable of supporting CD. Future research may want to compare and contrast varying CD technologies.

Finally, the expanded TAM model, rather than diffusion of innovation (DOI) theory, was proposed to measure potential XBRL adoption. The TAM is able to utilize intentions as an endogenous variable and DOI theory is not. According to Agarwal (2000, 90), DOI research specifically recognizes that institutionalization of a behavior is different from, and perhaps more important than, its initial manifestation. Therefore, since the premise of the current paper is adoption, the author deemed the TAM's focus on intentions toward XBRL as more appropriate than focusing on the institutionalization or use of XBRL as measured by DOI theory. After CD technologies are adopted by more organizations (government or corporate), future research should incorporate DOI theory and relevant theoretical frameworks (e.g., Gallivan 2001 and Attewell 1992) to analyze various assimilation/implementation impacts.

References

Adams, D.A.; Nelson R.R..; Todd P.A. (1992): Perceived Usefulness, Ease of Use, and Usage of Information Technology: A Replication, MIS Quarterly 16, 2, pp. 227-247.

Agarwal, R. (2000): Individual Acceptance of Information Technologies, in R. Zmud W. (ed.) Framing the Domains of IT Management: Projecting the Future...Through the Past, Cincinnati, OH: Pinnaflex Education Resources, pp. 85-104.

AICPA Special Committee on Financial Reporting (The Jenkins Committee) (1994): New York, NY: American Institute of Certified Public Accountants.

Al-Gahtani, S. (2001): The Applicability of TAM Outside North America: An Empirical Test in the United Kingdom, Information Resources Management Journal 14, 3, pp. 37-46.

Attewell, P. (1992): Technology Diffusion and Organizational Learning: The Case of Business Computing, Organization Science 3, 1, pp. 1-19.

Attewell P.; Rule J. (1984): Computing and Organizations: What We Know and What We Don't Know, Communications of the ACM 27, pp.1184-1192.

Benbasat, I.; Bergeron M.; Dexter A.S. (1993): Development and Adoption of Electronic Data Interchange Systems: A Case Study of the Liquor Distribution Branch of British Columbia, Proceedings of Administrative Sciences Association of Canada Twenty First Annual Conference, pp. 153-163.

Blackwell, R. (2003): Agencies Line Up Software for Bank Data Project, American Banker 168, 116, p. 4.

Carter, C.F.; Williams B.R. (1959): The Characteristics of Technically Progressive Firms, Journal of Industrial Economics 7, 2, 87-104.

Carter, M.E.; Soo B.S. (1999): The Relevance of Form 8-K Reports, Journal of Accounting Research 37, 1, pp. 119-132.

Cash, J.I.; Konsynski B.R. (1985): IS Redraws Competitive Boundaries, Harvard Business Review, pp. 134-142.

Clarke, C.T. (1991): Rationale and Development of a Scale to Measure Computer-Mediated Communication Apprehension, Doctorial Dissertation, Kent State University, Dissertation Abstract International, 52-04, p. A1129.

Cohen, W.M.; Levinthal D.A. (1990): Absorptive Capacity: A New Perspective on Learning and Innovation, Administrative Science Quarterly 35, pp. 128-152.

The CPA Letter (2002): AICPA 82, 9, pp. G1-2.

Davis, F.D. (1989): Perceived Usefulness, Perceived Ease of Use, and User Acceptance of Information Technology, MIS Quarterly 13, 3, pp. 319-340.

Davis, F.D.; Bagozzi R.P.; Warshaw, P.R. (1989): User Acceptance of Computer Technology: A Comparison of Two Theoretical Models, Management Science 35, pp. 982-1003.

Davis, F.D. (1993): User Acceptance of Information Technology: System Characteristics, User Perceptions and Behavioral Impacts, International Journal of Man-Machine Studies 38, pp. 475-487.

Deshmukh, A. (2004): XBRL, Communications of the Association for Information Systems, (13), pp. 196-219.

Duncan, R.B. (1974): Modifications in Decision Structure in Adapting to the Environment: Some Implications for Organizational Learning, Decision Sciences 5, pp. 705-25.

Editorial Staff (Dec. 6, 2004): AICPA Chair Call on Profession to Accept Change; Delivers Keynote Address at SEC-PCAOB Conference, PR Newswire.

Fichman, R.G. (1992): Information Technology Diffusion: A Review of Empirical Research, Proceedings of the 13th International Conference on Information Systems (ICIS), pp. 195-206.

Fichman, R.G. Kemerer C.F. (1997): The Assimilation of Software Process Innovations: An Organizational Learning Perspective, Management Science 43, 10, pp. 1345-1363.

Fichman, R.G. (2004): Going Beyond the Dominant Paradigm for Information Technology Innovation Research: Emerging Concepts and Methods, Journal of the Association for Information Systems 5, pp. 314-55.

Financial Accounting Standards Board (2000): Electronic Distribution of Business Reporting Information, Steering Committee Report Series, Business Reporting Research Project.

Flaherty, L.M., Pearce K.J., Rubin R.B. (1998): Internet and Face-to-Face Communication: Not Functional Alternatives, Communication Quarterly 46, 3, pp. 250-270.

Gallivan, M. J. (2001): Organizational Adoption and Assimilation of Complex Technological Innovations: Development and Application of a New Framework, Database for Advances in Information Systems 32, 3, pp. 51-85.

Garramone, G.M.; Harris A.C.; Anderson R. (1986): Uses of Political Computer Bulletin Boards, Journal of Broadcasting & Electronic Media 30, pp. 325-339.

George, G.; Zahra S.A.; Wheatley K.K.; Khan R. (2001): The Effects of Alliance Portfolio Characteristics and Absorptive Capacity on Performance: A Study of Biotechnology Firms, The Journal of High Technology Management Research 12, pp. 205-226.

Guithues Amrhein, D.; LeRouge C.; Pinsker R. (2006): REA and XBRL: Synergies for the 21st Century Business Reporting System, Working Paper, Saint Louis University.

Huber, G.P. (1990): A Theory of the Effects of Advanced Information Technologies on Organizational Design, Intelligence, and Decision Making, The Academy of Management Review 15, 1, pp. 47-71.

Hucklesby, M. (2003): Corporate Governance – X-factor Fast Speeding Up Financial Reporting, Management Magazine, 3 pages.

Hunton, J.; Wright A.; Wright S. (2003): The Supply and Demand for Continuous Reporting in Roohani S. (ed.) Trust and Data Assurances in Capital Markets: The Role of Technology Solutions, Smithfield, RI: PricewaterhouseCoopers, pp. 7-16.

Iacovou, C.L.; Benbasat I., Dexter A. S. (1995): Electronic Data Interchange and Small Organizations: Adoption and Impact of Technology, MIS Quarterly 19, 4, pp. 465-485.

Igbaria, M. et al. (1997): Personal Computing Acceptance Factors in Small Firms: A Structural Equation Model, MIS Quarterly, pp. 279-305.

Karahanna, E.; Straub D.W.; Chervany N.L. (1999): Information Technology Adoption Across Time: A Cross-sectional Comparison of Pre-adoption and Post-adoption Beliefs, MIS Quarterly 23, 2, pp. 183-213.

Korpela, M. (1996): Traditional Cultural or Political Economy? On the Root Causes of Organizational Obstacles of IT in Developing Countries, Information Technology for Development 7, pp. 29-42.

Li, S. (2005): The Impact of Information and Communication Technology on Relation-based Governance System, Journal of Information Technology for Development 11, 2, pp. 105-122.

Li, S.; Park S. H.; Li S. (2004): The Great Leap Forward: The Transition from Relation-based Governance to Rule-based Governance, Organizational Dynamics 33, 1, pp. 63-78.

Li, S.; Pinsker R. (2005): Modeling RBRT Adoption and its Effects on Cost of Capital, International Journal of Accounting Information Systems 6, 3, pp. 196-215.

Link, A.N.; Siegel D. S. (2002): Unions and Technology Adoption: A Qualitative Analysis of the Use of Real-time Control Systems in U.S. Coal Firms, Journal of Labor Research 23, 4, pp. 615-630.

Malhotra, A.; Gosain S.; El Sawy O.A. (2005): Absorptive Capacity Configurations in Supply Chains: Gearing for Partner-enabled Market Knowledge Creation, MIS Quarterly 29, 1, pp. 145-187.

Markus, M.L. (1987): Toward a "Critical Mass" Theory of Interactive Media, Communications Research 24, 5, pp. 491-511.

Perse, E.M.; Courtright J.A. (1993): Normative Images of Communication Media: Mass and Interpersonal Channels in the New Media Environment, Human Communication Research 19, pp. 485-503.

Peters, L. (2000): Is EDI Dead? The Future of the Internet in Supply Chain Management, Hospital Material Management Quarterly, pp. 42-47.

Pinsker, R.; Li S. (2006): Costs and Benefits of XBRL Adoption: Early Evidence, Working Paper, Old Dominion University.

PricewaterhouseCoopers (2002): The Trust Challenge: How the Management of Financial Institutions Can Lead the Rebuilding of Public Confidence, White paper.

Regulation Fair Disclosure (August 15, 2000): SEC Release 33-7881, Rules 101-103.

Rice, R.E. (1993): Media Appropriateness: Using Social Presence Theory to Compare Traditional and New Organizational Media, Human Communication Research 19, pp. 451-484.

Robey, D. (1977): Computers and Management Structure: Some Empirical Findings Re-examined, Human Relations 30, pp. 963-976.

Robey, D. (1979): Organizations, Managers, and the MIS: Report from an International Study, Presented at the Irvine Conference on Social Issues and Impacts of Computing, Lake Arrowhead, CA: 44 pages.

Rogers, E.M. (1983): Diffusion of Innovations (3rd Ed.), New York: Free Press.

Rubin, A.; Bantz C.R. (1987): Utility of Videocassette Recorders, American Behavioral Scientist 30, pp. 471-485.

Rubin, A.; Rubin R.B. (1985): Interface of Personal and Mediated Communication: A Research Agenda, Critical Studies in Mass Communication 2, pp. 36-53.

Steinfield, C.W. (1986): Computer-mediated Communication in an Organizational Setting: Explaining Task-related and Socioemotional Uses, Communication Yearbook 9, pp. 777-804.

Swanson, E.B.; Ramiller N. (2004): Innovating Mindfully with Information Technology, Working Paper, University of California Los Angeles.

Trombly, M. (2000): Value-chain Management, Computerworld, pp. 64-68. United State Securities and Exchange Commission (2002): The Sarbanes-Oxley Act.

Van den Bosch, F.; Volberda H.; deBoer M. (1999): Coevolution of Firm Absorptive Capacity and Knowledge Environment: Organizational Forms and Combinative Capabilities, Organization Science 10, 5, pp. 551-568.

Walther, J.B.; Burgoon J.K. (1992): Relational Communication in Computer-mediated Interaction, Human Communication Research 19, pp. 50-88.

Weidenbaum, M. (1996): The Chinese Family Business Enterprise, California Management Review 38, 4, pp. 141-157.

Williams, F.; Phillips A. F.; Lum P. (1985): Gratifications Associated with New Communication Technologies, in Rosengren, K.E.; Wenner L.A.; Palmgreen P. (eds.) Media Gratifications Research, Beverly Hills, CA: Sage.

Wilson, P. (July, 2003): XBRL Heralds New Era in Data Accountability, Vancouver Sun, page D4.

Xbrl.org. (2002): XBRL: Understanding the XML Standard for Business Reporting and Finance, White paper, www.xbrl.org.

Zahra, S.A.; George G. (2002): Absorptive Capacity: A Review, Reconceptualization, and Extension, The Academy of Management Review 27, 2, pp. 185-207.

Zhang, X.; Fan S.; Ximing C. (2002): The Path of Technology Diffusion: Which Neighbors to Learn From?, Contemporary Economic Policy 20, 4, pp. 470-478.

Economic Consequences of Internet Financial Reporting

Alfred Wagenhofer

University of Graz,
Austria

alfred.wagenhofer@uni-graz.at

Contents

1 Introduction[1,2]

The last fifteen years or so have seen enormous development of the Internet and an increasing acceptance by its users. Major characteristics of the Internet are that information can be accessed (almost) any time and everywhere, and generally at a low cost; the information is up-to-date; there are few limits on data availability; information can include dynamic presentations and multimedia; and there is the possibility of interactive information demand and supply. These developments have a significant effect on the dissemination of information and on the trading of goods, including shares, and thus on the organizational structures of how these activities are performed. They also open up new and astounding opportunities for financial disclosure that affect all interested parties, notably corporations, investors, auditors, and information intermediaries. These opportunities concern standard setters as well as regulators.

Various studies show that most listed corporations now disclose financial information on their websites, and that the level of disclosure has increased over the last years. (e.g., Lymer 1999; Lymer et al. 1999; Ettredge, Richardson, Scholz 2002; Debreceny, Gray, Rahman 2002; Trabelski, Labelle, Laurin 2004). The Internet has probably become the primary source for users searching for corporate financial reports. Companies invest substantial resources in the development of their websites, and come up with innovative ways to present financial information.

While the acceptance of Internet disclosure has increased, most of the information provided is still substantially the same that is available from other sources, too. There are many opportunities for this practice to change. Empirical studies suggest a decline in the value of traditional financial reports. (Lev, Zarowin 1999) Reducing boundaries for generating and disseminating information by Internet technologies may provide the opportunity to change the traditional financial reporting model. For instance, Elliott concludes that "Information technology (IT) is changing everything," (e.g. Elliot 1999) and Trites sees a shift from the *Pacioli paradigm* to the *Google paradigm* (Trites 2004).

With the advent of Extensible Business Reporting Language (XBRL) as a standardized data description format for financial reporting, there are many studies that describe this technology and promote the benefits to all preparers and users of financial reports.

[1] Helpful comments by Roger Debreceny, Andy Lymer, two anonymous reviewers, and participants at a workshop at The University of Sydney are gratefully acknowledged.

[2] This article is an updated version of an article published in Schmalenbach Business Review 55 (2003), pp. 262-279. Reprinted with friendly permission of the publisher.

(e.g., Zarowin, Harding 2000; PricewaterhouseCoopers 2002) Quite often, this literature misses potential negative effects that may also exist.

The effects of new information technologies on financial disclosure have been an issue for standard setters and accountants. (FASB 2000; Lymer et al. 1999; Trites 1999; ICAEW 1998) These studies explore potential future developments not only for disclosure, but also for radical changes of the current financial reporting model. For example, they include forecasts like this: "The annual report of the 21st century will not be annual and it will not be a report: it will be an up to date, informative, permanent dialogue."[3] However, the ballyhooed future directions remain vague.

Although visionary thoughts on new opportunities no one has dreamed of before provide an important impetus for financial reporting developments, it is also clear that technology alone does not drive the demand and supply of financial information. It is the preparers and users whose supply and use of the information defines the type and amount of financial information that is being produced and digested. Standard setters and regulators follow up to see if there is a demand for standardization based on changing demand and supply.

This paper attempts to shift the discussion of the effects of the Internet on financial reporting towards an economic framework. The contribution lies primarily in an analysis of the economic consequences the Internet developments have on financial disclosure. It shows that information technology does not change everything. The principles governing their economic effects remain widely unaffected, (Shapiro, Varian 1999) that is, financial disclosure is (still) governed by incentives and cost-benefit trade-offs. The paper applies insights from the financial disclosure literature on Internet financial reporting to analyze the potential effects on the demand and supply of financial information. However, I note at the outset that many issues that arise with Internet financial reporting are still in flux, so that the significance of these effects is difficult to ascertain at present.

The paper is organized as follows: The next section gives an overview of financial information flows within and outside the firm. Section 3 analyzes the direct cost effects of Internet financial reporting, and what they imply for financial disclosure and for voluntary disclosure incentives by firms. Section 4 examines the increased demand for standardization that comes from the use of the new information technologies. There is a particular focus on XBRL and its effects on financial disclosure and accounting

---

[3]   Alan Benjamin Obe, as quoted in ICAEW (1998), p. 17.

standards. Section 5 considers issues that arise from the desire to assure a high quality of Internet financial reporting. Section 6 contains a summary and conclusions.

2   Accounting Information Flows

Figure 1 depicts the typical financial information flows of corporations.[4] Beginning with the recording of transactions and business events in the books of the corporation at various hierarchical levels, a major information flow occurs within the corporation. The information is used for reporting and consolidation purposes of business units. Part of the information within the corporation is condensed by applying accounting standards and other regulation into statutory financial statements. The financial statements are audited by an independent auditor and are subject to enforcement by the appropriate national body. Other information, such as interim reports and information published in compliance with continuous reporting requirements are typically not audited or reviewed, but may be subject to enforcement or overview. Some corporate information, e.g., press conference material, is neither audited nor subject to enforcement. The information is then communicated to the users, who are either information intermediaries who use the corporate disclosures and other information to advise end users, or are end users themselves who use the information for their own decision-making.

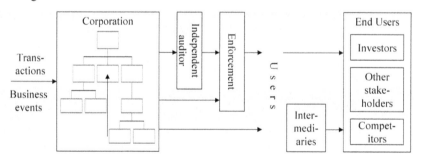

Figure 1: Accounting information flows

The Internet affects each of these information flows. The effects are twofold: First, the Internet changes the costs of the information collection, processing, and dissemination. Second, it increases the demand for standardization of information. I examine each of these two effects separately, although they are to some extent interdependent.

---

[4]   DiPiazza and Eccles (2002) discuss a corporate reporting supply chain which integrates similar elements.

The information cost change affects the cost-benefit trade-off of various processes and instruments. Existing processes will become less expensive, and the costs of new processes may fall below their expected benefit so that they are adopted. The second effect is why the Internet is often viewed as an enabling technology. It makes available many new possibilities of information gathering, processing, and disseminating to its users that were too costly or even impossible before.[5] However, it does not generate a new demand for information: the demand must already be there. Only the cost of satisfying that demand was too high before the new technology became available.

The Internet is independent of hardware but, nevertheless, requires a common format of the type of data they process. Standardized information is needed to fully exploit the opportunities of the Internet. XBRL provides such a standard for financial reporting. Its development and effects on financial reporting are considered in the subsequent section.

3   Effects of Information Cost Changes

3.1   Direct Effects of Cost Changes

The Internet offers easy access to firms' financial information. Firms can use this technology to reach more potential users than they can by other communication means. Placing financial disclosures on the Internet offers equal access to all users and reduces the information asymmetry between some institutional investors and others (*democratization of capital markets*).[6] This should also decrease the firms' cost of capital. (Easley, O'Hara 2004; Lambert, Leuz, Verrecchia 2006)

Speed of disclosure is enhanced by Internet disclosure. Disclosure and filing deadlines can become tighter. Information can be published at a time that is under full control by the firm. (DiPiazza, Eccles 2002) To alert users that new information has been put on the Internet, there are several *push* techniques, such as an email notice distributed to identified users. Speed is particularly important for continuous reporting requirements of stock price-relevant information during the financial year. The stewardship function of financial statements is less speed-sensitive, because financial statements are usually led by other disclosures, such as earnings forecasts.

---

[5]   DiPiazza and Eccles (2002) mention a cost saving in the production of business reports of up to 60 percent over traditional publishing methods.

[6]   However, Ordelheide (1999) argues that the resulting information overflow and the increasing dynamics of the capital markets can create a competitive advantage for professional analysts relative to private investors and thus increase information asymmetry for some time.

The easy availability of information may induce users to request more and more information, including assumptions, effects of alternative accounting methods, multidimensional properties of information (e.g., probability distributions), (Wallman 1996; Pellens, Fülbier, Gassen 1998) and all sorts of non-financial information. Information about intangibles and value drivers are natural candidates. This increased appetite for information raises the question of how much additional information firms are prepared to disclose. Besides the direct costs of auditing or reviewing such information, firms may be harmed by adverse actions of competitors and other parties that use this information. Moreover, additional disclosure raises legal concerns. In a litigious environment the legal costs can be substantial. If firms are to be motivated to experiment with new technologies and innovative disclosure practices, one way would be to extend safe-harbor rules for contents to Internet disclosures.[7] The reluctance of many firms to disclose *too much* is based on these negative effects.

By placing financial information on the firm's website, users can search, filter, retrieve, download, and even reconfigure such information at low cost in a timely fashion. But Internet financial reporting is not restricted to static texts and graphs. It allows for hyperlinks, search engines, multimedia, and interactivity.[8] For example, users may be allowed to customize the contents of financial reports to match their demands or to define user-specific trigger events for reports (Jensen, Xiao 2001). Even more use of interactivity would be a dialogue reporting by which users could specify information demands based on information they received previously. Users might be able to do their own sensitivity analyses and insert their own assumptions to measure assets and liabilities.[9]

Firms can learn from tracking users' information requests or specific user demands, which users can pose either anonymously or by filling in some kind of access identification. Access statistics are market-driven direct measures of the importance of information, and if interpreted carefully, can guide firms and also standard-setters to react to the demand revealed by the users' behavior. Software applications offered by a preparer on the Internet could allow firms to learn assumptions investors use in analyzing financial data.

---

[7] This suggestion is in the spirit of a recommendation by the Garten Task Force (2001), pp. 9-10, for more disclosure in general.

[8] For a survey of firms usage of such opportunities over 22 countries see Lymer et al. (1999), pp. 51-56.

[9] For example, current IFRSs (e.g., IAS 1, IAS 36, IFRS 7) require disclosure of key assumptions to determine asset values and the sensitivities of changes in the assumptions.

The Internet may also improve the availability of financial information within firms themselves. For example, many of the processes that occur in distant places can be automated and fed into a firm-wide information system. Reporting and consolidation is improved and speeded up (*fast close*). One opportunity is to increase reporting frequency from annual or quarterly to monthly, weekly, daily, or even (almost) instant financial statements.[10] The Internet is a perquisite for high-frequency reporting, as the information should be provided immediately after the announcement release and will lose value fast if delivered to users too late relative to the length of the period it covers. A consequence of more frequent reporting could be that the users' focus on quarterly earnings may vanish, and with it the incentives of firms to manage them. However, it would require a major change in most accounting systems because events, such as updates of market prices, estimates, and judgments, would need to be entered on a real-time basis as well. Of course, economic questions such as the optimal length of a reporting period emerge, but are not yet well understood.

In economic terms, although the Internet does not affect the objectives of the firm, i.e., maximizing the expected utility of (the representatives of) the firm's owners, it may have a significant effect on the constraints of the maximization problem. Thus, the usual cost-benefit trade-offs apply in deciding how to perform information processes, only the opportunities are (generally) expanded due to a relaxation in the constraints. The result is that existing processes may become less costly, newly available alternatives may replace the used processes, or new processes may be adopted due to a favorable cost-benefit ratio. Expanding the feasible set of processes cannot be harmful in a setting if there are no countervailing incentives. That is, the Internet opens up new disclosure opportunities, but the cost-benefit trade-off is relevant whether or not a firm takes up the opportunities.[11]

This discussion assumes that the Internet reduces the direct information costs of firms. However, firms may actually incur higher costs, albeit accompanied by additional benefits of the information source. Cost increases can result from investment in the design and maintenance of a website that includes financial information. Much of the information on the Internet currently complements other information sources. For example, financial reports are both printed as usual and provided via the firm's website, which is costly. This practice is about to change. There are some developments un-

---

[10] The usual example is Cisco Systems which is said to be able to close its books in hours. See, e.g. Eccles et al. (2001), p. 309.

[11] Trabelski, Labelle, and Laurin (2004) find significant differences in disclosures of *traditional* financial reporting and internet financial reporting, where the latter provides more information.

derway to substitute printed material for Internet-disclosed information. For example, in the U.K., if agreed to by a firm's shareholders, the reporting regime can be changed to allow companies to fulfill their statutory reporting requirements entirely in electronic form and to permit information delivery on a *by request only* basis. Regulation FD (Fair Disclosure) in the U.S. also pushes for more use of the Internet in lieu of printed material, because Internet disclosure offers availability to all interested users on the same terms.

The cost reduction aspect has been considered by some regulators for their filing requirements. The SEC requires electronic filings to its EDGAR system, and makes the information publicly available over the Internet. In 2005, it allowed voluntary XBRL filing on EDGAR to assess this technology.[12] Japan started a similar pilot project. The European Union requires member states to set up electronic filings and encourages (but not requires) them to take part in an electronic network across states to simplify user access to corporate information. Austria allows XML (extensible markup language) based filings of financial statements to the public registry. Initiatives such as these greatly increase the accessibility of financial disclosures of companies and benefit users. The economic reason for such a regulation is the expectation that the benefit of users exceeds the costs incurred by firms.

3.2 Effects on Voluntary Disclosure Incentives

Simple cost-benefit trade-offs do not capture potential interactions between the firm and users. In fact, financial disclosure decisions follow a complex cost-benefit trade-off in which the firm must consider the information endowment and strategic reactions of the users that is brought about by the firm's change in the information costs.

Potential effects of the Internet on financial disclosure can be analyzed by using results from the voluntary disclosure literature. As a benchmark, consider a setting in which a firm, which is interested in a high current share price, is endowed with some piece of information and can make a verified disclosure to the capital market. The capital market holds rational expectations, that is, it is aware of the fact that the firm possesses the information and reacts to the disclosure (or non-disclosure) in a way so that it is not

---

[12] Bhattacharya and Premuroso (2006) find significant differences between adopters and non-adopters of XBRL reporting. They suggest that adopters demonstrate superior corporate governance and higher future operating performance.

misled, on average. The unraveling principle states that in such a setting, the only equilibrium is full disclosure of the firm's information.[13]

Introducing a cost of disseminating information introduces partial disclosure, in that only relatively favorable information is disclosed. The effect of a decrease in this cost is an increase in financial disclosure in equilibrium.[14] More disclosure generally occurs in the region of less favorable information. Thus, the cost decrease triggers the disclosure of relatively less favorable news.

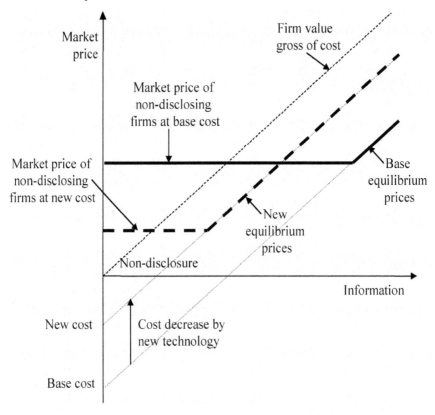

Figure 2: Disclosure equilibrium with different disclosure costs[15]

---

[13] See, e.g., Milgrom (1981). Intuitively, this equilibrium is supported by skeptical beliefs of the capital market in case information is withheld: The market assumes the worst information in case the firm does not disclose.

[14] See Verrecchia (1983). If users are uncertain about the disclosure objective of the firm, Einhorn (2006) shows that this result holds in aggregate, but not necessarily for individual firms.

[15] The figure is adapted from Wagenhofer and Ewert (2003), p. 293.

Figure 2 shows the structure of such an equilibrium and the effects of a change in the cost. The equilibrium prices for the base case of high cost are shown in solid lines. Due to the high cost, only few firms find it beneficial to disclose their information.

Suppose the cost decreases to the new cost shown in Figure 2. The new equilibrium (in broken lines) is such that more firms now have an incentive to disclose their information. However, a comparison of the equilibrium prices reveals that the cost decrease is not to every firm's advantage. Only firms with highly favorable information gain from the cost reduction.

In many situations, ex ante each firm may experience a disadvantage from the information-cost decrease. The reason is that the information cost is a dead-weight loss in this setting, a loss that can be avoided if the firm does not disclose. Essentially, the cost decrease leads to more information about firms in the capital market but may lower the average market prices.[16] Thus, investors might not benefit from the increased disclosure level.

Another insight from such a model is that more precise information is more likely to be disclosed for a given cost,[17] which implies that a cost decrease will (ceteris paribus) increase the likelihood of a disclosure of additional, but less precise, information. The reason is that more firms find it worthwhile to separate and disclose their information due to the reduced cost of doing so; the equilibrium market price of non-disclosing firms adjusts accordingly to a lower level.

A different cost that is affected by the Internet is the cost of information acquisition. Lower costs tend to result in more information acquisition and to more disclosure in equilibrium, both in the level of information and of bad news (e.g., Dye 1985; Wagenhofer 1990). If users are uncertain about the cost of disclosure, more disclosure by peers may indicate reduced costs, which will generate the same effect. Similar to the case of disclosure costs, the ex ante effect of a decrease in information acquisition costs is ambiguous. Lower costs motivate more firms to acquire the information; this behavior is anticipated by the users who, given non-disclosure, revise the equilibrium

---

[16] The total effect depends on the probability distribution of the information, the cost change, the risk aversion of the investors, and how they use the information. For example, consider a setting in which the expected market price is equal to the private information which is uniformly distributed over [0, 1] and let k denote the disclosure cost. Then the equilibrium is such that there is disclosure over the interval $[2k, 1]$ for $k < 0.5$. Suppose the base cost is $k = 0.4$, then, ex ante, disclosure occurs with probability of 0.2, and the dead weight loss of disclosure is $0.2k = 0.08$. Reducing k to, say, 0.3 increases the probability of disclosure to 0.4, and the dead weight loss is $0.4k = 0.12$. In fact, the dead weight loss is greatest for $k = 0.25$.

[17] See Verrecchia (1990); this result depends to some extent on the shape of the cost function (see Richardson 2001).

price downwards, which induces more firms to disclose. Firms that possess unfavorable information and do not disclose in the equilibrium with high costs will find that they either disclose in the equilibrium with low cost or, if they still do not disclose, the equilibrium price goes down. They will lose from the lower information acquisition cost.

More disclosure usually increases the information about firms in the capital market. However, this statement is not unambiguously true: It depends on potential reactions by the market participants to the increased financial disclosure by firms. Many investors acquire their own information, which is reflected in the market prices of the firms. More public disclosure typically reduces the incentives to acquire private information. Depending on the structure of private information markets, investors may gain or lose ex ante from a firm's disclosure (Bushman 1991).

Users incur a cost of information acquisition. Lower costs increase the usage of that information because more users will find it worthwhile to acquire the information. This potentially improves market efficiency, effectively implying a lower cost of capital on average.[18] However, the comparative competitive advantages of analysts may decline.

4   Standardization of Financial Information

4.1   Development of XBRL

Although many people think that increased computerization offers more flexibility in various processes, generally the opposite apparently happens. Software is designed to capture standard processes that are anticipated by the software developer. Usually, a departure from such processes is difficult, if not impossible. Computerization of information processes also requires machine-readable data formats. These formats make it difficult to insert new items or leave open items that developers assume are required information. For use within firms, data warehouse systems have been introduced to combine different databases with differing formats, which enables the firm to use the databases jointly. It is more difficult to create some kind of common understanding of processes, and particularly data across firms. Since financial disclosures are used by many different users, standardization of financial information may have high external benefits.

---

[18]   See, e.g., Grossman, Stiglitz (1980) for an analysis in a noisy rational expectations equilibrium model.

In fact, beginning in 1999, a standardization of financial reporting began on a world-wide scale. Extensible Business Reporting Language (XBRL) is based on extensible markup language (XML), an Internet document description language of which HTML is another subset. XBRL is a market-driven approach undertaken by the private efforts of accounting organizations, individual firms, and other interested parties[19] (Debreceny, Gray 2001).

XBRL includes several layers of descriptions of the source data (meta data). The taxonomies include a schema and link bases. The schema defines unique specifications or tags of individual financial reporting data. Link bases provide hierarchies of data, calculation schemes, references to the respective standard, and different languages. In 2000, the first taxonomy for financial statements based on U.S. GAAP was developed. It is currently the only fully approved taxonomy for U.S. financial reporting. In late 2002, IFRS primary financial statements taxonomy was published that departs in its formal structure somewhat from the original U.S. GAAP taxonomy. Meanwhile, Germany, IFRS, and Spain have final acknowledged taxonomies, and several other countries work on local taxonomies. The taxonomies for primary financial statements include some 3,000 elements that capture individual items in a typical financial report, including the balance sheet, income statement, statement of changes in owners' equity, cash flow statement, notes, and accountant's report.

A direct cost advantage of XBRL is that financial statement information on the financial reporting level needs to be prepared only once. This information can then be reused in various formats, such as a published financial report in print or on the Internet, filing with a stock exchange or supervisor, loan documents, and also in audit schedules. The multiple uses of data avoid transferring data into different formats, a costly, time-consuming, and potentially inaccurate process.[20] Tagging financial statement information using XBRL taxonomy is a complicated task, but it can be automated easily as output from standard accounting software packages.

Specifying tags for financial statement data is but one objective of XBRL. Another is to develop a taxonomy for raw business transactions and events that are recorded in the accounting and book-keeping systems. The XBRL General Ledger taxonomy aims to achieve a unified and technology-independent data transfer within companies. This development could make consolidation easier and faster, particularly if newly acquired subsidiaries are involved. It could also improve corporate reporting by allowing users

---

[19] For a description of the bodies developing and supporting XBRL see also www.xbrl.org.
[20] See PricewaterhouseCoopers (2002) for a detailed discussion of the potential benefits of XBRL.

to drill down to the level of raw data which is usually not possible in data warehouse software. Data can also easily be exchanged with the companies' contracting partners, a function that is reminiscent of the various forms of electronic data interchange (EDI) between suppliers and retailers.

Given all these possibilities, it is interesting to note that after more than five years on the market, only few companies have yet begun to use XBRL, even though many companies closely observe its development and have been even involved in the XBRL consortium.[21] It may be that the individual benefits to firms are not significant if there is no standard for using XBRL. A regulatory demand for using XBRL may trigger a positive network effect that implies increasing benefits the more users apply it.[22] The following implications of XBRL on financial reporting should be read in the light of the low adoption as yet.

4.2   Implications for Financial Disclosure

The information contained in the XBRL tags enables investors, with the help of specialized software (*intelligent* or *smart* agents), to automatically extract and download these data without manually searching the Internet.[23] For example, data can be automatically loaded into a specific investor's model or tool, such as a spreadsheet program, and then analyzed.

The changing user approaches to financial information may have several implications. First, it is likely that quantitative information will become more important than it already is. Qualitative information and soft facts are difficult to process even though, for example, the IFRS taxonomy includes a significant component that is qualitative in nature. Second, the enhanced accessibility of bits and pieces of the full information may mean that investors will read only the selected pieces of information, without considering related information or the context in which the information appears. Firms could be advised to formulate information in more comprehensive block. Third, the pressure to provide comparable, *apples-to-apples* information will increase. Users can better identify strategic measurement or disclosures when comparing them across firms. The tendency to gather only specific pieces of information is likely to generate a demand to provide convenience translations of financial statements or use a "common" presentation currency, to use a *common* language, to use *common* accounting

---

[21] Bhattacharya and Premuroso (2006) identify 46 firms, of which 19 are domiciled in the U.S.

[22] For a discussion of network effects in the standardization of financial reporting see, e.g., Währisch (2001), pp. 60-64.

[23] Demonstrations of such opportunities can be found under http://www.xbrl.org/Demos/ and http://www.microsoft.com/office/solutions/xbrl.

methods, and to fill in all the information for which tags exist. Comparing financial statements prepared under different GAAP is cumbersome, and therefore, XBRL usage will increase the pressure on companies to report under a single GAAP world-wide, whatever this standard may eventually turn out to be.

More opportunities abound. One is to let investors self-define accounting methods or accounting standards that can then be used to calculate a company's financial statements. The firm could prepare the results for certain alternative assumptions or under alternative accounting methods, or provide more basic information so that investor requests can be calculated from the original data. With XBRL, it could become easier to get to the details of the differences. In fact, a scenario might be to allow access to unfiltered tagged raw data.[24] Investors would be able to select, manipulate, and aggregate the raw data in whatever way they wish. However, it is unlikely that firms will find that the benefits of providing such detailed information are worth the cost. Survey results of preparers suggest that firms are reluctant to provide such detailed data, mainly for fear of putting themselves at a competitive disadvantage.[25]

A key criterion for the usefulness of a XBRL taxonomy is its comprehensiveness. Since investors will often utilize XBRL to extract comparable information across companies, similar events or information should be assigned the same tags and different events or information should bear different tags. However, there are limits to becoming more specific. The more tags that are available for closely related information, the less useful is the taxonomy for the investor. Experience in applying the IFRS taxonomy in practice indicates that firms use highly idiosyncratic financial information layouts, not only in the notes but also in the income statement and other financial statements. Therefore, standardization of the formats will probably increase, even though XBRL, technically, deemphasizes the issue of the layout. As the word *extensible* in the XBRL acronym suggests, the data provider is free to add to or modify elements of a taxonomy. Doing so has the disadvantage that such information is unlikely to be searched or requested by users who would find it difficult to follow up individual specifications, hence, much of the standardization benefit to vanish. For example, voluntary disclosure incentives may decrease. Therefore, formal standardization implies a demand for the standardization of information contents as well. Standardizing contents is not simple for financial statement information, but it is even more difficult for

---

[24]   See, e.g., Wallman (1997). This idea goes back to the fundamentals of financial accounting in the *events versus value* debate (e.g., Sorter 1969) and in cost accounting (e.g., Laßmann 1968).
[25]   See, e.g., Trites (1999), pp. 45-46, Xiao, Jones, and Lymer (2002), p. 258.

non-financial information, which is often highly firm-specific, such as performance drivers, key measures, strategies, and descriptions of operations.

The XBRL consortium that develops the taxonomies maintains that XBRL does not affect the contents of financial statements at all, but that it merely takes up the required disclosures in an accounting system and categorizes them into a comprehensive set of tags. Seen from the implications for firms and users, creating a taxonomy is not quite so innocuous, due to the implications on firms' disclosure policies. A XBRL taxonomy can be seen as a huge checklist for information, because it shows clearly what information a firm is expected to make available. Thus, there is a trade-off between the comprehensiveness of a taxonomy that allows more firm-specific information, and standardization that reduces firm-specific content but improves on cross-sectional comparability.

4.3   Effects on Accounting Standards

A direct implication of XBRL on financial reporting is that it renders unimportant the structure and sequence of the presentation of financial information. Many standard setters, mainly those from continental Europe, have traditionally given high priority to a strict balance sheet and income statement layout. On the other hand, the IASB and the FASB do not require a strict layout of the financial statements. Under XBRL, tagged information can be found by the appropriate software no matter where it is placed in a document. Therefore, users can define their own layout and automatically feed a company's financial disclosures into it. For example, experimental evidence indicates that users are better able to integrate related information that appears in different places in the financial statements. (Hodge, Kennedy, Maines 2004). However, as noted above, users are likely to demand more standardized contents, which imply a higher degree of standardization of the layout for items that follow logical consistency.

XBRL's de facto standardization of contents should be of particular interest to accounting standard setters. The common aim of the XBRL consortium seems to be to provide as much national taxonomy as possible to cover different countries and industries. National taxonomies might satisfy the demand of national authorities so that they may be eager to adopt XBRL as the standard for statutory filings. However, national taxonomies do not correspond to the increasing demand for standardization in the capital markets. Cross-sectional comparability could be better served by a common (base) taxonomy. The IFRSs could be a candidate for such a base taxonomy, and in fact the Consortium apparently goes in this direction. It is no coincidence that the IASB has a strong interest in XBRL and is actively involved in the XBRL consortium. Taxonomies for national GAAP could include a subset of tags that are country-specific. Such an approach could work with additional disclosures, however, it would be more difficult with recognition and measurement requirements, because many accounting rules are not upwards compatible. A base taxonomy with national supplements is an obvious concept from an information systems perspective, but not necessarily optimal from an economic perspective. It would lead to monopolizing the base standard, although there are good reasons for allowing a controlled competition between different standards[26] (Sunder 2002; Benston et al. 2003, Benston et al. 2006).

Users could urge standard setters to reduce the number of options provided by accounting standards, or even to eliminate options altogether. Restricting options would make it easier to process the financial information as reported, because the taxonomy applied is clear from the data contained in the XBRL instance file. The particular accounting option used in a certain context is perhaps less obvious and requires more consideration in processing the data.

Considering the scenario in which firms provide access to raw data, investors would be able to access an XBRL-based financial accounting database that records all raw business events, and could apply their own accounting standards. As a consequence, the role of standard setters would diminish. Standard setters would compete with analysts and private for-profit firms to provide models that read XBRL raw data and transform them into decision-relevant summary information for investors.[27] The criterion for competitive advantage would be to provide the best solutions for investors who make decisions based on company information.

I can only speculate what type of standards would survive the market test. It might be standards that require only a little additional information usually not included in the raw business data. A perfect example would be pure cash flow statements that can easily be derived from business data. However, accruals usually carry much more information about properties of business transactions. It is difficult to imagine that such developments could seriously question the (marginal) usefulness of financial statements.

---

[26] See, e.g., Sunder (2002), Benston et al. (2003), pp. 61-65, Benston et al. (2006), Ch. 10.
[27] In some sense, there is already competition going on. An example is Standard & Poor's definition of *core earnings*. Moreover, many firms provide pro forma earnings that differ from related GAAP earnings.

5   Information Quality

The quality of financial disclosures on the Internet is an important issue. Unreliable financial information on the Internet is less relevant or irrelevant for rational users, and can have a detrimental impact on other users. Financial information generally has a higher degree of trustworthiness than other information because it is embedded in corporate governance mechanisms, and it is subject to auditing and enforcement. A major advantage of the Internet is its flexibility, which, however, creates a disadvantage for credibility and authenticity. Data can be easily changed, often without leaving a trace, particularly if the website is dynamically linked with an underlying database. New information can be communicated not only by adding that information, but also by replacing the original information. For example, in the light of new events, why not revise a previous forecast in the latest directors' report? What about just changing the wording in the financial statements, at least for a few critical days?

Often, it is not so much the fact that data can be manipulated by a company, rather is it the conscious selection of which data a firm provides via the Internet. Hyperlinks can be included to point to various other sources, including the auditor's report, which may or may not be appropriate in the context, or to external sources like a favorable analyst report. With XBRL, firms may have incentives to become creative in their tagging: For example, because investors will be tempted to work with the data provided by the extraction software, and without double-checking all details, a company that wishes to hide a certain piece of information may well attempt to not tag it, to place it in a certain tag, or to define an individual tag. To assure the quality of disclosures, the auditor would have to check whether the assignment of tags was meticulously performed.

Another issue affecting information quality is the security of the website. It may be difficult to control who has access to the website or its underlying database. Needless to say, fraud, hostile intruders, and hackers can and do find holes in the security net and alter data without knowledge of the company.

Issues like these suggest that financial disclosure provided via the Internet is less credible than is information from other company sources. The credibility is not only of concern to companies and users, but also to auditors and regulators. As Debreceny and Gray describe it, "the auditor's report becomes part of the chaotic morass of information that characterizes the web" (Debreceny, Gray 1999, p. 336).

One way to cope with these concerns is to restrict the opportunities the Internet offers to those that are less affected by such possibilities. For example, auditors may decide not to allow links to and from the auditor's report, or to require that it be stored on the auditor's own or on an official registrar's website. Actually, the most common practice is to provide the annual report in a read-only facsimile version (e.g., in Adobe's PDF format). Such formats can be interpreted as assuring the Internet user of the boundaries and quality of the information.

If firms were to produce real-time reports or allow users to access raw data, auditors would have to change their audit procedures from mainly outcome-related to continuous, process-related audits. (Alles et al. 2000) That is, since the data are dynamically changed during the course of the business, the audit would have to attest to the system of data entry rather than the result. This system includes the processes, preparation, and integrity of the data (Wallman 1997, p. 111). The auditor could also be asked to actively monitor the client's website or to keep track of changes of particular pages. Currently, there are no auditing standards that adequately address these issues.[28] For example, the AICPA maintains that websites are not *documents*, which implies that auditors are not required to read such information.[29] Therefore, it is important that financial information on the Internet is understood to not purport to be of the same quality as the printed *official* version.

The lack of public standards leaves room for private initiatives to increase trustworthiness. An example could be the certification of the website, similar to WebTrust. WebTrust awards a seal to a company's website if the website follows certain business standards, mainly giving assurance to customers in e-commerce. XML, a standard of which XBRL is a specific subset, provides a digital signature to authorize information. Extensible Assurance Reporting Language (XARL) is another tool to aid in the assurance of the integrity and reliability of financial information (Boritz, No 2005).

Some stock exchanges and regulators have issued guidelines which include certain principles that financial disclosure on the Internet should follow. The French Commission des Opérations de Bourse was probably the first such organization. For Minitel, a precursor of the Internet that had been popular in France, it issued recommendations for disclosure of listed corporations already in 1993. The recommendations were revised to address the use of the Internet in 1999. In the same year, the Toronto Stock Exchange issued guidelines that aimed at encouraging companies to use the Internet to provide financial information, and it defined principles, some of which were considered obligatory. A research study by the Canadian Institute of Chartered Accountants also includes recommendations for standards (Trites 1999). The (then) IASC followed

---

[28] See also Küting, Dawo, and Heiden (2001), pp. 72-80.
[29] AUS 9550. For a discussion whether this will hold in courts see Debreceny and Gray (1999), p. 344.

suit and published a discussion paper in which it provided detailed guidelines as a code of best practice (Lymer et al. 1999, pp. 62-66). The IASB did not take up its predecessor's suggestion to develop a reporting standard based on these guidelines. Instead, the IASB halted the project in 2001, arguing that it was not concerned with the contents of financial information but was closer to corporate governance issues so that the IFAC might be better equipped to work on the issue. In fact, the IFAC staff prepared a paper which includes general guidelines and principles for reporting on the Internet (IFAC 2002). Currently, there are no guidelines for financial disclosure on the Internet in the U.S. despite all the effort put into discussing related issues (FASB 2000).

In the future, we can expect to see increasing regulation of financial disclosure on the Internet. As the history of accounting regulation suggests, a higher degree of regulation has almost always been triggered by financial scandals. In a Delphi study, an expert from academia noted that "The first Internet reporting scandal has yet to take place, but if it does, it is likely to provide a significant spur to the development of regulation."[30]

It remains to be seen whether national regulation can be an efficient means of disclosure regulation, or whether there is a need for a global standard. Since the Internet is truly global, e.g., the location of the company or the institution responsible for the content, the location of the server, and the location of users are likely to differ, and hence the jurisdictions that apply, there may be a need to coordinate standards. Regulation would end the current experimentation stage, and with it some of the possibilities for innovation based on current, or currently perceivable, future technology. Moreover, we should keep in mind that technology moves faster than regulators can (Litan, Wallison 2000).

6   Conclusions

Philip D. Ameen of General Electric predicted in 2001 that "Debates about how pension surplus or derivatives or leases affect 'net earnings' will seem as amusing then as the handwritten ledgers of the 1900's seem to us now."[31] In contrast to that prediction, this paper argues that the rise of the Internet and its increasing use for financial reporting does not change the fundamentals of financial accounting and disclosure. Changes in financial reporting are triggered by fundamental changes in how business

---

[30]   Xiao, Jones and Lymer (2002), p. 261.
[31]   Testimony on behalf of the FEI before the U.S. House of Representatives Subcommittee on Capital Markets, Insurance & Government Sponsored Enterprises on June 7, 2001 (http://www.iasplus.com /resource/ameen.pdf).

is performed, not by the way how transactions and events are recorded.[32] The Internet developments certainly remove some barriers to financial disclosure and offer new opportunities that had not been worth the cost earlier on. But there must be an economic demand for such disclosures in the first place. It is not created by modern information technologies.

This paper studies the economic consequences the Internet has on financial reporting. It analyzes the effects of a change of the information costs, and shows that more disclosure is the consequence of declining disclosure costs and greater user information demands. However, because of market price adjustments occurring due to the changed environment and firms' strategic disclosure responses, these consequences are not necessarily always beneficial in a capital market setting.

The paper also discusses that the increasing use of Internet financial reporting increases the demand for standardization, of which the XBRL is the most notable product. Although the XBRL developers maintain that they model only a meta-language for existing disclosure standards and practice, it is likely that a widespread adoption of XBRL will in fact also standardize the contents of financial disclosure. Thus, the contents and form of disclosure cannot be separated.

Financial reporting on the Internet creates concerns about the quality of the information. The technological flexibility the Internet provides for the firms that generate the disclosures may be easily misused, and may therefore create a demand for more and different auditing services and more regulation. These factors are another cost that should be considered alongside other effects.

As a consequence, simple generalized statements about the overwhelming benefits of the Internet and XBRL are not well founded in economic theory, but require a more thorough consideration of the costs and benefits of financial reporting. This paper provides some general insights into the trade-offs involved but certainly does not resolve all the issues that are important in this regard.

References

Alles, M.; Kogan, A.; Miklos A. Vasarhelyi (2000): Accounting in 2015, The CPA Journal, November.

---

[32] However, the accounting may well determine whether or not transactions are performed. For instance, it is said that Enron and others entered into long-term futures contracts mainly to increase accounting discretion, as these contracts are measured at fair value.

Benston, G.; Bromwich Mi.; Litan, R. E.; Wagenhofer A. (2003): Following the Money – The Enron Failure and the State of Corporate Disclosure, Washington, D.C.

Benston, G.; Bromwich Mi.; Litan, R. E.; Wagenhofer A. (2006): Worldwide Financial Reporting: The Development and Future of Accounting Standards, New York et al.

Bhattacharya, S.; Premuroso R. F. (2006): Do Early Members of XBRL International Signal Superior Corporate Governance and Future Operating Performance?, Working Paper, Florida Atlantic University, May.

Boritz, J. E.; No G. W. (2005): Security in XML-based Financial Reporting Services on the Internet, Journal of Accounting and Public Policy, pp. 11-35.

Bushman, R. M. (1991): Public disclosure and the structure of private information markets, Journal of Accounting Research, pp. 261-276.

Debreceny, Roger, Gray, G. L. (1999): Financial Reporting on the Internet and the External Audit, European Accounting Review, pp.335-350.

Debreceny, Roger, Gray, G. L. (2001): The Production and Use of Semantically Rich Accounting Reports on the Internet: XML and XBRL, International Journal of Accounting Information Systems 2, pp. 47-74.

Debreceny, Roger, Gray, G. L.; Rahman A. (2002): The Determinants of Internet Financial Reporting, Journal of Accounting and Public Policy, pp. 371-394.

DiPiazza, S. A., Eccles, R. G. (2002): Building Public Trust – The Future of Corporate Reporting, New York et al., pp. 11-138.

Dye, R. A. (1985): Disclosure of Nonproprietary Information, Journal of Accounting Research, 123-145.

Easley, D.; O'Hara M. (2004): Information and the Cost of Capital, Journal of Finance, pp. 1553-1583.

Eccles, R G.; Herz, R. H.; Keegan, E. M.; Phillips, D. M. H. (2001): The Value Reporting Revolution, New York et al.

Einhorn, E. (2006): Voluntary Disclosure under Uncertainty about the Reporting Objective, Journal of Accounting and Economics, forthcoming.

Elliott, R. K. (1992): The Third Wave Breaks on the Shores of Accounting, Accounting Horizons, June, pp. 61-85.

Ettredge, M.; Richardson, V. J.; Scholz S. (2002): Dissemination of Information for Investors at Corporate Web Sites, Journal of Accounting and Public Policy, pp. 357-369.

FASB (2000): Business Reporting Research Project: Electronic Distribution of Business Reporting Information (http://www.fasb.org).

Garten Task Force (2001): Strengthening Financial Markets: Do Investors Have the Information They Need?, Report of an SEC-Inspired Task Force, May.

Grossman, S. J.; Stiglitz J. E. (1980): On the Impossibility of Informationally Efficient Markets, American Economic Review 70, pp. 393-408.

Hodge, F. D., Kennedy J. J.; Maines, L. A. (2004): Does Search-Facilitating Technology Improve the Transparency of Financial Reporting?, The Accounting Review, pp. 687-703.

ICAEW (Ed.) (1998): The 21st Century Annual Report, London.

IFAC (2002): Financial Reporting on the Internet, New York.

Jensen, R. E.; Zezhong Xiao J. (2001): Customized Financial Reporting, Networked Databases, and Distributed File Sharing, Accounting Horizons, September, 209-222.

Küting, K.; Dawo S.; Heiden (2001): Internet und externe Rechnungslegung, Heidelberg.

Lambert, R. A.; Leuz, C.; Verrecchia R. E. (2006): Information Asymmetry, Information Precision, and the Cost of Capital, Journal of Accounting Research (forthcoming).

Laßmann, G. (1968): Die Kosten- und Erlösrechnung als Instrument der Planung und Kontrolle in Industriebetrieben, Düsseldorf.

Lev, B; Zarowin, P. (1999): The Boundaries of Financial Reporting and How to Extend Them, Journal of Accounting Research, pp. 353-385.

Litan, R. E.; Wallison P. J. (2000): The GAAP Gap – Corporate Disclosure in the Internet Age, Washington, D.C.

Lymer, A. (Ed.) (1999): Special Section: The Internet and Corporate Reporting in Europe, European Accounting Review, pp. 287-396.

Lymer, A.; Debreceny, R.; Gray G. L.; Rahman. A. (1999): Business Reporting on the Internet, IASC Discussion Paper, London, November.

Milgrom, P. R. (1981): Good News and Bad News. Representation Theorems and Applications, Bell Journal of Economics, pp. 380-391.

Ordelheide, D. (1999): Rechnungslegung im digitalen Zeitalter, in: Gebhardt, Günther, Bernhard Pellens (Eds.): Rechnungswesen und Kapitalmarkt, Zeitschrift für betriebswirtschaftliche Forschung, Sonderheft 41, pp. 229-253.

Pellens, B.; Fülbier, R. U., Gassen J. (1998): Unternehmenspublizität unter veränderten Marktbedingungen, in: Börsig, Clemens, Adolf G. Coenenberg (Eds.): Controlling und Rechnungswesen im internationalen Wettbewerb, Stuttgart, pp 55-69.

PricewaterhouseCoopers (2002): Corporate Communications for the 21st Century, London.

Richardson, S. (2001): Discretionary Disclosure: A Note, Abacus, pp. 233-247.

Shapiro, C., Varian, H. R. (1999): Information Rules. A Strategic Guide to the Network Economy, Boston (MA), p. 206.

Sorter, G. H. (1969): An Events-Based Approach to Basic Accounting Theory, The Accounting Review, pp. 12-19.

Sunder, S.(2002): Regulatory Competition Among Accounting Standards Within and Across International Boundaries, Journal of Accounting and Public Policy, pp. 219-234.

Trabelski, S.; Réal L.; Laurin C. (2004): The Management of Financial Disclosure on Corporate Websites: A Conceptual Model, Canadian Accounting Perspectives, pp. 235-259.

Trites, G. D. (1999): The Impact of Technology on Financial and Business Reporting, Toronto.

Trites, G. D. (2004): Decline of the Age of Pacioli: The Impact of E-Business on Accounting and Accounting Education, Canadian Accounting Perspectives, pp. 171-177.

Verrecchia, R. E. (1983): Discretionary Disclosure, Journal of Accounting and Economics 5, 179-194.

Verrecchia, R. E. (1990): Information Quality and Discretionary Disclosure, Journal of Accounting and Economics 12, pp. 365-380.

Wagenhofer, A, (1990): Informationspolitik im Jahresabschluß, Heidelberg, pp. 36-50.

Wagenhofer, A.; Ewert, R. (2003): Externe Unternehmensrechnung, Berlin et al.

Währisch, M. (2001): The Evolution of International Accounting Systems, Frankfurt a.M. et al.

Wallman, S. M.H. (1996): The Future of Accounting and Financial Reporting, Part II: The Colorized Approach, Accounting Horizons, June, pp. 138-148.

Wallman, S. M. H. (1997): The Future of Accounting and Financial Reporting, Part IV: "Access" Accounting, Accounting Horizons, June, pp. 103-116.

Xiao, Z.; Jones J. M., Lymer, A. (2002): Immediate Trends in Internet Reporting, European Accounting Review, pp. 245-275.

Zarowin, S.; Harding, W. E. (2000): Finally, Business Talks the Same Language, Journal of Accountancy, July, pp. 24-30.

Domain Implications

How Do Firms Address Multiple Taxonomy Issues?

Zane Swanson, George Durler, William Remington

Emporia State University,
USA

swansonz@emporia.edu
mdurler@emporia.edu
wremingt@emporia.edu

Contents

1   Introduction

As a matter of course in international business, multinational firms produce reports according to different taxonomies for the same entity. However, the relation between US and IFRS taxonomies is nontrivial. There are some exact correspondences of accounts and some accounts which lack congruence. This issue is complicated by the need to have different industry taxonomies applicable to different reporting needs in different countries. The source of the differences is the different regulatory accounting approaches to economic events. This paper addresses these taxonomy issues, both generally and with a case example of a specific firm. Investors, companies, and regulators have the need to reconcile statements produced under alternative taxonomies. This problem is not restricted to this one issue. For example government authorities create XBRL taxonomies for banking purposes and then need to reconcile with generally used Generally Accepted Accounting Principles (GAAP) taxonomies from different jurisdictions.

2   Taxonomy Propagation Issues

This section addresses the basic foundation of XBRL taxonomies in information system terms. Taxonomies are defining elements for XBRL instance documents. The taxonomy defines the valid elements (tags) to be employed. This structure can be compared to the DTD which defines the content of an XML document, or to the schema which defines the context of a database.

The potential for enhanced and simplified comparability of financial reports is one of the key strengths of XBRL. The notion of a single fixed taxonomy would greatly improve the prospect of comparability. Unfortunately, the existence of multiple taxonomies dramatically undermines the concept of comparability. How can statements produced using different taxonomies be compared? This leads to an even larger question: How can disparate taxonomies be integrated?

We have some guidance in this effort from the parallel field of database theory (Attaluri 1995) and to some extent from XML. In developing queries to be drawn from multiple databases, the problem of semantic heterogeneity emerges (Lee 2003). Combining elements from different schemata leads to four different kinds of conflicts:

1. Naming conflict. The same item has different names in different schema.

2. Structural conflict. The same item is structured differently in the two schema

3. Identifier (primary key) conflict. Different identifiers are used as the identifier for the same conceptual item.

4. Constraint conflict. The same item may carry different constraints.

There are potential resolutions to each of these conflicts. Hakimpour (2005) and Nicolle (2003) approached the problem from the viewpoint of ontologies. He says that one should examine the ontology that underlies the schema. To the extent that the ontologies coincide, common elements can be discovered, regardless of the conflict in the schema. In the simplest and most encompassing approach we can look to the notion of *union compatibility*. This states that attributes of different relations are *union compatible* if they are drawn from the same domain (i.e. the same kind of data). Domains can be very broad or very narrow. One domain can include another. Thus, it is not if the elements have the same data type or if they have the same name, but it must be that they represent the same kind of data. This *sameness* will always exist if we advance the definition of the domain to be very broad. But that might not be very useful. This is an important concept for taxonomies because combining elements from different taxonomies would be very like a *union*.

As an example of the application of domains, consider the following list, drawn from the domain *apples* jonathan, macintosh, delicious, gala. All appear to fit in the domain of *apples*. Consider a second list, drawn from the domain of *oranges*, valencia, navel, earlygold, itaborai. Now, of course, one cannot mix apples and oranges. But, if we could envision a domain called *fruit*, then all eight of these items could be valid members. It is simply a matter of defining a domain sufficiently broad to include all of the items in question.

How does this example apply to taxonomies? One must use a parallel strategy. Items are placed in a chart of accounts (and later in financial reports) so that they can precisely define what they represent, and so that they can be grouped together with items of similar representation (Schmitt 2001).

Consider *depreciation expense* and *depletion expense*. They are quite different items, and yet they have similar impact on financial reports (i.e. they both offset against income). One would never suggest that they be combined, but it might be proper to find them both in a similar position in an Income Statement.

The problem is analyzing multiple financial statements that are not based on the same taxonomy. One solution would be to develop a composite taxonomy that contains all of the elements of the subject taxonomies. This composite taxonomy would be structured so that the disparate contributing elements would be placed in appropriate position in the composite taxonomy and would contribute to whatever combined category where they both belonged. Then, by limiting our analysis or comparison to higher aggregation, we could achieve comparability.

3   US and IFRS Taxonomy Similarities and Differences

3.1   General Situation

The Financial Accounting Standards Board (FASB) in the USA and the International Accounting Standards Board (IASB) are discussing comparability of financial statements prepared under different standards (FASB Press Release 7/6/06, FASB Press Release 5/22/06, FASB Press Release 2/27/2006, FASB News Release 06/01/05). While both IASB and FASB are discussing convergence of accounting standards as a means of providing comparability between international companies, the reality is that such convergence could take years to achieve, if ever.

There are several major accounting issues with respect to the two major XBRL reporting taxonomies which are the US and International Financial Reporting System (IFRS). Over time, the United States has developed a GAAP framework that US companies are to follow in order to list on US stock exchanges. The Financial Accounting Standards Board (FASB) promulgates GAAP for US public companies. Auditors note exceptions from GAAP on their reports. The SEC causes firms to address GAAP reporting problems and prosecutes companies with fraudulent reporting. Consistent with the US GAAP reporting requirements, the US GAAP taxonomy has been developed. A detailed version of the taxonomy can be found on the XBRL.org website (www.xbrl.org). It is important to remember that XBRL taxonomies facilitate the categorization of firm information according to a uniform chart of accounts, but XBRL does not prescribe the GAAP. Thus, a GAAP has the force of law in the various reporting jurisdictions, but XBRL taxonomy applicable to a reporting jurisdiction is not necessarily legally mandated for company use.

The International Accounting Standards Board (IASB) formulates the IFRS. As of 2006, the current IFRS taxonomy is located at http://xbrl.iasb.org/int/fr/ifrs/gp/2005-05-15. An important consequence for IASB's multinational character is that its dictates do not have the force of law unless a reporting jurisdiction makes it so. In 2002, IFRS was decreed by the Parliament and Council of the European Union to be GAAP starting in 2005 for European companies listed on stock exchanges. A significant portion of the rest of the world is adopting the IFRS standards because of the globalization of financial markets.

The US XBRL taxonomy is different from the IFRS XBRL taxonomy, because the US GAAP is different from the IFRS GAAP (Ernst & Young 2005). Some taxonomy elements are similar in the two regimes, but many are different. Some elements are present in one taxonomy but not in the other. The reason for the differences is that different accounting rules can cause the same economic event and to be reported differently. The only way that US and IFRS XBRL taxonomies will be equivalent is when/if the US and IAS harmonize the GAAP standards. The momentum has shifted over time and currently there is movement in the direction of one global accounting set of regulations. In 2002 the FASB and IASB agreed in a memorandum of understanding that all new GAAP standards will be harmonized (i.e., Norwalk Agreement). Also, some previous standards have been harmonized (e.g., FASB has dropped pooling from consolidation accounting).

For the foreseeable future, there will be differences between US and IFRS GAAP because the ruling bodies are not coming to terms with issues particularly with respect to fair value accounting in regards to reserve accounts and revaluing assets. Another area of difference exists in financial instrument accounting treatments. Other major GAAP differences are in the areas such as fixed assets, LIFO inventory, and income taxes. Cultural values drive accounting values (Radebaugh, Gray and Black 2005). Considerable research has identified the sources of these differences. The forces of globalization (e.g., internet securities market trading) are trending the GAAP regimes towards harmonization. Further, accounting is a reflection of internal and external economics of firms which are operating globally. Investors are the prime factors in the globalization of financial reporting because they can easily access the Internet and as a consequence desire reports that are comparable across countries. The ultimate consequence can be anticipated to be a global GAAP which will permit a single global XBRL taxonomy, but not for many years.

Even with a single global taxonomy, there will be differences between companies' XBRL reporting because there will be accounting differences from industry and specific firm characteristics. The challenge will be to incorporate the relevant XBRL accounts without creating confusion. If one follows the tenets discussed above, then the conversion between US and IFRS GAAPs can be depicted in Figure 1.

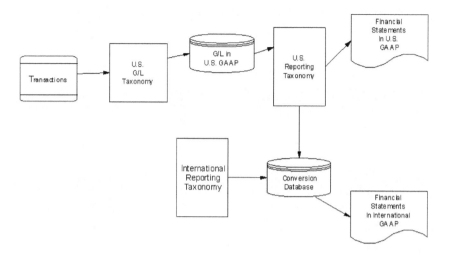

Figure 1: Reporting Taxonomies

3.2 Hypothetical Approach to Firm XBRL Information Structure

An alternative to standards convergence is to use XBRL to convert financial data from one set of standards to the other. In this approach companies would employ XBRL to create financial data tagged using a financial reporting taxonomy under a given GAAP and *translate* it into financial data using the other taxonomy. This translation is done by matching up the elements for each taxonomy to the same or similar elements in the other taxonomy and using software to substitute the existing tag with the tag from the other. For example, the tag for an item tagged as inventory using the U.S. GAAP Reporting taxonomy would be replaced with the tag for inventory in the IASC GAAP taxonomy. An XBRL tagged financial statement created using a U.S. GAAP taxonomy could then be translated into an International GAAP tagged financial statement simply by running the data through the conversion software. Such an approach would not overcome measurement differences in the standards, however.

A method of making these replacements might be as follows: A database would be created matching each tag in the two taxonomies. This database would be updated for changes in the taxonomies and for taxonomy extensions. The XML file containing the XBRL tagged information would be read by the translating software, a match for each tag would be found in the database, and the information would be written to a new XML file with the new tags. This would be a straightforward method. The programming for the translating software is simple and similar to programs which have been used for many years. The difficulty in this method is creating the database of matched tag pairs from the different taxonomies. Since different accounting standards were used in creating the two taxonomies there are tags in each that simply do not have a match in the other. Creation of the database thus becomes labor intensive with someone arbitrarily judging what to do when tags can't be matched. A further problem occurs even when it appears there are what appears to be matching tags. The basis for the information using those tags may not be the same due to differences in valuation methods. An example of this approach, developed by the IASB is at http://213.52.229.67 /ifrs_us_convergence/index.htm.

Is there an alternative approach using XBRL which may still achieve an effective conversion from one GAAP standard to another? Possibly, but the conversion must be done before creating the financial statements using either GAAP taxonomy. Instead of converting data that has already been tagged using a reporting taxonomy, the conversion must take place at a more fundamental level in the processing of financial transactions into financial information. The conversion occurs at the General Ledger level. See Figure 2.

All companies have essentially similar *give and get* transactions regardless of their size, location of operations, or GAAP they use in preparing financial statements. Companies purchase goods to use or to resell, giving up cash or creating obligations in return.

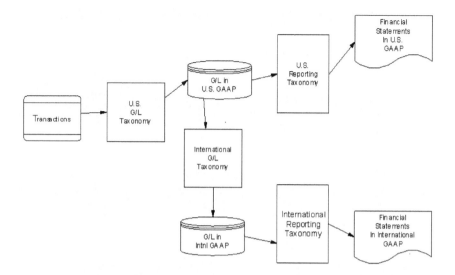

Figure 2: General Ledger Taxonomy

Companies sell goods or services receiving cash or promises to pay in exchange. Companies assign valuations to resources they own, or have a right to use, and the exchanges which occur with other companies. Traditionally, these transactions were recorded into journals and ledgers based on the GAAP standards used by the company. Using XBRL General Ledger taxonomies it is possible to tag economic events as they are initially recorded. This tagged data can then be used to prepare XBRL tagged financial statements based on U.S. GAAP, International GAAP, or any other GAAP for which XBRL taxonomy exists. Since all transactions have the same economic *give and get* basis the XBRL General Ledger taxonomies are more similar to each other than corresponding reporting taxonomies The lower the level in the financial processing the more similar the taxonomies are likely to be due to the more fundamental nature of what is being tagged. Even valuations of resources have similar characteristics since either the initial valuation or valuation changes must be recorded somehow into the accounting system in order to incorporate them into the financial statements.

Thus, the taxonomy conversion database matches up pairs of tags from General Ledger taxonomies instead of reporting taxonomies. Instead of reading in tagged information from financial statements the conversion program uses data from a company's General Ledger tagged database of transactions. The GL XBRL tag based on one set of standards is replaced with the GL XBRL tag from the other set of standards. There will still be some dissimilarities between the two taxonomies, but there should be fewer conceptual differences thus making the creation of the paired tags database easier to create and maintain. Once the *new* database of tagged data is created financial statements can be prepared using the corresponding reporting XBRL taxonomy in the same manner as would have been done if the database had been created with that set of standards.

The disadvantage of this method is that it cannot use published financial statements as the source of information to be converted. The conversion must occur within a company instead of by external analysts, unless a company is willing to provide public access to its General Ledger data. This is access most companies would be unwilling to grant. It also requires that two XBRL tagged General Ledger databases be maintained by the company. However, given the relatively low cost of data storage and the ability to use automated software to create XBRL tagged financial statement from XBRL tagged general ledgers, companies may find it advantageous to provide multiple XBRL tagged financial statements prepared with different sets of GAAP standards in order to reduce their overall cost of capital by having access to international securities markets.

4   Specific Case Analysis of BHP Billiton

In this section, a case analysis will be provided of BHP Billiton taxonomies. BHP Billiton is an appropriate target company to review because it is listed in the US (where US GAAP is practiced) and Australia (where IFRS GAAP is now practiced). With respect to the previous section, the taxonomy issues are visualized in Figure 3 which gives an overview picture. The key issues for any company that wishes to supply statements with XBRL tags at the account line items is what information can be represented with the general economy-level reporting taxonomy and what account items will need to be represented by industry or firm specific taxonomies.

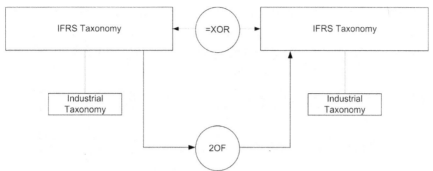

Figure 3: IFRS and US General and Industry Taxonomies Reconciliation

The advantage of investigating an actual company is the ability to place in context the disclosure issues in terms of US and Australian (IFRS) XBRL taxonomies. As of the time of this writing, the data available concerned a transition period where BHP Billiton was preparing to adopt IFRS in Australia, but a comparison with the adoption period showed no line item name differences applicable to XBRL conventions, further, company management indicated that accounting procedures were IFRS compliant in advance of Australia's IFRS adoption.

The discussion covers the Income Statement, Balance Sheet and a reconciliation of the Australian and U.S. GAAP as per the U.S. SEC 20-F reconciliation report. Also, this case analysis gives the opportunity to investigate the issues of extensions required in terms of industry taxonomies and firm specific taxonomy information. Some work had been done in the United States on a taxonomy for entities with oil and gas producing activities, but no approved or acknowledged version is currently available. One of the authors is the principal investigator and generally assigned the XBRL descriptions which are presented here. BHP Billiton did not designate or review any of the XBRL classifications. In most, but not all, cases, the author was able to assign XBRL descriptions. In the situations where no XBRL tag from the IFRS or US GAAP seemed appropriate a *?* is noted.

A comparison of BHP Billiton Australian GAAP versus US GAAP taxonomy reporting at the level of the Income Statement is shown in Table 1. Most of the line items have differences in terminology for the same type of line account (e.g., the revenue accounts). With respect to depreciation, the US GAAP has much more detail than the Australian GAAP. Relatively few accounts match monetary figures between the taxonomies. The classifications according to the different GAAPs are one aspect, but another is simply different accounting regulation treatments.

While BHP Billiton is a natural resource company, it is interesting to find that the Income Statement did not require any industry specific or firm specific XBRL account designations. There are two interpretations possible. One is that the general industry taxonomy covers the major summarization of accounts. The other interpretation is that BHP Billiton does not engage in such specialized business practices that the financial statements will require unique material accounts in order to present factual information to investors. Due to the size of BHP Billiton, the latter explanation is more likely.

Table 1: Comparative BHP Billiton Income Statements under U.S. and Australian GAAP

From group combined financials			From 20-F notes		
Australian account name-Original AUS GAAP	IFRS taxonomy XBRL name	AUS$ 2005	US account name-20F US GAAP	US taxonomy XBRL name	US$ 2005
Operating revenue	Consolidated Revenue	29649	Sales revenue	SalesRevenue Net	29587
Non-operating revenue	OtherOperating IncomeTotal ByFunction	1458			
		31107			
Expenses from ordinary activities, excluding depreciation, amortisation and borrowing costs	CostOfSalesBy Function	20697	Cost of sales	CostGoodsSold	-19496
			Loss on termination of operations (a)	GainLoss Disposition Assets	-387
Share of net profit of joint venture and associated entities accounted for using the equity method	Consolidated ShareOfProfit LossFromEquity Accounted Investments	564			
Depreciation and amortisation	Depreciation And Amortisation	1994	Depreciation and amortisation	Depreciation Amortization	-2082
			Goodwill impairment	Impairment Goodwill	
			General and administrative expenses	General Administrative Expenses	-192
			Operating income	OperatingProfit	7430
			Other income	OtherIncome	579
			Interest income	InterestIncome	107
Borrowing costs	InterestExpense	499	Interest expense	InterestExpense	-302

Profit from ordinary activities before income tax		8481			
			Net foreign exchange loss/(gain)	Foreign Currency ExchangeGains Losses	126
			Income before tax, minority interests and equity in net earnings of affiliates	EarningsBefore InterestTaxes	7940
Income tax expense attributable to ordinary activities	IncomeTax ExpenseIncome	2240	Taxation expense	Current Income-Tax ExpenseBenefit	-1836
Net profit		6241			
Outside equity interests in net profit of controlled entities	ProfitLoss AttributableTo MinorityInterest	232	Share of profits of affiliated companies	RevenueAffiliates	517
Net profit attributable to members of the BHP Billiton Group		6009			
Net exchange fluctuations on translation of foreign currency net assets and					
foreign currency interest bearing liabilities net of tax	Foreign Currency Exchange Increase Decrease Total	7			
			Minority interests	Minority Interest NetTaxEffect	-233
Total changes in equity other than those resulting from transactions with owners		6016	Net income from Continuing Operations	NetIncome	6388

A comparison of BHP Billiton Australian IFRS GAAP taxonomy Balance Sheet reporting is shown in Table 2. The XBRL cross referencing between Balance Sheet accounts is much more straightforward with the key exceptions (noted by ?) in the stockholders' equity section. The concepts of ownership are based on law and social value judgments which differ by culture.

A number of line items are similar before adjustment, but accounting regulatory differences require adjustments. Regulatory issues concerning intangibles are the source of large differences. The property, plant and equipment accounts also differ considerably. The author had *a problem* with the tax accounts. While this issue would seem general, no IFRS XBRL account names appeared appropriate. This issue does not seem like something that would require an industry or firm specific, but perhaps a revisit to the general industry taxonomy.

Table 2: Comparative BHP Billiton Balance Sheets under U.S. and Australian GAAP

AUS. Account Title	IFRS XBRL Tag		U.S. Account Title	US XBRL Tag	Un-adjusted 6/30/ 2005 US$M	Adjust-ments 6/30/20 05 US$M	US GAAP 6/30/2005 US$
Assets			Assets				
Current assets			Current assets				
Cash	Cash And Cash Equiva-lents	1418	Cash	CashAnd Cash Equivalents	1418		1418
			Restricted cash	Restricted Cash		85	85
Recei-vables	TradeAnd Other Receiv-ables Net Cur-rent	490	Recei-vables	Receivab-lesNet	3450	-2	3448
Other financial assets	Other Financial Assets Current	212	Other financial assets	ShortT erm Investments	212	54	266
Inven-tories	Inven-tories	2542	Invento-ries	Inven-toriesNet	2465		2465
Other assets	OtherAs-setsCur-rent	160	Other assets	Other Cur-rent Assets	160		160
Total current assets		7822	Total current assets	Total Current Assets	7705	137	7842
Non-current assets			Non-current assets				
Recei-vables	LoansAnd Recei-vables-Non Cur-rent	619	Recei-vables	Noncurrent-Notes Re-ceivable	619	-143	476
Invest-ments accounted for using the equity method	Equity Method Ac-counted Invest-ments Total	1525	Invest-ments accounted for using the equity method	LongTerm Investments	1525	908	2433

Other financial assets	Other Financia-lAssets Non Current	97	Other financial assets	Invest-mentsLong-Term Other	97	109	206
Invento-ries	Other Invento-ries	103	Invento-ries	Other Inven-tories	103	77	180
Property, plant and equip-ment	Property PlantAnd Equip-mentNet	30347	Property, plant and equip-ment?	Property Plant Equipment-Net	30347	2084	32431
Intangible assets	Intangible AssetsNet	513	Intangible assets?	Intangible AssetsFini-teLivedNet		49	49
			Good-will?	Intangible Assets-GoodwillNet	17	2593	2610
Deferred tax assets	Deferred TaxAssets	660	Deferred tax as-sets?	Deferred TaxAsset Noncurrent	1110	32	1142
Other assets	OtherAs-setsNon-Current	424	Other assets	OtherAs-setsCurrent-NonCurrent	424	-146	278
Total non-current assets		34288	Total non-current assets?	Noncurren-tAssets	34242	5563	39805
Total assets		42110	Total assets?	Assets	41947	5700	47647
Liabilities and share-share-holders' equity			Liabilities and share-share-holders' equity				
Current liabilities			Current liabilities				
Payables	Trade-Payab-lesCurrent	4091	Payables?	Ac-countsPaya-ble	4051		4051
Interest bearing liabilities	Interest-Bearing Borro-wingsCur rent	1500	Interest bearing liabilities	OtherShort-TermBor-rowings	1500		1500
Tax lia-bilities	Current-Tax-Payables	842	Tax lia-bilities	AccruedTax-es	842	18	860
Other provisions	Provi-sionsCur-rent	1226	Other provi-sions?	OtherCurren-tLiabilities	2104	2	2106
Total current liabilities		7659	Total current liabilities	CurrentLia-bilities	8497	20	8517

Non-current liabilities			Non-current liabilities				
Payables	TradePayablesNonCurrent	162	Payables	OtherLongTermDebt	162		162
Interest bearing liabilities	Interest bearing liabilities	9626	Interest bearing liabilities	LongTermDebt	9626	-4	9622
Tax liabilities	Deferred Tax Liabilities	1318	Tax liabilities?	DeferredTaxLiability Noncurrent	1192	1440	2632
Other provisions	Other Provisions NonCurrent	4981	Other provisions	Other Noncurrent Liabilities	4981	-617	4364
Total non-current liabilities		16087	Total non-current liabilities	NoncurrentLiabilities	15961	819	16780
Total liabilities		23746	Total liabilities	Liabilities	24458	839	25297
			Equity minority interests	MinorityInterest	336	10	346
Shareholders' equity			Shareholders' equity				
Contributed equity – BHP Billiton Limited ?	ShareCapitalTotal	1611					
Called up share capital – BHP Billiton Plc?	?	1752					
			Paid in capital?	CommonStockValue	3363	5174	8537
			Other equity items?	ComprehensiveIncomeEnding AccumulatedBalancesEachType	417	-19	398
Reserves	OtherReserves	638					
Retained profits	RetainedEarningsAccumulatedLosses	14022	Retained profits?	RetainedEarnings	13381	-304	13077

Outside equity interests?	Minori-tyInterest	341					
			Interest in shares of BHP Billiton?	TreasuryS-tockValu-eTotal	-8		-8
Total share-holders' equity		18364	Total share-holders' equity	Stockholder-sEquity	17153	4851	22004
			Total liabilities and share-holders' equity	Total Liabilities and Stockholders' Equity	41947	5700	47647

A reconciliation of the US and Australian GAAP is shown in Table 3. It is a 20-F report required by the SEC in order to list securities on an US exchange. The key point about Table 3 is the major differences between Australian GAAP and US GAAP as they would require transformations using XBRL and industry / firm specific taxonomies. These differences can be categorized in the following areas according to the relevant GAAP.

Table 3: 20-F Reconciliation of Income

Attributable profit as reported under Australian GAAP	6398
add/(deduct)	
Estimated adjustment required to accord with US GAAP:	
Fair value adjustment on acquisition of BHP Billiton Plc Group – depreciation, amortisation, impairments and other asset movements	-282
Employee compensation costs	60
Depreciation – write-downs	-5
Depreciation – revaluations	4
Depreciation – reserves	-9
Fair value accounting for derivatives	302
Fair value adjustment on acquisition of WMC Resources Ltd	-20
Exploration, evaluation and development expenditure	-38
Start-up costs	5
Pension plans	-24
Other post-retirement benefits	1
Employee Share Plan loans	-7
Goodwill	-2
Profit on asset sales	2
Taxation effect of above adjustments	287
Other taxation adjustments	-284
Total adjustment	-10
Net income of BHP Billiton Group under US GAAP	6388

An overall analysis of the BHP Billiton U.S. and Australian taxonomies indicates some similarities and dissimilarities. It is interesting to note that the Balance Sheet as a statement of position shows considerable similarity, but the Income Statement as a statement of performance shows greater dissimilarities. These differences are reflective of the thinking of accounting standard setters towards revenue and expense recognition. In part this is driven by social value judgments. In particular, the US regulators do not permit reserve account usage. Only in the case of established external markets does US GAAP permit upward changes in fair values, but IFRS does.

A limitation of the analysis is that one of the authors prepared the application of the XBRL taxonomies to the financial statements. If the company accountants were to do this work, they will have greater access to firm accounting information applicable to the XBRL account classifications. Also, company accountants would be more knowledgeable about classifying BHP Billiton accounts in terms of industry and company specific taxonomies. However, company accountants might wish to give industry or firm specific account names to *Income Statement line items*, because they perceive that they are distinguishing company value from the rest of the firms in their industry. There may be an issue of comparability versus specificity. From a XBRL system perspective, the combination of multiple taxonomies always leads to validation concerns. The main GAAP taxonomies have been validated, but industry and firm specific taxonomies will need to be validated with respect to being well formed and having a valid schema by a XBRL parser. Fortunately, these parsers are in existence. Correcting a taxonomy becomes a process of elimination of errors.

While the specific assignment of values to account line items is a matter of judgment at the firm level, there are some useful resources available at the XBRL.org web site for US GAAP and at the IASB.org web site for IFRS GAAP. Both sites have taxonomy documentation which links current standards to the individual line items. In the case of the BHP Billiton, line item accounts are specific to the firm's economic activities. Financial statements are only meaningful in the context of their GAAP. The explanation of the GAAP is found in the financial statement footnotes. Both US and IFRS GAAP taxonomies have footnote items. While the current case analysis did not link together the footnotes from the two GAAP taxonomies with respect to the financial statements, ultimately accountants/financial analysts have to establish that relation in order to have comparability which is a key objective in financial reporting.

5 Conclusions

This chapter addresses taxonomy issues that accountants and systems analysts face in implementing XBRL in multi-jurisdiction situations where different taxonomies may be necessary for the same firm. General database concepts are related to XBRL design issues. Alternative approaches to XBRL system design for multiple taxonomy situations are discussed. The application of XBRL to BHP Billiton is investigated with respect to multiple taxonomies and XBRL tag definition issues.

References

Attaluri, G. K.; Bradshaw D. P.; Coburn, N.; Larson, P. A.;Martin, P.; Silbershatz, A. Slonim, J.; Zhu, Q. (1995): The CORDS Multidatabase Project, IBM Systems Journal, 34 (1), pp. 39-62.

Ernst & Young (2005): IFRS/US GAAP Comparison, Ernst & Young LLP,United Kingdom.

FASB Press Release 7/6/06 (2006): US FASB and IASB Publish First Draft Chapters of Joint Conceptual Framework, Press Release.

FASB Press Release 5/22/06 (2006): Representatives of the Financial Accounting Standards Board and the Accounting Standards Board of Japan Meet In Pursuit of Global Convergence, Press Release.

FASB Press Release 2/27/06 (2006): FASB and IASB Reaffirm Commitment to Enhance Consistency, Comparability and Efficiency in Global Capital Markets, Press Release.

FASB News Release 06/01/05 (2005): FASB Issues Accounting Standard That Improves the Reporting of Accounting Changes as Part of Convergence Effort with IASB Press Release.

Hakimpour, F.; Geppert, A. (2005): Resolution of Semantic Heterogeneity in Database Schema Integration using formal Ontologies, Information and Technology Management, 6.

Hoffman, C. (2006): Financial Reporting Using XBRL IFRS and US GAAP Edition, Lulu.

Lee, M. L.; Wang Ling, T. (2003): A Methodology for Structural Conflict Resolution in the Integration of Entity-Relationship Schemas, Knowledge and Information Systems, 5,

Nicolle, C.; Yetongnon, K.; Simon, J.-C. (2003): XML Integration and Toolkit for B2B Applications, Journal of Database Management, 14(4).

Radebaugh L.; Gray S.; Black E. (2005): International Accounting and Multinational Enterprises, 6, Wiley.

Schmitt, I.; Saake, G. (2005): A Comprehensive Database Schema Integration Method based on the Theory of Formal Concepts, Acta Informatica, 41 (7/8).

XBRL as eXtensible Reporting Language for EU Reporting

Maciej Piechocki, André Gräning, Harald Kienegger

Technische Universität Bergakademie Freiberg, Germany

{maciej.piechocki\andre.graening\harald.kienegger}@bwl.tu-freiberg.de

Contents

1   Introduction

The eXtensible Business Reporting Language (XBRL) is a metadata representation language designed for a wide range of business reporting environments. Whilst primarily aimed at financial reporting, today XBRL is in use in not only for typical financial reporting domain, but also in various other business reporting scenarios. So for example, the *Committee of European Banking Supervisors* (CEBS) in its *Common Reporting* (COREP) taxonomy uses XBRL for reporting of solvency information for financial institutions (Boixo, Flores 2005). Another example is the *EUROSTAT initiative* that is analyzing the use of XBRL for statistical purposes for gathering business related information. Nonethless, each of these scenarios do not cross the border of what traditionally could be regarded as business reporting that is closely related to financial information. One of the possible reasons for this can be related to the profile of the participants of the XBRL International consortium that is responsible for the development of the language. Traditionally, the significant majority of these participants come from the financial reporting and related domains (XBRL 2006a). That is why it is important to evaluate XBRL use as a more universal metadata language. Observing the recent developments concerning XBRL in the European Union (EU) it can be clearly stated that due to its extensibility the XBRL standard is very useful in the many scenarios where the international reporting needs to be implemented at international and national levels. Usually the regulations are interpreted in paper form and often employ proprietary reporting solutions are implemented to enable data gathering. The innovative approach of the CEBS, with the European COREP XBRL taxonomy being extended on the level of European member stated, demonstrates the potential for standardisation and harmonisation of business reporting.

In our research, we first construct a set of criteria against which XBRL as an *eXtensible Reporting Language* (XRL) can be evaluated. Although in this paper we apply the criteria to EU regulations it is clearly possible to generalise them for a broader spectrum of reporting. Analysing the CEBS approach we test how far XBRL can be used in very untypical domains other than traditional business or financial reporting thus answering the question if XBRL can be treated as eXtensible Reporting Language. In order to do so we chose the domain of energy performance of building reporting and modelled the scenario using XBRL standard. Finally in order to evaluate the XBRL use as XRL we applied the set of criteria constructed at the beginning of the analysis.

The paper proceeds as follows. The introduction of the problem domain and the research questions are addressed in the first section. The second section deals with the construction of a set of criteria appropriate for further research. The third section introduces XBRL as a standard based on the eXtensible Markup Language (XML) family. The basic terms as XBRL taxonomies, taxonomy extensions as well as instance documents are discussed. The fourth section describes the current situation of the case study domain. It introduces the legal basis, as well as the implementation of the 2002/91/EG guideline on the *Energy Performance of Buildings* which is explained by means of the example of the implementation in Germany. Finally in this section XBRL is discussed as the proposed solution of the identified issues. The fifth section provides an evaluation of the introduced XBRL solution in the given scenario. The paper ends with a short conclusion summarising and generalising the suggested approach for other reporting scenarios thus answering the research question about applicability of XBRL as eXtensible Reporting Language.

2 Criteria of the Reporting Standards in the EU

The investigation of the designated issues requires a set of criteria that enables methodical analysis of the problem domain. With the help of such criteria the later evaluation of the XBRL use as a broader *XRL* can be conducted. Although many authors (e.g. Heinrich, Lehner 2005; Krcmar 2005) refer to the concept of a general reporting domain, the literature provides no clear set of criteria defining the reporting domain. Therefore, we have designed a set of criteria relevant to the context of our research. The selected criteria are twofold. Firstly, they refer to the qualities of reporting within the EU thereby implying the applicability of the researched standards in this area. Secondly, we employ a set of software quality norms we derive from the well-accepted DIN ISO 9126 standard (Schlenker 1998). We have selected the appropriate norms for this study.

The European Union has established basic principles which apply to each member of the community. The two primary principles are *transparency* (Europe 2006b) and the *harmonization* (Europe 2006a) of the actions amongst the member states. Transparency should ensure primarily that the Union is open to public scrutiny and accountable for its work (Europe 2006c). The harmonization of the actions concerns alignment of the European Union economic objectives at the policy level with the operational realities within the member states. Furthermore *standardization* (Wurster 2007) is a substantial criterion for the community since it leads to common action amongst the

member states. Based on standardized concepts it is possible to overcome existing lin-
guistic and cultural differences. The standardization leads also to lowering of transaction costs, which is particularly interesting for potential investors within European
domestic markets (König 1997). We applied all three criteria, transparency, harmonization and standardization, for our research due to their high relevance to the reporting
processes in the EU.

Furthermore in order to analyze the technological layer of the reporting solution the
DIN ISO 9126 (Deutsches Institut für Normung accepted International Organization
for Standardization norm) is applied. DIN ISO 9126 is a standard which defines software quality criteria. The standard contains six main criteria with sublevels in order to
gain an abstract conclusion about software quality. The overall DIN ISO 9126 criteria
are functionality, reliability, usability, efficiency, changeability and transferability
(DIN 1991). In our research we reduced the number of criteria to two that are most
relevant from the reporting viewpoint of view. We selected the *changeability* and
transferability for the further analysis. Although the remaining four DIN ISO 9126
criteria could be also further considered they refer very strong to the software quality
and it is difficult to apply them as the reporting criteria.

First of the accepted DIN ISO 9126 criteria is the so-called changeability of the reporting software. Changeability is the overall term for describing the effort to realize
changes within the software. Changes are classified as corrections, improvements or
just modifications of the reporting software. Within the sublevels analyzability, mod-
ifiability and verifiability of the reporting standard can be assessed. The changeability
criteria are also of particular concern to the European Union because of the broad
range different member states, each having different cultural foundations and legal
requirements. Incorporating these requirements leads to changes and adjustments in
the reference to reporting domain.

The second criterion selected from the DIN ISO 9126 is the quality of data communication to the authorities and between the member states. Although DIN ISO 9126 refers to the criterion as transferability we applied the simplified term electronic
processing. The rising need for electronic information processing from authorities,
investors and other information users should be taken into consideration at this stage in
the reporting domain.

Finally we decided to incorporate one more criterion not directly discussed at either
the EU level or in DIN ISO 9126. It refers to the network effects and partially to already mention standardization (Buxmann, König 1998). This criterion concerns the

openness of the reporting solution. The sublevels such as accessibility to the standard, industry support as well as lack of proprietary barriers are considered here. It impacts the reporting standard quality on the one hand and the market acceptance on the other hand. Open solutions can be regarded as a strong alternative to proprietary solutions.

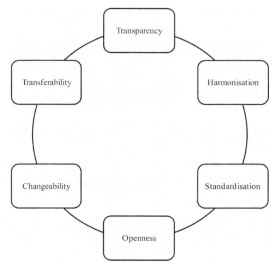

Figure 1: Selected set of criteria for reporting standards in the EU

The described criteria presented in diagram 1 are the subject of this research. They are at basis for input to the case study conducted for the EDPB and our subsequent evalua-tion. The basis for the evaluation of the criteria is the level of their fulfilment. Neither EU literature nor DIN ISO 9126 clearly states how to evaluate the described criteria. Therefore in this paper we have adopted a simplified evaluation scheme in three stag-es. The highest stage (+) informs the complete fulfilment of the analysed criteria. In case the criteria fulfilment level is insufficient the middle stage (o) is assigned. The third stage (-) represents the situation when the criteria is not fulfilled or not con-cerned. The evaluation base is the conducted analysis and constructed case study. On the basis of experiences from the case study the stages are assigned to each of the indi-vidual criteria.

3   XBRL as Standard for Business Reporting

XML is generally accepted as a de facto standard for electronic data transfer. The XML standard is developed by the World Wide Web Consortium (W3C) offers users a multitude of application possibilities (Weitzel et al. 2001). Many software applications support XML based standards either natively or as a data interchange protocol. For example, the EML (Environmental Markup Language) was developed as common language for environmental sciences for description of environmental objects (Tochtermann, Riekert 2001). Another example is the development of the CIM XML (Common Information Model) for representing power system models which represents a step into standardization of interchange protocols (de Vos, Widergren, Zhu 2001). Arguably, one of the most significant developments in the reporting domain remains XBRL (Hoffman 2006).

The technical analysis of the XBRL is the substantial subject of the second section. The discussion starts with the introduction to XBRL specification which is the basis documentation for the language.[1] In the first part of the section the focus is on XBRL for financial reporting (XBRL FR) which is regarded as the core XBRL technology (Hoffmann 2006; Boritz, Won 2005, 13). The definitions and critical analysis of terms such as XBRL taxonomies, taxonomy extensions and instance documents together with the analysis of the issues concerning the current XBRL specification (Engel et al. 2005) build the next part of the section. Another core XBRL application apart from the mentioned FR adaptation is XBRL GL[2]. XBRL GL plays an important role in the internal reporting domain by standardising a format for the transport of journal entries, General Ledger (GL) and trail balances (Ramin et al. 2006; hAonghusa 2005, 74; Kranich, Schmitz 2003, 80) between co-operating systems. Although recently introduced, the XBRL Dimension Taxonomies (XDT) is gaining importance. We excluded this class of taxonomies from our research scope due to their complexity and the fact that its modularity is not useful in the context of the case study. Nonetheless, *XBRL Dimension Taxonomies* will be an important further research line.

3.1 Technological Foundation of the XBRL Standard

XBRL was first named the eXtensible Financial Reporting Markup Language (XFRML), but soon the XBRL community agreed that the language could have broader use and adjusted its name to incorporate various business reporting aspects (Garbelotto, Hannon 2005, 57; Hoffman 2006, 45; XBRL 2006b). Combining the XBRL definition from the XBRL specification and the definition of financial reporting from Wagenhofer and Ewert (Wagenhofer, Ewert 2003, 4) the core financial reporting aspects of XBRL (XBRL FR) can be described as: "XBRL for financial reporting com-

---

[1] XBRL is de facto standard for digital business reporting so the terms language and standard are used interchangeably (Bergeron 2003, 15-16).

[2] Both XBRL FR and XBRL GL are based on the XBRL Specification.

promises all XBRL enabled information systems oriented towards external users such as investors, creditors, customers, suppliers, competitors and public".

Table1 explains the basic terms in XBRL FR area which are taxonomies and instance documents. XBRL taxonomies reflect the underlying financial reporting principles in form of different Generally Accepted Accounting Principles (GAAP)[3] encoded using standardized XBRL vocabulary. The instance documents essentially reflect the financial statements of an entity, but in digital and tractable form.

Table 1: Relation between Traditional Reporting and XBRL FR

	Underlying accounting principles	Financial report
Traditional reporting	GAAP	Paper, PDF or HTML[4] financial report
XBRL FR	GAAP based XBRL taxonomy	Instance document

Figure 2 provides a more detailed view of the XBRL FR framework. Basic terms including taxonomy, taxonomy extension, instance document and Discoverable Taxonomy Set (DTS) are visualised together with relations between them.

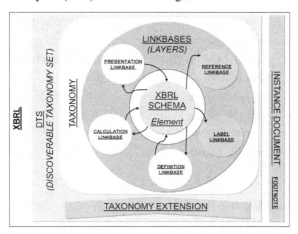

Figure 2: XBRL Financial Reporting Framework (IASCF 2006)

A taxonomy in general terms means a catalogue or set of rules for information classification. In XBRL, a taxonomy is a dictionary, containing computer-readable definitions of business reporting terms as well as relationships between them and links connecting

---

[3] Although division between principle, rule and definition based accounting standards exists between different GAAPs the statements reflects the IFRS view as principle based accounting standard.

[4] Formats such as HTML and PDF are not treated as digital format even though being application consumable. HTML and PDF are not describing the reported facts in a standardized way using for example tags.

them to human-readable resources. A typical taxonomy consists of a schema (or schemas) and linkbases. A set of taxonomies that can be discovered[5] from one entry point schema is called Discoverable Taxonomy Set (DTS) (Engel et al. 2005; Hoffman 2006, 77; IASCF 2006).

Taxonomy extensions[6] add concepts and modify the relationships among the concepts in the base taxonomies that they extend. They are created to support specialised reporting requirements in specific accounting jurisdictions, in specific industries, or for specific companies. Taxonomy extensions consist of a set of taxonomy schemas and/or linkbases that augment a DTS that references the base taxonomies (IASCF 2006). An instance document is a business report in XBRL format. It contains tagged business facts, together with the context in which they appear and unit description (Engel et al. 2005; IASCF 2006) and is referring the tags to the elements specified in the taxonomy.

Apart from the XBRL Specification 2.1 there are associated governing documents that define the rules for XBRL FR vocabulary and taxonomies architecture. The most important for creation of taxonomies is the Financial Reporting Taxonomy Architecture (FRTA). FRTA states a set of 104[7] rules concerning best practices of taxonomy creation (Hamscher et al. 2005, 4-5). Another set of rules is the nascent Financial Reporting Instance Standards[8] (FRIS) that exists for the creation of instance documents and facilitate the analysis and comparison of XBRL financial reporting data by computer applications and human readers[9] (Goodhand, Hamscher 2004, 1). Finally, underlying principles for modelling of financial reporting taxonomy were created by Hoffmann (Hoffman 2006, 265-355). So called patterns are a collection of twenty modelling rules which help to create standardized taxonomies which are FRTA valid.

Different taxonomies are required for different financial reporting purposes. National jurisdictions may need their own financial reporting taxonomies to reflect their local accounting regulations. Many different organisations, including regulators, specific industries or even companies, may require taxonomies to cover their own business reporting needs. The current research considers taxonomies with the potential use in the European area with special focus on business reporting in Germany. Therefore the dis-

---

[5] DTS discovery is a technical term and means traversing over related XBRL schemas and linkbases (Engel et al. 2005).
[6] The term taxonomy extension is used interchangeably with the term extension taxonomy (Hoffman 2006, 110; Teixeira et al. 2003, 1-2).
[7] The number of FRTA rules is changing because of the ongoing Domain Working Group (DWG) enhancements to the document.
[8] FRIS opposite to FRTA is not completely approved by the XBRL International consortium.
[9] FRTA and FRIS similarly to XBRL Specification are accompanied by conformance suits in order to achieve greater software compatibility (Wallis 2004; Wallis 2005a).

cussed taxonomies are *International Financial Reporting Standards General Purpose* (IFRS-GP), *United States Generally Accepted Accounting Principles* (US GAAP)[10] and *German Accounting Principles* (GermanAP).

The XBRL GL taxonomy is intended to provide a standardized format for representing the data fields found in accounting and operation systems and transactional reports that will allow organizations to tag journal entries, accounting master files, historical status reports in XBRL and the underlying detail for financial reporting taxonomies (XBRL 2005). XBRL GL is not a separate specification, but is based on the XBRL Specification 2.1. However, XBRL GL is not related to the FRTA and FRIS governance documents and conformance suites. The XII published as a draft the proposed XBRL GL Instance Standards (GLIS) to facilitate the analysis and comparison of XBRL GL data by computer applications and human readers (Wallis 2005b, 3) as well as GL Taxonomy Framework Technical Architecture (GLFTA) establishing rules and conventions that assist in comprehension, usage and performance among different journal focussed taxonomies (Wallis 2005c, i). From the technical point of view XBRL GL is a stand-alone taxonomy, suitable for the needs of representing basic accounting databases and transactions. The most important features of the XBRL GL taxonomy according to XII are:

- multi-GAAP, drill-up to multi-XBRL reporting taxonomies capability;

- being a standard format to move unposted and posted GL information back and forth from branch offices to consolidating systems, budgeting and forecasting tools and reporting tools;

- being a standard format to move information from client systems to auditor system;

- being a tool for representing detail drill-down for performance measurement reporting items; .

- creating possibilities for any type of mandatory audit trail (XBRL 2006b).

The first part of this section analyses and summarises the XBRL standard from the technical point of view. We conduct our research using the available XBRL governing documents and literature. Also the practical experiences with the XBRL taxonomy development are reflected in the research results.

---

[10] According to the assumptions of the thesis and focus on the profit-generating entities in the commerce and industry and not financial or insurance area only the US GAAP Commerce and Industry (CI) taxonomy is taken into consideration.

3.2 Application of the XBRL as eXtensible Reporting Language

In this section we analyse the technical aspects explained above and their correspondence to more general reporting scenarios. It has to be considered, that only minor details constrains XBRL to business or financial reporting only. The direct indication of business or financial reporting character is represented mainly through particular data types including the *monetary item* data type and the *balance* attribute with the values debit or credit, which is coupled to the monetary item data type. On the other hand, XBRL utilises a number of general data types and attributes known from XML schema thus enabling the creation of a very wide range of data elements. Further, the described five kinds of linkbases do not imply the financial reporting character and can be easily adapted for the use of different domains.

The section 2.1 analysed two groups of taxonomies. The XBRL FR taxonomies are clearly financial reporting oriented and none of the existing taxonomies, such as IFRS, US GAAP or German GAAP, seems to fulfil the general requirements of other domains. Nevertheless it is possible to build a taxonomy for other than financial or business reporting purposes, based on the experiences and rules from XBRL FR. The second described taxonomy, XBRL GL, is a highly specialised expression of data fields found in accounting and operation systems and transactional reports. Although theoretically possible to develop XBRL GL-like taxonomy for other needs, the experiences in this area are restricted to this one taxonomy only. At present, it is not immediately adaptable to other reporting domains.

Furthermore, analysing the usability of XBRL for other domains, it is important to consider a clear distinction between the domain data model and a metadata model in XBRL. Besides considering facts in isolation, XBRL is capable of processing contextual knowledge and additional information about facts (IASCF 2006). This capability not only offers advantages for the financial sector but also for the other reporting scenarios, which will be demonstrated using the case study in the next section (Engel et al. 2005). Taxonomies and instance documents enable users of XBRL to save general information detached from facts. A single taxonomy can be used for several instance documents, which is an advantage of XBRL and the explanation for the separation of data from metadata. Also the possibility to create taxonomy extensions gains on importance in scenarios where an international reporting regulation is implemented on the national level, which is a very common case in the EU.

4   Case Study with Reporting of Energy Performance of Buildings

In the subsequent section we introduce a case study based on the EDPB. This domain was selected due to its lack of relation to traditional XBRL financial and business reporting domains. Also the construction of the case study is assuming the set of criteria constructed in the second section.

Originally initiated as an economic union, the European Union (EU) is continually harmonising and standardising its economic sectors. The introduction of International Financial Reporting Standards (IFRS) for EU corporations together with the Basel II for EU financial institutions form a foundation which enables monitoring and evaluation of performance and risks of entities within the international world of finance. Meanwhile due to scarce of energy resources, the consumption of energy is also an important topic in the EU. This growing awareness of energy consumption within the EU creates a demand to measure and compare energy consumption. Directive 2002/91/EG on the Energy Performance of Buildings (EDPB) determines the minimum energy efficiency of buildings together with necessary basic measures. However, achieving a high level of legal standardisation, each member country is left to make their own judgments as far as technical harmonisation is concerned. This situation leads to different implementations of the directive across the member states and complicates comparability across the EU. We chose the EDPB for our case study mainly due to the high comparability to the Basel II reporting and XBRL taxonomies COREP (Common Reporting) and FINREP (Financial Reporting) developed for this reasons and adjusted to the national level within EU member states. The EDPB is a good basis for consideration of reporting of a completely different character than financial reporting domain.

The European Commission (EC) determined to consider environmental protection in its collective policy and legislation in Article 6 of the EWG treaty (Guideline 2003). Guideline 2002/91/EG on the Energy Performance of Buildings is based on the insight that energy consumption has to be reduced in order to save scarce resources. Article 1 of above mentioned directive states the following objectives:

- a general framework for the calculation of the energy performance of existing buildings has to be provided;

- prescribed minimum requirements for the energy performance of new buildings have to be applied;

- establishment of so called "energy passes" for real estate. Member states should implement the guideline in their countries and discuss measures to guarantee minimum requirements on energy performance.

The legal framework for the adoption of the guideline is first described. This should enable the reader to understand the implementation of the guideline. Building on this insight, the reasons for the necessity of an EC-wide standard for energy reporting are the explained.

4.1   Legal Framework

According to Article 15 of Guideline 2002/91/EG, administrative and legal specifications were required to become effective on January, 4 2006 (Guideline 2003). Based on Guideline 2002/91/EG the Deutsche Energie-Agentur GmbH (dena) initiated a field test prior to the establishment of the German Energieeinsparverordnung (EnEV, based on guideline 2002/91/EG). This field test was aimed at testing methods of calculation of energy consumption for their suitability for daily use. Figure 3 shows the involved parties spanning from the EC to the national legislation bodies. Moreover, it displays the technical implementation and application by German authorities, which issue energy passes. On November 17 2006, the German ministery of transport and the German secretary for trade and industry, who are members of the advisory board of *dena*, advised the adoption of energy passes. In the future, each owner of real estate will be obliged by *Energieeinsparverordnung* to show the energy pass of a building, in the case of a future sale. The energy pass contains data on the building's energy consumption, as well as further climatic information. The energy pass acts as an instrument for owners of real estate to prove the energy consumption of their property. On the other hand, identified inefficiencies concerning energy consumption of a building can be corrected, in order to improve the energy balance of a building (Bundesministerium 2006).

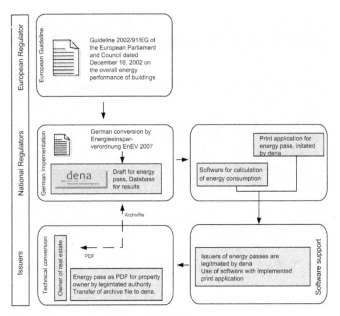

Figure 3: Laws and guidelines of the EDPB

During the field test, which was conducted by *dena*, a simplified graphical form for the energy pass was developed (Gebäudeenergiepass 2006). Additionally, *dena* assigned programmers to develop a verified printing application, which is implemented as a standard in specific software. Every producer of the software, who is concerned with the adoption of the 2002/91/EG guideline, is obliged to integrate above mentioned printing application into their software, to ensure required uniformity (Guideline 2003). All required data are imported from the different programmes into the dena application. According to dena, it is possible to process for one third of the data directly after the import. These data contain pictures of buildings, consumption dates as well as further information that is not provided by calculation software. The integrity of data is supervised by a check routine. Mistakes are displayed in an information window. The actual energy pass is generated in *PDF* and archived. The PDF file corresponds to the energy pass and remains with the property owner(s). The archive file contains all facts concerning energy effectiveness of a real estate. The archive file can be sent to dena anonymously. In addition, it is possible to select the files which should be transmitted to *dena*. There is no legal obligation to transfer data to dena. Data received by *dena* is stored in a database and allows statistical analysis (ROWA). An expert, legitimated by *dena*, examines the condition of buildings. In course of the field test several hundred issuers of energy passes signed in to the database installed on *dena's* websites.

This section presents the legal framework which is the basis for the case study developed in the subsequent sections. In order to conduct the case study the emerging issues are identified and discussed in the next section.

4.2   Emerging Issues

The law of energy performance of buildings includes arguments derived from Article 5 of the EWG treaty. The basic principles for the requirements and objectives of the guideline are determined by the common base of the EC according to Article 5 of the EWG treaty. Member states are required to realise the guidelines. Thus, every member state is able to decide on a system, which fulfils the minimum requirements of the guideline within in the scope of their possibilities. It was abandoned to use strict rules for the implementation of the treaty. That way, the heterogeneous member states are able to adopt the guidelines according to their own capabilities (EnEV).

The objective of this minimum standard is to create transparency of the calculation of energy efficiency throughout the EC. All permitted methods of calculation, positive influences on the calculation and a notice on classification of buildings according to Article 3 of the 2002/91/EG guideline can be found in the Appendix of this guideline (Guideline 2003).

While the framework for calculation provides a background for common calculation, it cannot be regarded as full harmonisation of the 2002/91/EG guideline. Further there is no definition of DIN or ISO standards that would ensure conforming implementation of the guideline 2002/91/EG throughout the EC. Thus, member states are given the possibility to implement the 2002/91/EG guideline according to their own interpretation of the rules stated in the appendix. The application of different interpretations of the appendix will lead to a lack of transparency within the EU.

In addition to the political issues a number of economic issues arise. Despite the economic harmonisation of the EU as constituted by the *Rome Treaties* (Pelkman 2006), it cannot be ensured that the overall energy performance stated in an energy pass in France, for example, corresponds to the overall energy performance of a similar building stated in an energy pass issued in Poland. Hence, an energy pass can only be regarded as general information for investors in public or private property. This problem is caused by the lack of standardisation in implementation of the 2002/91/EG guideline.

Another challenge arises in the practical implementation of the 2002/91/EG guideline. Several software producers provide different proprietary software solutions for issuers of energy passes (Hansen 1997). These software solutions also prevent further standardisation and harmonisation. Furthermore changeability of software has to be considered. Laws and regulations build the foundation of the energy pass. In case of a change in laws and regulations, every existing software application has to be adjusted according to the changes under high efforts and costs. Provided that it could be implemented into existing systems easily, a standard software solution would potentially generate efficiency advantages. The majority of existing software solutions for the calculation of energy performance are based on the model Rechenkern IBP-189599 Kernel developed by *Fraunhofer Institute for Building Physics* (Fraunhofer). This model closes the gap between simple statistical methods and complex building simulations. The core of the model is offered to software producers for implementation in their software. To ensure transparency, the source code is accessible on the Internet (Rechenkern 2006). The source code is accessible for every publisher of energy performance calculation software and therewith offers a standardized solution. Therefore, it could be implemented as a standard, while the complete software solution including the printing application, offered by *dena* is protected by the copyright law.

In order to issue an energy pass in Germany apart from mandatory performance indicators, the printing application offered by *dena* is required. As mentioned above, this printing application was developed to establish a uniform design for energy passes in Germany. Nevertheless, this application represents a proprietary solution. For the time being, it is impossible to create standardized energy passes throughout the EU. An open standard could lead to increased transparency, harmonisation and to a unified European solution. Moreover, the application offered by *dena* enables anonymous data transfer from issuers of energy passes to dena. However, the transmission of unified data to a central European evaluation entity requires a unified standard for data transmission, which would also increase the independency from the software producers. Figure 4 depicts problematic areas of guideline 2002/91/EG spanning from European to national level and from technical to implementation issues. Harmonisation and standardisation issues arise between the European and the national level. Proprietary software solutions evoke dependencies between national level (here Germany) and technical domain. This leads to the conclusion that there is a lack of open standards which could assure the implementation of minimum requirements of guideline 2002/91/EG. In addition, there is a transparency problem, which complicates the comparison of results. Furthermore, there are difficulties concerning the automatic processing of data. Data can only be transmitted by generating an archive file.

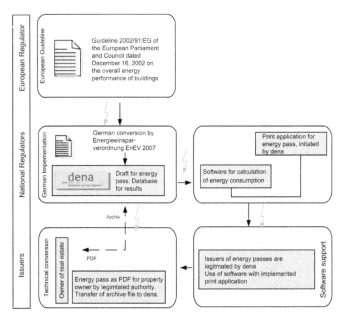

Figure 4: Identified problem areas

In the following discussion, the issues addressed are addressed by adopting a systematic approach using an open XBRL metadata standard. Utilization of XBRL offers an alternative solution to the problems discussed in this section as well as make progress in standardisation of energy passes.

4.3   XBRL as a Technology Enabler for EDPB

As mentioned above, there are restrictions concerning data transfer, standardisation and harmonisation. Further complications arise from different legal interpretations of the guidelines, differentiated application in member states as well as from comparability of results. Increasing internationalisation of markets intensifies these issues. XBRL taxonomies enable the interrelation and the addition of information, which support users in creating and using taxonomies. The data stored in the instance documents are only facts which neither have any inherent relationships nor have any hierarchical order. They are a collection of inputted data (as in XML). The XBRL schema file, as a part of the taxonomy, allows the definition of individual positions (IASCF 2006). It is possible to define numerical and alphanumerical values and to relate these to dates or periods of time. Furthermore, the definition of tuples or single elements is possible. Tuples are tables with known headlines and an unknown number of value lines. Later in an instance document a tuple could represent for example all apartments in one building along with their energy consumption. The several positions are listed in the schema file.

An example for such a concept for EPDC purposes is *BedarfHeizOel*. This represents the position *Heating Oil Consumption*. As this is a machine-readable notation it may seem confusing to human readers. This notation directly leads to linkbases which are central parts of taxonomy. Taxonomies solve the issues addressed defining not only the concepts but also relationship among them and relationships to human understandable descriptions. Figure 5 displays the structure of a taxonomy as already explained in connection with the instance documents. Furthermore, it depicts the three linkbases applied in our case study explained below. One can distinguish between two different types of linkbases within taxonomy documentation linkbases and relation linkbases. Documentation linkbases connect concepts with reference data while relation linkbases combine several concepts. Thus, a semantic connection between the separate concepts is possible. The so called label linkbase represents one documentation linkbase. Concepts defined in a scheme can be assigned to labels and terms, which can be understood by human users. This facilitates the use of the taxonomy and its application for all users. Moreover, it is possible to assign multiple terms to one concept. In respect of energy passes, this consideration is very meaningful as it is a European application that is used in a variety of different languages.

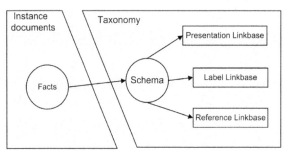

Figure 5: Data- and Metadata Concept

The concept *BedarfHeizOel*, for example, could be used on the one hand by the label *Heizoelbedarf* in German and on the other hand by the label *Heating Oil Consumption* in English. This allows a pan-European comprehension of the taxonomy. The example chosen, only contains two languages although it is possible to integrate an infinite number of languages. The presentation linkbase is another linkbase that can be applied in the presented taxonomy. It enables a structured and hierarchical presentation of data. The presentation linkbase represents a relation linkbase, which combines several elements together. The parent-child relation enables an explicit classification of concepts. For example, it is possible to classify the concepts heating demand, water demand or primary energy demand as children of the concept evaluation measures. Moreover the element order attribute allows an exposure of the elements based on legal restrictions. A unified display and a definite hierarchy of concepts (figure 6) lead to enhanced understanding and usability of the taxonomy (IASCF 2006).

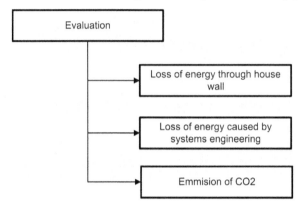

Figure 6: Selection from the presentation linkbase

Another implemented linkbase is the reference linkbase. It allocates legal foundations to concepts. Thus, every user is able to see which law defines each position. The concept-reference relation connects a concept to the corresponding legal basis. This allows users to refer to the legal basis every time, which is a valid feature concerning the transparency of the required data.

To model all fundamental concepts, the core taxonomy has to be developed. Core taxonomies are fundamental concepts, which are available for application in every member state in the EU. Not only financial and goods markets are subject to the effects of internationalisation. The market for real estate is also increasingly becoming the target of international private equity firms.

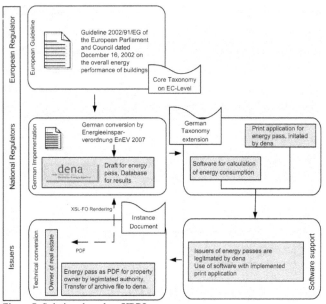

Figure 7: Solutions based on XBRL

This emphasises the importance of a unified European standard for the compilation of energy performance data. Given this standard, investors are able to compare invest-ment alternatives. As shown in figure 7, it has to be taken in consideration that the tax-onomy must be valid for all European states. Moreover, it creates the basis for interna-tional comparisons, which enables comparisons despite of national interpretations. This basis is the core taxonomy, which should be provided by the authorities of EU member states. Country specific characteristics can be considered by the application of taxonomy extensions.

In Germany, *dena* should provide the taxonomy extension to potential software pro-ducers or implement it into its existing printing application. Thus, issuers of energy passes are free to choose to use software with or without a printing application. Issuers of an energy passes may transform data to PDF by using XSL-FO. Therewith, the data are made accessible for potential investors in the same visual format. Furthermore, an interface could be applied, to integrate instance documents into the dena database for evaluation. This could be characterized as a harmonisation of energy reporting, adapted by a unified public standard. On the one hand, the application of a non-proprietary solution enhances establishment of a standard. On the other hand, users are offered a broad range of extensions. In this field, XBRL represents an adequate exam-ple upon which enhancements can be discussed.

In previous sections, the possibility of electronic data processing was discussed. A customised version of XBRL also allows the user to process data electronically. Time savings are the central advantage realised by electronic data transfer. Furthermore, manual data input is automated while data quality remains equal.

5   Evaluation of Proposed Solution

The constructed case study demonstrates that XBRL is able to convert the minimum requirements of the 2002/91/EG guideline represented by the energy pass in the standardized form. In this section we evaluate the use of XBRL as a general reporting solution in the form of a XRL based on the criteria defined in the second section. The evaluation is based on a graphical approach, which should clarify the advantages and disadvantages of the open XBRL standard. Additionally, improvements enabled by the use of XBRL are described. Figure 8 depicts the criteria standardisation, transparency, harmonisation as well as the issue of open versus closed standards and the possibility of automatic data processing as well as changeability.

The CEBS example shows that *transparency* can be improved using XBRL. Uniformity is ensured by a given schema, which is considered to have a positive influence on the transparency of data. Thus, results are comparable for all national levels and provide clarity of data to potential investors. Also in our case study the level of transparency is increased implying a positive return from application of XBRL to the knowledge domain. So the overall evaluation of the criterion is positive (+).

Concerning *harmonisation*, representing the second criterion, no improvement can be determined. Harmonisation refers to all the economic processes between member states. It is difficult to determine the effect on this criterion only by referring to the reporting domain. Also as we evaluated this criterion as neutral (o) it should be considered that taxonomy extensions imply harmonisation in a much broader sense.

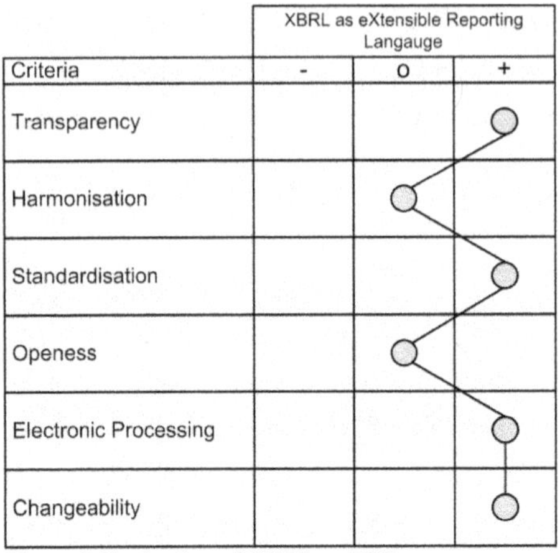

Criteria	XBRL as eXtensible Reporting Langauge		
	-	o	+
Transparency			O
Harmonisation		O	
Standardisation			O
Openess		O	
Electronic Processing			O
Changeability			O

Figure 8: Evaluation of XBRL as XRL

Certainly, a unified standard for overall reporting is desirable. Nevertheless XBRL has no direct influence on economic processes. XBRL is only able to illustrate economic processes, but does not help to improve them. However, XBRL *standardizes* illustration of processes, which is subject of the third criterion. XBRL offers taxonomies and instances to provide an identical framework for reporting of entities from all member states of the EU. This application could also be applied to the existing German printing application. XBRL as an open standard can be implemented in existing systems independent from data and programming languages (Guideline 2003). Moreover, it allows authorities easier analysis of the reported data. The analysis supports further decisions making.

The fourth aspect is characterised by the discussion about *open vs. closed standards.* As already mentioned, XBRL is an extensible reporting technology. This means each member state can add new elements to an existing European solution, without violating the main concepts. The open standard allows developing a customized version of the taxonomy for the national level, to meet all national reporting requirements. In contrast, a closed standard could only be customized by the legal owner of the copyright of a standard. If all 25 member states of the EU started to develop own national standards, the above mentioned problems would occur again. Faced with these issues, the application of an open standard is advantageous for the European overall reporting concept.

Another criterion was *electronic processing* of data. By using XBRL, data transfer could be implemented as the background application. All data can be exported via an XML interface and subsequently be imported into a database. The process of selecting and making data anonymous for transmission becomes obsolete, as these steps can be implemented directly. Simultaneously XBRL enables publishing data in various data portals. Existing data can be updated by using XBRL dynamically.

The final aspect of evaluation concerns the *changeability* criterion. Changeability of existing systems includes monetary and time aspects. As depicted, modifications in law have to be implemented into existing systems. All the software concerning reporting has to be adjusted, if a proprietary solution is applied. In contrast, if a standard such as XBRL is used, solely the core taxonomy would have to be modified. As taxonomy extensions refer to the core taxonomy the software solutions adapt the changes automatically. Therefore, the conformance to all minimum requirements beside country specific characteristics is guaranteed. Thus, financial and timely aspects are less affected by a standard than by a proprietary solution. Changes in the core taxonomy require only one change. Proprietary software, in contrast, has to be adjusted in all versions. Especially fundamental changes require high financial and time effort.

Above research demonstrates that an open standard, such as XBRL could serve as a solution for standardized reporting and automatic data processing in untypical for XBRL scenarios. In addition, section four demonstrates advantages in using a core European taxonomy. National taxonomy extensions provide better support concerning changeability, compared to proprietary solutions. Improved changeability could be advantageous in turn of harmonisation of reporting and the associated European-wide comparability of reporting entities. Unified energy reporting as prescribed by the 2002/91/EG guideline can only be achieved by the use of a standard, as well as attending economic harmonisation according to EWG treaty. Indeed, XBRL is capable to conform to the guidelines. As it is not mandatory to use the finance specific features of the language, it is also possible to refer to this application as a generic XRL. This aspect allows its application apart from the financial and business sector. The broad spectrum of application enables the implementation of the language in many areas and does not restrict the user to specific (proprietary) solutions. Metadata and accordingly, contextual knowledge facilitate the usage of the standard. On the other hand international comparability is supported. Furthermore electronic processing and further use of the same data is promoted.

6 Conclusions

In the current paper we analysed use of XBRL in non-typical area for this standard. We used the *European Directive on Energy Performance of Buildings* in a case study in order to evaluate the use of this standard for general reporting and evaluate its potential according to the EU and DIN ISO based set of criteria. The section two introduces the criteria used for later research. The third section provides an overview of XBRL together with analysis of XBRL Financial Reporting and XBRL Global Ledger. We chose the XBRL FR as the basis for our further modelling. In the third section we presented the existing issues in the EDPB domain. On this basis we developed a case study creating excerpt of the European EDPB taxonomy and its German extension and tested it with use of sample instance documents. Finally we evaluated the solution with a set of selected criteria.

The conducted research indicates that XBRL use in other than business or financial reporting domains provides a series of advantages indicated in our evaluation. However we constructed the excerpt only so the full taxonomy for EDPB could be further developed and used in this specific domain. Furthermore it would be an interesting research line to test XBRL in various different domains and different reporting scenarios. We decided to use XBRL FR as the data model for EDPB nevertheless the use of more data centric XBRL GL approach of multidimensional XBRL Dimensions Taxonomies (XDT) approach could be further investigated.

References

Bergeron, B. (2003): Essentials of XBRL - Financial Reporting in the 21st Century, John Wiley & Sons, New Jersey.

Boritz, J. E.; Won, G. N. (2005): Security in XML-based financial reporting services on the Internet, in: Journal of Accounting and Public Policy, No. 24, pp. 11-35.

Boixo, I.; Flores, F. (2005): New Technical and Normative Challenges for XBRL: Multidimensionality in the COREP Taxonomy, in: The International Journal of Digital Accounting Research 5(9).

Bundesministerium für Wirtschaft und Technologie (2006): Tiefensee und Glos bringen Energieausweise für Gebäude und Wohnungen auf den Weg, http://www.bmvbs. de/pressemitteilung-,302.980291/Tiefensee-und-Glos-bringen- Ene.htm, downloaded 2006-23-11.

Buxmann, P.; König, W. (1998): Das Standardisierungsproblem: Zur ökonomischen Auswahl von Standards in Informationssystemen, in: Wirtschaftsinformatik 40 2, p. 122-128.

Deutsche Energie-Agentur GmbH (dena): http://www.deutsche-energie-agentur.de /page/fileadmin/DeNA/dokumente/Unternehmen/dena-Kurzdarstellung.pdf, downloaded 2006-11-28.

de Vos, A.; Widergren S. E.; Zhu, J. (2001): XML for CIM Model Exchange, in: Power Industry Computer Applications, 2001. PICA 2001. Innovative Computing for Power - Electric Energy Meets the Market. 22nd IEEE Power Engineering Society International Conference, IEEE Press.

DIN ISO 9126 (1991): Informationstechnik-Beurteilen von Software-Produkten, Qualitätsmerkmale und Leitfaden zu deren Verwendung, Beuth Verlag, Berlin.

EnEV-online (without year): http://software.enev-online.de/software/index.htm, downloaded 2006-11-26.

Engel, P.; Hamscher, W.; Shuetrim, G.; vun Kannon, D.; Wallis, H. (2005): Extensible Business Reporting Language (XBRL) 2.1, http://www.xbrl.org/Specification/XBRL-RECOMMENDATION-2003-12-31+Corrected-Errata-2005-11-07.htm, download in November 2006, pp. 13-17.

Europe (2006a) (Anonymous): Transparency Initiative, http://www.euractiv.com/en/ pa/transparency-initiative/article-140650, EurActiv, downloaded 2007-03-24.

Europe (2006b) (Anonymous): Technical Harmonization, http://europa.eu/scadplus/ leg/en/s06011.htm, downloaded 2007-04-06.

Europe (2006c) (Anonymous): Green Paper 'European Transparency Initative', http://ec.europa.eu/commission_barroso/kallas/doc/eti_communication_20070321_en. pdf, downloaded 2007-04-06.

Fraunhofer-Institut für Bauphysik (without year): http://www.ibp.fhg.de, downloaded 2006-29-11.

Garbellotto, G.; Hannon, N. (005): Why XBRL Is a "Business" Reporting Language, in: Strategic Finance, May, pp. 57-61.

Gebäudeenergiepass (2006): http://www.gebaeudeenergiepass.de/page/index.php?id= 1632, downloaded 2006-11-20.

Goodhand, M.; Hamscher, W (2004): Financial Reporting Instance Standard 1.0, XBRL International, http://xbrl.org/technical/guidance/FRIS-PWD-2004-11-14.zip, downloaded 2007-04-12.

172 Maciej Piechocki, André Gräning, Harald Kienegger

Guideline (2003): Richtlinie zur Gesamtenergieeffizienz von Gebäuden, http://eur-lex.europa.eu/LexUriServ/site/de/oj/2003/l_001/l_00120030104de00650071.pdf, in: Amtsblatt der europäischen Gemeinschaft 2003, downloaded 2006-11-28.

Hamscher, W.; Goodhand, M.; Hoffmann, C.; Homer, B.; Macdonald, J.; Shuetrim, G.; Wallis, H. (2005): Financial Reporting Taxonomies Architecture 1.0, XBRL International, http://www.xbrl.org/technical/guidance/FRTA-RECOMMENDATION-2005-04-25+corrected-errata-2006-03-20.rtf, downloaded 2007-04-12.

hAonghusa, C. O. (2005): The Journal Taxonomy, in: Accountancy Ireland, Vol. 37, No. 5, October, pp. 72-74.

Hansen, H.R. (1997): Arbeitsbuch Wirtschaftsinformatik Lexikon, Aufgaben und Lösungen, At: Bea, F.X., Dichtl, E., Schweitzer, M. (Hrsg.): Grundwissen der Ökonomie. Lucius & Lucius, Stuttgart, p. 276.

Heinrich, L.J.; Lehner, F. (2005): Informationsmanagement, R. Oldenbourg Verlag, München.

Hoffmann, C. (2006): Financial Reporting Using XBRL: IFRS and US GAAP, Edition 1, Lulu, p. 16-45.

International Accounting Standards Committee Foundation (2006): XBRL Fundamentals, http://www.iasb.org/XBRL/about_xbrl/fundamentals_xbrl.html, downloaded 2006-11-23.

Kranich, P.; Schmitz, H. (2003): Die Extensible Business Reporting Language - Standard, Taxonomien und Entwicklungsperspektiven, in: Wirtschaftsinformatik, No. 45, pp. 77-80.

König, W. (1997): zur Qualität und Durchsetzung von Standards – diskutiert am Beispiel von STEP, in: Wirtschaftsinformatik 39 1, p. 82-83.

Krcmar, H. (2005): Informationsmanagement, 4th Edition, Springer, Berlin, Heidelberg.

Pelkman, J. (2006): European Integration Methods and Economic Analysis, Pearson Education, Harlow (England), p. 20 ff.

Ramin, K. P.; Kesselmeyer B.; Ott S. (2006): XBRL im Internal Financial Reporting von Unternehmensgruppen, in: Zeitschrift für internationale und kapitalmarktorientierte Rechnungslegung, No. 3, http://www.kesselmeyer.com/blog/wp-conent/uploads/2006/03/XBRL%20Internal%20Financial%20Reporting%20KRSOBK%20060301%20Lang.pdf, downloaded 2007-04-12, pp. 1-14.

Rechenkern zur DIN V 18599 (2006): http://www.ibp18599kernel.de/, downloaded 2006-11-28.

ROWA-SoftGmbH, Lignadata GmbH (without year): http://rowagmbh.de/Daten/Erste Schritte.pdf, downloaded 2006-11-26.

Schlenker U. (1998): Datenmodellierung für das Data Warehouse- Vergleich und Bewertung konzeptioneller und logischer Methoden, http://www.ub.uni-konstanz.de/v13 /volltexte/1999/187/pdf/187_1.pdf, p. 26, download in June 2006.

Teixeira, A.; Hoffmann, C.; Macdonald, J. (2003): Taxonomy Mapping: The Process of Creating Extension Taxonomies, http://www.iasb.org/xbrl/images/xbrllab/past_ projects/CreatingExtensionTaxonomiesDraft2003-03-24.pdf, downloaded 2006-11-26.

Tochtermann, K.; Riekert, W.-F. (2001): Neue Methoden für das Wissensmanagement im Umweltschutz - 4. Workshop des GI-Arbeitskreises Hypermedia im Umweltschutz und Workshop 3 der GI-Initiative Environmental Markup Language, Metropolis, Marburg.

Wagenhofer, A.; Ewert, R. (2003): Externe Unternehmensrechung, Springer.

Wallis, H. (2005a): FRTA 1.0 Conformance Suit, XBRL International, http://www .xbrl.org/technical/guidance/FRTA-CONF-RECOMMENDATION-2005-04-25.rtf, downloaded 2007-04-12.

Wallis, H. (2005b): XBRL GL Instance Standards 1.0, XBRL International, http:/ /www.xbrl.org/int/gl/2005-11-07/GLIS-CR-2005-11-07.rtf, downloaded 2007-04-12.

Wallis, H. (2005c): GL Taxonomy Framework Technical Architecture 1.0, XBRL International, http://www.xbrl.org/int/gl/2005-11-07/GLTFTA-CR-2005-11-07.rtf, downloaded 2007-04-12.

Weitzel, T.; Harder, T.; Buxmann, P. (2001): Electronic Business und EDI mit XML, 1. Aufl., dpunkt, Heidelberg.

Wurster, Th. (2007): AmCham: Gemeinsame technische Standards in der EU und den USA würden Milliarden sparen /Wirtschaft unterstützt Merkels Vorstoß für engere Kooperation, Tagesspiegel-Online.

XBRL International (2005): XBRL GL 2005, http://www.xbrl.org/int/gl/2005-11-07/gl-2005-11-07.htm, downloaded 2007-04-12.

XBRL International (2006a): XBRL's History, http://www.xbrl.org/history.aspx, downloaded 2007-04-12.

XBRL International (2006b): XBRL GL Key Features, http://www.xbrl.org/GLKey Features/, downloaded 2007-04-12.

Technical Implications

XBRL and Business Intelligence
– From Business Reporting to Advanced Analysis –

Peter Chamoni

University of Duisburg-Essen
Germany

peter.chamoni@uni-due.de

Contents

1 Introduction

There are several reasons to join the two concepts of business intelligence (BI) and eXtensible Business Reporting Language (XBRL). Both concepts have in common the support and automation of the management process of reporting and analyzing business information. Whereas XBRL tries to describe the meaning of business data and to standardize data exchange, BI seeks to analyze and report these decision-relevant data. Both come from different perspectives, XBRL from semantic description of data within an XML environment and BI from search of knowledge in data. In a naïve way we can understand XBRL as an automated process of business reporting and therefore as a part of BI. Otherwise BI provides a broad set of algorithms to explore the structure and meaning of data. All the data scrubbing and pre-processing (extract, transform and load: ETL) has to do with the mapping of meta data and can be neglected when we leverage clean and meaningful (XBRL-) data. So why not use the semantic layer and taxonomy of XBRL to go beyond reporting and do more in-depth analysis of financial transactions as can be found in a general ledger? Real-time control of business processes is currently hyped within the data warehousing industry. As every business process should possibly be traced in the accounts of a company a constant flow of financial data in XBRL-format into a BI-system will be necessary for a continuous control of operations, for early fraud detection and BI as a source of compliance systems. The intelligent real-time enterprise of the future will be based on these technologies. The objective of this paper is therefore to point out what future research must be done to develop analytical applications with a high degree of *intelligence* and very low reaction time based on XBRL and BI.

A short description of business intelligence (section 2) will be followed by the presentation of a five-stage maturity model for the classification of BI-solutions (section 3). Next will be the introduction of a research framework to enhance BI-systems with XBRL (section 4) and a brief summary (section 5).

2 Business Intelligence

The development of concepts and solutions for management support systems can be seen as an evolutionary process within the last thirty years. While system concepts such as management information systems (MIS), decision support systems (DSS) or executive information systems (EIS) were more or less successful and accepted by the management we have seen data warehouses emerging during the last ten years which now provide solid foundations for data analysis. These consolidated data sources for analytical use give a new insight into relevant market data or internal business data like time series of financial metrics. The aim of these systems is to process decision relevant information in a timely and problem-adequate way. The intuitive information access and the implementation of decision models to derive proposals for problem solutions are most important. The basic architecture of management support systems contains a data base, a tool box of methods, a model base and a report base. The implementation of business intelligence[1] within an enterprise's incorporates a set of applications (Anandarajan 2004) which assist in understanding value chains and customer behaviour for better planning and coordination of business activities. We assert that a high degree of transparency of the actual status of business provides more accurate control over key business processes which in turn leads to higher profitability.

The technological implementation of business intelligence includes a selection of tools and applications with decision-support characteristics. In a wider sense it includes all system components which serve for the extraction, processing and storage of operational data with the overall aim to generate information and knowledge. In particular, these systems provide functions for the analysis and presentation of business data in an integrated fashion. Another way to define business intelligence can be found in a process-oriented approach. Under this approach we understand business intelligence as the process of finding knowledge about opportunities and perspectives derived from fragmented and non-homogenous data about the enterprise, markets and competitors (Grothe 2000). The drivers for upcoming developments can be found in risk management, financial reporting, customer relationship management and business performance measurement.

Following the above-mentioned definition of business intelligence we assign all components which help to select, process, store, analyze and present decision-relevant data to this concept. Following the classification of (Gluchowski 2006) we describe a BI-platform as constituting a multi-layer architecture with two main function blocks to facilitate data provision and data access. The up-flow and integration of data from different sources through an ETL-process into an persistent data warehouse is one of the key elements of business intelligence. Besides the storage of decision-relevant data in a multidimensional cube it is crucial that data flow be efficiently organized into a hub-and-spoke architecures (Kimbal et al. 1998).

---

[1] Business Intelligence as processed information of interest to management about the present or future environment in which the business is operating is already known since the mid nineteen-sixties (e.g. Cassady 1964 or Greene 1966).

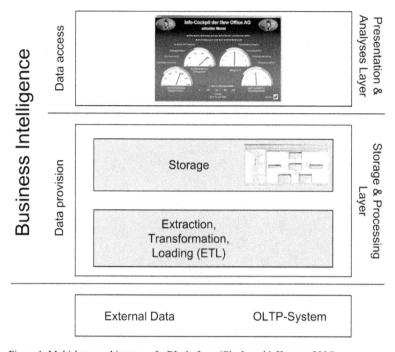

Figure 1: Multi-layer architecture of a BI-platform (Gluchowski, Kemper 2006)

This usually is managed by the use of metadata which represent the semantic layer of data storage as well as data flow. Therefore we find a key initial application field for XBRL is within BI because XBRL improves the semantic description of financial and other business reporting data and helps to map sources into a data warehouse.

The kernel of BI can be found in the presentation and analysis layer. Reporting, ad-hoc-analysis and the use of sophisticated models and methods are the generic base systems that bring the power to build decision support upon data management systems. Figure 2 shows the complete classification (Gluchowski, Kemper 2006) of all three groups of BI-tools. Business applications such as balanced scorecard, risk management, legal consolidation or compliance belong to concept-oriented systems and can be constructed with elements of the generic base system. Management cockpits and portals are the BI user interfaces and give access to these applications. The contribution of XBRL in this area is a semantically enrichted data transport in favor of generic base systems (reporting) and may be used to build presentation and access systems.

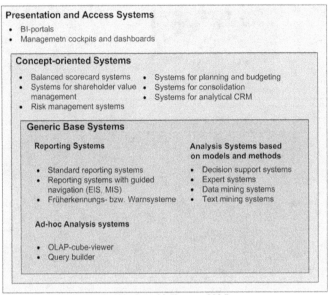

Figure 2: Shell of BI-tools (Gluchowski, Kemper 2006)

3   Business Intelligence Maturity Model

The phenomenon of business intelligence can best be judged in a holistic way. There are different perspectives which describe the maturity of BI-solutions. Within the framework of $biMM^®$ (business intelligence maturity model) we decide to choose three main perspectives which are business content, information technology and organisation (Chamoni, Gluchowski 2004). Along these perspectives we identify a sequence of different stages (figure 3):

The first stage of evolution is characterized by rigid evaluations of business facts which are presented in periodic reports. Further analysis is difficult or impossible because these standard reports only result from derivation of business figures. They are restricted to applications of special departments and often bound to operational transaction systems. The second stage provides OLAP (online analytical processing) for multi-dimensional business analysis and gives power users, according to Dr. Codd's the OLAP rule, flexibility and a high degree of interaction.

stage 1: predfined reporting	stage 2: functional data warehouse	stage 3: enterprise-wide data warehouse	stage 4: advanced analytics	stage 5: Active knowledge processing
standard reports with redundant content	Silo approach	Standard reports with common semantic for whole enterprise	closed-loop-applications	deal-time data warehouse
poor capability to analyse data	Ad-hoc-analsys		advanced methods for analyse (data& textmining)	data sreaming
	Common semantic for department	Simple forcasts		Qualitive/ unstructured data
reports for single departments		Integration of external data	trend extrapolation	concept of roles
no common semantic			comples scenarios for planning	active decision support
			use of decison models	embedded analytics

Figure 3: Stages of BI-maturity

Still valid only for departments on this stage these local data silos come along with multi-dimensional data bases which make navigation and visualisation easy for the user. A multi-dimensional data model enforces clear commitment to a common semantic. Updates of OLAP-cubes are automated so that the management of departments can concentrate on the solving of business problems. Ad-hoc reports of time series and Excel front-ends provide powerful tools for decision support.

The third stage claims to build an enterprise-wide data warehouse with high availability and integration. The setting of standards and the definition of overall semantics leads to consistent information pools which are the source for standard reporting and forecasts. Once an enterprise-wide data warehouse is established it is easy to add external market data to enhance the analytical power of BI.

More advanced capabilities of BI can be found on the fourth stage. Data mining and text mining as well as simulation and trend extrapolation are elements of advanced analytics. Results of these procedures are directly pushed into the OLTP-systems so that a closed loop between analytical and operational processes is formed.

Last but not least we find the fifth stage of the maturity model which can be described by a very high level of integration. Well structured data and time series of business metrics are combined with the content of documents. This means that concepts of BI and knowledge management come together and give more insight into relevant business objects. Moreover, we no longer update data in a periodic ETL-process, but use event-based triggers to feed the analytical applications with real-time information. Because of this synchronous signal processing and push mechanism a short response time becomes possible and opens the field for new control applications. The significance of these reactive BI-solutions is significant. The impact on XBRL will be shown in the following section.

4   Research Framework for BI and XBRL

The eXtensible Business Reporting Language (XBRL) is an emerging standard based on XML which will improve the accuracy, reliability and transparency of business and financial reporting (Engel et al. 2006). It is an electronic tagging format which allows to exchange business information like financial statements, balance sheets or income statements across different platforms. Not only the reporting of business information to investors or analysts becomes easier but also the automated analysis and comparison of business data from different sources. Originally, XBRL was developed to support the reporting supply chain along the activities of production, verification, delivery and analysis of business data (Nutz, Strauß 2002). The main components of XBRL are taxonomies, instance documents and context information as illustrated in figure 4.

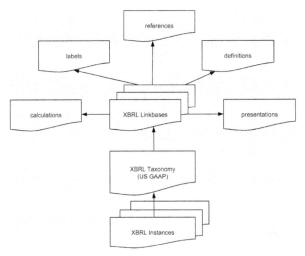

Figure 4: Components of XBRL specification

XBRL instances are the central documents which can be produced in ERP systems by using and setting references to the structure of a predefined XBRL taxonomy. These taxonomies are formal frameworks to describe the necessary elements and their rela-tionships of Generally Accepted Accounting Principles (GAAP). In terms of BI we can understand this as a meta data layer where concepts (e. g. assets) are structured in a multidimensional way with links to definitions, labels, calculations, references and presentations (Felden 2006). Instances stand for facts which are extracted from accounting systems and represent actual transaction data. Every instance is defined by multidimensional concepts of one or more specific taxonomies and therefore also multidimensional in nature. It seems obvious that the definition and description of business objects have to be done in this way. So it is little wonder that BI and XBRL are founded on a similar basis. One of the main differences is that XBRL instances are normally snapshots of single data points whereas fact tables in BI systems represent time series.

There is only a slim literature about the similarity and the mutual dependency of BI and XBRL. From the perspective of BI content one has to distinguish between information sources mapped into data warehouses, analysis models and the results of analysis (knowledge).

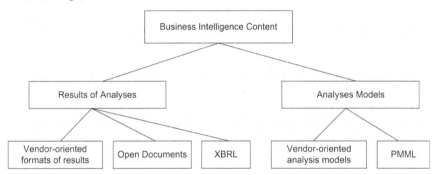

Figure 5: XBRL as category of BI content (Kemper et al. 2004)

On the one hand *Predictive Modelling Markup Language* (PMML) (Schwalm, Bange 2004) can be used to document data mining models whereas on the other hand XBRL can help to pump data into BI systems and also describe the results of business analysis for further use (Kemper et al. 2004, illustrated in figure 5). At present, there is only evidence for integration between BI and XBRL in the first level of BI maturity. Taxonomies (e.g. XBRL GL) are built in the source layer and used in reporting systems in the presentation layer (see figure. 6). This can only be the first step to bring together both concepts. In order to suggest a framework for future research work we use the following matrix to structure the relevant problem domains. The different BI tasks (ETL, data warehouse, analysis, presentation) form the rows and the maturity stages form the columns of the table in figure 6:

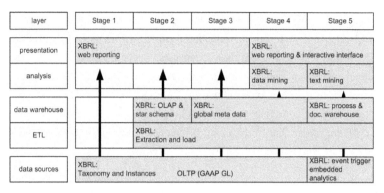

Figure 6: XBRL in BI maturity stages

On the first stage we find standard financial reporting as part of a BI environment that is fed with XBRL encoded data provided by a variety of sources such as internal OLTP accounting systems or external information pools. In this first stage, XBRL has no impact on extraction and loading algorithms and on data warehouse structures or business analysis. Therefore financial reporting can be implemented in a straightforward fashion and no more research needs to be done as we do not find any BI-infrastructure on this stage. XBRL standards and specific taxonomies have to be settled and promoted.

Taking ETL processes and data warehouses into account we identify several tasks that will be necessary to reach the second stage of maturity. Firstly, we have to couple XBRL taxonomies with the meta data of the ETL layer. Secondly, we must use these taxonomies as input for the multidimensional data models (OLAP) in the data warehouse layer. This will be one possible way to integrate heterogenous sources of financial data into arbitrary BI systems. In particularly, the modeling concepts of star schema, snowflake or galaxies have to be matched with different kinds of XBRL taxonomies. Once the integration on the meta level has been established there is no obstacle to deliver financial information in an accurate, timely and transparent way to business users for analysis.

In the third stage we have to consider that all decision-relevant information stored in BI systems should be harmonized and approved by the whole enterprise or group of envolved analysts. This means that business content has to be defined by a global repository within a data warehouse. With reference to this repository the data warehouse reflects the *single point of truth* of enterprise-wide information. At least for financial information XBRL can provide a widely accepted and highly standardized reference for cross-industry meta data. For incoming and outgoing financial data streams this reference should be incorporated by BI systems. So, XBRL also meets the demand of adding external data sources to a companies data warehouse. Research has to be done in order to find out how XBRL can enhance the global meta data in complex data warehouse enviornments.

As stated previously we find in the fourth stage of BI maturity, advanced models and methods including predictive analytics, financial forecasting and planning as well as closed-loop applications. This implies that XBRL instances and taxonomies must be available on the analysis layer as input for decision models. Data mining or Knowledge Discovery in Databases are well known processes to gain insight into the structure of business data and to discover potential interesting and relevant patterns in financial data. Following the requirements in the USA of Sarbanes-Oxley (SOX) for enterprises to maintain internal control over financial reporting and other complementary concepts of enterprise compliance, control or auditing these algorithms will help to automate the management of control techniques. Once irregularities have been found it is easy to trace them back to the back-end systems or down to the root of accounting records. The loop can be closed and a continuous control flow will be established. The impact on further research lies on the integration of logical models (e. g. decision trees and PMML) and XBRL taxonomies. How may XBRL influence decision models and how does an *intelligent* algorithm find business knowledge in a stream of XBRL instances?

Even more open questions arise in the fifth stage where we observe real-time data warehouses having small latency times. A stream of structured and unstructured data has to be analysed so that pro-active decision support will become a commodity. Sophisticated analytics have to be embedded into transaction systems or even into EAI or SOA platforms to succeed in implementing active knowledge processing (Schelp 2006). Hence event triggers will control the correct performance of financial transactions according to logical models and report deviations via XBRL statements to a process warehouse.

Following the idea of knowledge warehousing we have to combine document management and text mining to explore the content of unknown documents. This can be improved by taxonomies or ontologies which give a valid model of specific knowledge domains. XBRL taxonomies may be a start point to build a global data warehouse kernel of qualitative and quantitative financial information throughout international corporations.

Last but not least, we have to examine whether there may be a possible extension of XBRL taxonomies to hold and incorporate not only results of BI analysis but also of predictive models. This would bring XBRL beyond a standard of financial data interchange and would form a first step to active process control with elements of XBRL. Anyway there are yet a lot of topics to cover and further research in this field is a real challenge.

5   Conclusions

Business Intelligence and XBRL are founded on a similar basis. Both concepts have a foundation in the communication and understanding of business information. Therefore it is not surprising that an integration of both architectures and especially the convergence of taxonomies will bring benefits to business applications. We pointed out that along the path of BI maturity there are several stages where XBRL may enhance the funcionality of decision support systems. Vice versa there is a direct implication for the extension of XBRL when BI technologies meet taxonomies of financial data or of other business information. It is worthwhile to study in more detail the opportunities of integration of BI and XBRL as we need more automated and flexible systems for intelligent financial and business reporting.

Critical research questions can be found throughout the different stages of maturity in three fields. First we have to study the mapping between XBRL taxonomies (ontologies) and multi-dimensional global data models of BI-systems. A second research field is the integration of XBRL semantics and the description of logical models derived from data or text mining. Last but not least one can imagine that XBRL will be an important knowledge representation language to implement trigger mechanisms and embedded analytics in sensitive business processes.

References

Anandarajan, M.; Anandarajan, A.; Srinivasan, C. A. (2004): Business Intelligence Techniques, Berlin, p. 18f.

Cassady Jr., R. (1964): The Intelligence Function and Business Completion, in: California Management Review 6 (3), pp. 85-93.

Chamoni, P.; Gluchowski, P. (2004): Integrationstrends bei Business-Intelligence-Systemen, Empirische Untersuchung auf Basis des Business Intelligence Maturity Model, in: Wirtschaftsinformatik, 2-2004.

Engel, P.; Hamscher, W.; Shuetrim, G.; vun Kannon, D.; Wallis, H. (2006): Extensible Business Reporting Language (XBRL) 2.1, http://www.xbrl.org/SpecRemmondations, 2006, download 2007-03-20.

Felden, C. (2006): Business Intelligence und XBRL. Ein Format für alle Daten, BI-Spektrum, 03-2006, pp. 32-34.

Gluchowski, P.; Kemper, H.-G. (2006): Quo Vadis Business Intelligence, in: BI-Spektrum, 01-2006, pp. 12-19.

Grothe, M.; Gentsch, P. (2000): Business Intelligence. Aus Informationen Wettbewerbsvorteile gewinnen, München, p. 11.

Greene, Richard M. (1966): Business Intelligence and Espionage, ed. Homewood 111, Dow Jones-Irwin, Inc.

Kemper, H.-G.; Mehanna, W.; Unger, C. (2004): Business Intelligence – Grundlagen und prakische Anwendungen, Wiesbaden.

Kimball, R.; Reeves, M.; Ross, M.; Thornthwaite, W. (1998): The Data Warehouse Lifecycle Toolkit – Expert Methods for designing, Developing and Deploying Data Warehouses, New York.

Nutz, A.; Strauß, M. (2002): eXtensible Business Reporting Language (XBRL) - Konzept und praktischer Einsatz, Concept and practical implementation of the eXtensible Business Reporting Language (XBRL), Wirtschaftsinformatik 44, 5-2002, pp. 447-457.

Schelp, J. (2006): "Real"-Time Warehousing und EAI, in: Chamoni, P.; Gluchowski, P. (Ed) Analytische Informationssysteme, 3. ed., Berlin.

Schwalm, S.; Bange, C. (2004): Einsatzpotenziale von XML in Business-Intelligence-Systemen, in: Wirtschaftsinformatik 46, 1-2004, pp. 5-14.

Multidimensional XBRL

Carsten Felden

Technische Universität Bergakademie Freiberg (Sachsen)
Germany

carsten.felden@bwl.tu-freiberg.de

Contents

1 Introduction

The complexity of data warehouse models based on the entity-relationship-model was one of the biggest driving forces behind multidimensional modelling. Designed models should be easily understood by a business expert and easily analyzed by the final user. Nevertheless, the evolution of the dimensional paradigm has showed that the business world is complex and it is necessary to introduce new concepts to the models to allow a greater level of representation. These include bridge tables, heterogeneous dimensions and factless fact tables (Kimball, Ross 2002). As a result, the designed model lacks the desired simplicity and does not yet guarantee the representation of all the semantics of the domain. This paper explores an alternative design of data warehouses that allows the creation of a model that reflects in a greater proportion the semantic of the business world and that can be exploited by the final user through different analysis tools. The alternative, based on XBRL Dimensional Taxonomies (XDT), is shown through a comparison with a dimensional model and the level of semantic representation. We explore all the limitations and ease of use derived from this standard reporting language, eXtensible Business Reporting Language (XBRL). The objective is to show a dimensional and a XDT design and stressing out the semantic richness of each approach. In order to do so, the article will explore briefly the background of a dimensional understanding of a problem domain in the second section. Then it will show dimensional XBRL as a more semantically approach to model a dimensional reality in the third section. To show this, the fourth section contains an example that will be applied in a real case study. Finally, the article will point out an analysis of multidimensional XDT approach. The implementation of multidimensionality is, however, an initial point for further research activities. Due to this reason, the conclusion gives some further directions for research which are based on multidimensional approaches.

2 Dimensionality of Reporting

The collection, reduction and selection of relevant information for analytical tasks can only occur on the basis of consistent company-wide data retention. Due to heterogeneous legacy systems a systematic bringing together of relevant databases is necessary (Lusti 2002). The data warehouse concept is an attempt to efficiently manage and collect relevant information derived from the vast amount of data contained in transaction systems (Lehner 2003). Some authors define a data warehouse as a collection of data (e.g. Bauer, Günzel 2001; Devlin 1997; Lehner 2003). Others define data warehousing as a process of assembling and managing data from various sources for the purpose of gaining a single detailed view of the company's activities (Inmon 2002; Lusti 2002; Chamoni 1998). Whether there is an understanding of a collection of data or process, the system has to deal with a huge amount of data for analytical tasks, which implies challenges in its construction, management, and usage. Commonly, data warehouse data are stored in an n-dimensional space, allowing their study in terms of facts subject of analysis and dimensions showing the different points of view a user can have (Bauer, Günzel 2001). The following section presents the background of the data warehouse concept as an already accepted approach for analytical information systems and focuses on the dimensionality of reporting to give a broad understand about the problem domain.

2.1   The Data Warehouse Concept

Devlin was the inventor in the mid 1980s of the idea to have a data storage for a huge amount of data available that should give support for analyzing data (Devlin 1997). Inmon identified four characteristics of a data warehouse, which are represented in his formal definition: "... a data warehouse is a subject oriented, integrated, non-volatile and time variant collection of data in support of management's decisions." (Inmon 2002) The structure of a data warehouse is radically different from the structure of operational databases. A data warehouse differs due to the distinct objective of an operational database by the type of the entered data and their supply. The core of a data warehouse is a database, in which data from different operational systems are historically saved in different levels of aggregation.

2.2   Dimensionality

Due to the fact that, as a rule, analysts make complex queries and demand intuitive working with the database, a multidimensional data model seems appropriate. Each combination of dimensions, e.g. region, time, or customer, characterizes a possible analyst's query. The complexity of a multidimensional structure is the result of the amount and the type of dimensions. Dimensions can be seen as the highest reduction level of data (Codd 1970). Therefore, two types of dimensions can be differentiated. On the one hand, all elements of a dimension are equal; this means they all have the same granularity. On the other hand, there is a hierarchical relationship between them (Bulos 1996, pp. 33). One example is the time dimension. This dimension is the result of hierarchical aggregation starting from day to month, to quarter, and to year.

A multidimensional data model needs describing elements which can denote the characteristic properties of the underlying database structures. Basic elements of a multidimensional database design are sets of related dimension elements which are organized by aggregating and disaggregating operators. A multidimensional data space is spanned by the characterizing data (=dimensions). Business measures are loaded from the transactional systems according to the mapping between both systems and their synchronization (Chamoni 1998, p. 233; Holthuis 1999, p. 122). Individual user queries represent manipulations within the multidimensional space, whereby the access of the business measures can be realized via the dimensions, because the dimensions are nothing else then classes of real world objects (Chamoni, Gluchowski 1999, p. 402; Gluchowski 1997, pp. 62). For example a product dimension represents all of a company's product types. The positions that can be queried within a dimension are specific real world objects which can be grouped, because of a semantically relationship between these objects (Gabriel, Gluchowski 1998, p. 495).

From a geometric point of view, a multidimensional data model can be seen as a cube with three dimensions. If we have more than three dimensions, the multidimensional structure is called a hypercube. Such multidimensional structures are the basic idea of Online Analytical Processing (OLAP) to reflect analyst's queries (Schinzer, Bange 1999, p. 55). OLAP supports multidimensional querying in an integrated data warehouse database (Chamoni, Gluchowski 1999, p. 403). Following figure 1 shows a multidimensional structure.

Hypercube

Slicing/Dicing

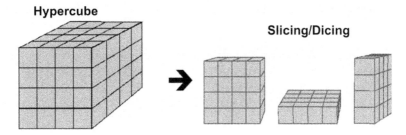

Figure 1: Multidimensional data structure (Bissantz 1999, p. 381)

Each cell of the cube contains business measures which are called fact data or more briefly facts. Their meaning is determined by the characterizing dimensions of the cube structure. Querying such a database can be done by using the operations slicing, dicing, pivoting, and drill down (Chamoni 1998, p. 234). The complexity of an underlying hypercube results from the number and type of dimensions (Gabriel, Gluchowski 1998, p. 496).

This kind of data structure can be realized in a non-multidimensional database. Should it be an implementation of a multidimensional data space according to the relational data model, the most used modelling technique is called the star schema (Raden 1996). It is based on the entity-relationship model in order to support multidimensional analysis in a relational framework (Nußdorfer 1998, p. 18). Due to the idea of tables in such a relational model, two kinds of tables can be differentiated: fact tables and dimension tables. Fact tables contain quantitative and businesslike data which can be retrieved by database queries. Dimension tables contain characterizing elements of fact data. Relationships exist just between fact and dimension tables. There are no relationships between dimension tables (Poe et al. 1998, pp. 192).

Multidimensional concepts and relationships are useful for analytical tasks. It should not imply, however, that other data modeling concepts should be ignored. Almost all existing multidimensional models are limited to model isolated subjects of analysis, because the data warehouse architecture is typically semantically impoverished. Moreover, besides the lack of semantic relationships there is no agreement on the definition and properties of multidimensional concepts. All models merely impose the properties and structure of aggregation hierarchies in the analysis dimensions. Another important issue in multidimensional modeling is the implementation of aggregability or summarizability. The data schemas should show how data of a given granularity can give rise to data of coarsest granularity.

The importance of aggregation hierarchies is recognized. Thus, most multidimensional models provide mechanism to define them. Nevertheless, none of the authors proved nor justified the characteristics of those hierarchies. Based on the structure of aggregation hierarchies and data dependencies, the structure of the fact data has been studied.

In recent years, several multidimensional models appeared. Each of those models uses a different nomenclature and was conceived for a different purpose so that their comparison becomes difficult. There is a need for a framework in favor of the comparison of such different models.

It is quite common in analytical tasks that information used or obtained from the study of a given subject is valuable for the analysis of another subject. However, existing models do not pay enough attention to this and allow representing isolated star schemas. A variation of the three-levels ANSI-SPARC architecture is presented to facilitate it.

3   Dimensional XBRL

The eventuality of realizing a dimensional XBRL data storage demands a data model which defines the existing elements in its different expressions. There exists no graphical modeling technique in the field of XBRL such as already known in database or software engineering. The graphical modeling technique employed in this paper refers to the elements of the XBRL Dimensions 1.0 specification (Hernández-Ros, Wallis 2006). The rules shown are appropriate to design a model graphically and to implement the model as a set of taxonomies. Effectively, XDT demands a sequential order of modeling and implementing a real world problem. Due to this reason there are four so called arcroles, namely:

- all or notAll (primary item – hypercube);

- hypercube-dimension;

- dimension-domain;

- domain-member.

Figure 2 shows the usage of these arcroles and dimension types.

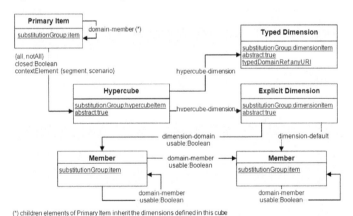

(*) children elements of Primary Item inherit the dimensions defined in this cube

Figure 2: Dependencies in XDT (Hernández-Ros, Wallis 2006, p. 7)

The characterizing dimensions of a hypercube are described by the four arcroles. Additionally, the dimension's domain and domain members are visualized. Figure 2 shows the different arcroles between the elements. An element is grouped into a substitution group. Depending on the situation whether an element is a hypercube, dimension, or a member, it can be modelled as a hypercubeItem, a dimensionItem, or just as an item.[1] The representation of the relationship shows the kind of arcroles between the individual elements.

Primary items represent business fact data. These facts are linked to all other elements. Due to the arcroles, all and notAll has to show the existing relationship between a primary item and the concerned hypercube. All is used, if all dimensions of a hypercube are related to a primary item. NotAll is used, if all dimensions of a hypercube are definitively not linked to a primary item (Hernández-Ros, Wallis 2006). Due to the reason that not each element has to be linked to a hypercube, the arcrole domain-member is to be used not just within domain taxonomies, but also within the primary taxonomies. This offers the possibility to link a full tree hierarchy of primary items to the respective hypercube.

The modelled dimension types of figure 2 are so-called explicit Dimensions. These dimensions are explicitly described. This means, in favor of the shown example, that all dimension members are grouped to exactly one dimension and to no other.

Another and second condition of a dimension is a so called typed dimension. This kind of dimension is used if the amount of members is too large so that it cannot be called an explicit Dimension. An example is the storage of all longitudes and latitudes within a geographical dimension. Such a dimension would contain an unsupportable quantity of numeric values. This effect can be reduced by using a typed dimension. The content is to be defined in another XML-file, whereby XBRL:typedDomainRef is referencing this file (Hernández-Ros, Wallis 2006, p. 19).

4   Example

There is a need for an approach to realize a multidimensional integration and evaluation of data which, on the one hand, represents the real world problem domain and, on the other hand, defines the storage of the data.

4.1   Setting the Sample Data Set

There are not many data sources available which can be used for such a multidimensional usage. Business reports of international operating enterprises seem to be an appropriate research basis, because they are constantly and via open access available in the World Wide Web. The segment reports within these enterprise reports are present-

---

[1] Item is a standard element of XBRL.

ing separated business measures according to the enterprise's branches and regions. This reflects already a dimensional point of view onto the used data set.

We are going to use the segment reports of *RWE Energie AG* (RWE), *Energie Baden-Württemberg* (EnBW), and *Vattenfall Group* (Vattenfall) as examples of industry-specific data. Each of these enterprises are using the accounting standard IFRS.[2] The measures used are inter-company revenue, external revenue, total revenue, and segment revenue of each enterprise. The segment reports are separated, according to the information stated before, according to the branches and regions. It has to be stated that the used segment reports are just taking the most recent three years into account, commencing from 2005.

4.2   Multidimensional ADAPT-Model for the Energy Industry

ADAPT is a modeling technique in favor of developing multidimensional data structures. The modeled dimensions are reflecting the time, the specific regions (in which the enterprises have business activities), and the individual business segments, for example *RWE Power* and *RWE nPower* of *RWE Energie AG*.

---

[2] IFRS is an international accounting standard which requires segment reports.

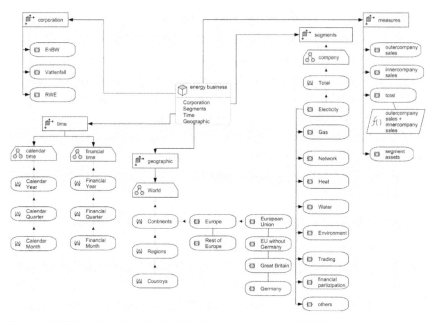

Figure 3: Multidimensional Data Model of the Energy Industry using ADAPT

As seen in figure 3, the time dimension is modelled as an aggregated dimension and subdivided into year, quarter, and month as a hierarchical expression. It has to be stated that this hierarchy exists within this model for the sake of completeness, because the used reports are just reflecting a single year. It is important to understand that a differentiation into fiscal time and legal time is necessary. A fiscal year can, for example, cover the interval 1 April to 31 March of the following year. A year according to legal time is in principle 01 January to 31 December. The necessity of this differentiated point of view results from the situation that time is not typically obeyed in XBRL-model (as seen in XBRL-model later). XBRL itself describe time aspects typically not within a model, but together with the measures in a so called instance document. It is necessary to keep this differentiation in mind to be able to compare both developed models according to their content.

The ADAPT-model contains the fact data in the measure dimension which is stored in the hypercube. The intercompany revenue reflects the sum of the revenues between the enterprise's segments. The sum of external and intercompany revenue is the total revenue of the segments. The enterprise earnings result from the summarized earnings of each segment of an enterprise. To show the segment reports of each region, external revenue and total revenue are summarized to calculate the enterprise earnings. Such calculation information is modelled by a calculation symbol, whereby fact data are marked as dimension members.

The segments of individual enterprises are often identical, but they can sometimes have varying names. Due to the reason it seems to be useful to define categories in which comparable segments of an enterprise are stored. The different segment labels are generalized and distributed to the different categories. All segments are modelled by aggregating dimensions and linked to the enterprise as a single dimension member. The geographical region in which the enterprises have business activities are hierarchy elements of continents, regions, and countries. In the following the same problem do-main is modelled as XDT.

4.3   Multidimensional XBRL-Model for the Energy Industry

The developed model, shown in figure 4, displays a hypercube with two so-called di-mension taxonomies (dimension taxonomy region and dimension taxonomy segment), a primary taxonomy and a template taxonomy. These taxonomies are necessary in fa-vor of the technical functionality of the implemented dimensional XBRL data model.

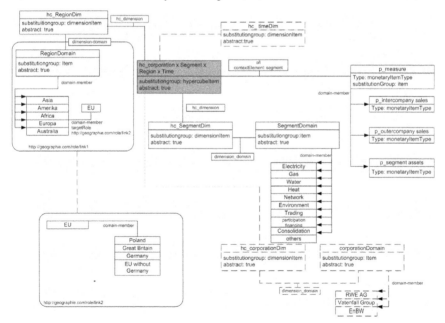

Figure 4: Multidimensional Data Model of the Energy Industry using XDT

Figure 4 shows the elements of the taxonomies, arcroles and the hierarchical measure structure. Context of the template taxonomy is the hypercube *hc_Segment_region*, the dimension *RegionDim*, *SegmentDim* and miscellaneous arcroles which represent a logical linkage between the model elements. The arcroles defer to the two domains *EnterpriseRegion* and *EnterpriseSegment* and to all primary items of the primary taxonomy (*p_measures*). The result of this modelling is a relationship of the template taxonomy to all other taxonomies in this model.

The modelling of the dimensions *RegionDim* displays the relationship between the individual members. The initial point is a hierarchical ranking which is comparable to the hierarchy of the illustrated ADAPT approach. Each segment report of the relevant enterprise has a structure that contains a hierarchy element Europe, a hierarchy element *European Union*, and *RestOfEurope*. The individual elements of XDT are described as follows: the continent Europe has a member *European Union* (as member of *enterprise region*). Such a member can have further member, e. g. Poland and Germany. Another necessary dimension is the segment dimension (*SegmentDim*). As shown before, the used labels of the segments are according to the implemented categories. Due to this reason, the XBRL-model is also using these categories. *SegmentDim* results out of the domain *segment_enterprise*. All members are sub-organized to these segments. The business measures are modelled as a part of the primary taxonomy. The relationship between the hypercube and the primary taxonomy is specified by the arcrole all. This means that all primary items can be linked to all dimension members of *RegionDim* and to the dimensions itself. This declaration is essential for the following evaluation. As already stated, time aspects are not modelled in an individual dimension. They are reflecting the contextual information in an instance document for all the captured data.

5   Evaluation and Findings

It is essential to set appropriate evaluation criteria in order to compare the different modelling techniques. We use the standard DIN ISO 9126, which defines software quality criteria, as the baseline. The standard contains six criteria and levels in order to gain an abstract conclusion about software quality. Some defined criteria are not taken into account, because they are not relevant for this research. Software quality aspects are not sufficient when we are analysing multidimensionality. Due to this reason it is appropriate to use Codd's twelve OLAP rules as an enhancement of the six criteria. This has to be done with the limitation that Codd's rules are strongly related to proprietary analytical software tools. We propose, therefore, the restriction of the five criteria which are already known as *Fast Analysis Shared Multidimensional Integration*

(FASMI). These five aspects fit within the boundaries DIN standard so that they can be used for the following evaluation.

5.1 Evaluation Criteria

Figure 5 shows the categories taken from the DIN standard and their relevant features.

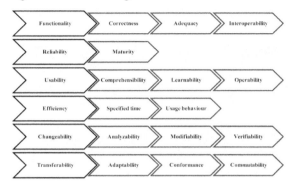

Figure 5: Evaluation criteria according to DIN ISO 9126 (Schlenker 1998, p. 26)

Firstly, it has to be examined whether the technique generates correct results, that the modeling-technique delivers appropriate construction elements and that there is an interaction support for distributed information systems to evaluate the *functionality* of a conceptual modeling technique. Furthermore, the multidimensional point of view has to be considered. This aspect is included in the FASMI criterion *multidimensionality*. *Reliability* is the system's ability to be a standard solution in a specific problem domain. A criterion to validate reliability is the maturity level of the standard. For example, the *Gartner Group Lifecycle*-evaluation (Fenn, Linden 2005) is such a validation. Useability describes the modelling effort due to the respective technique. This is validated by using the criteria comprehensibility, learnability, and operability. FASMI, for example, is using these criteria in the context of *Analysis* and *Shared* as well. There is a need for appropriate query and retrieval mechanisms to use OLAP-systems without a specific knowledge about the underlying database. *Efficiency* is describing the proficiency level of the method used and the amount of system resources. Commonly, the criteria specified time and runtime behaviour are used to evaluate this criterion. Resources are reflecting the used system volume, storage volume, and model size. *Changeability* is the headline for describing the effort to realize changes within the model. Changes are corrections, improvements or just modifications of the model. The evaluation is done by using the criteria analyzability, changeability, and evaluation ability. *Transferability*, the final DIN category, describes the model's ability to be transferred (on a conceptual, logical, and physical layer) from one architecture to another. Adaptability, conformity, and compatibility are the used criteria.

5.2   Evaluation of the XDT-Modeling Technique

The following figure illustrates the evaluation of the used modeling techniques.

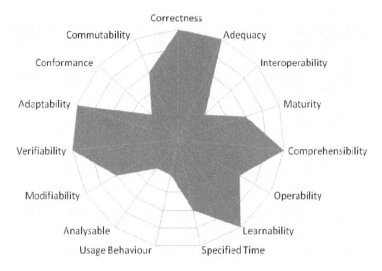

Figure 6: Evaluation result

The evaluation of the category *Functionality* shows that we can use XDT to establish a multidimensional model which contains all functionalities which are necessary to implement a data warehouse. Also all other necessary elements could be modelled as well. In total, the FASMI criterion *Multidimensionality* is fulfilled. The relationships between dimensions and their respective hypercube (as business measure storage) are described by the usage of arcroles (e. g. domain member). Furthermore, hierarchies are displayed explicitly. XDT does not have the ability to interrelate with different systems. XBRL is, however, an analogue to XML platform independent. Due to this reason, usage in different systems is theoretically possible.

Reliability is the second evaluated criterion. Reliability is a relevant aspect in context of the standardization of XBRL and according the standardization of the XDT. It is an important issue for potential users that a used technique is reliable – otherwise, it could not get any acceptance in the market as a condition for being a communication standard. A content wise establishment of such a reporting standard which also shows the maturity of XDT is not to be seen, yet. There are existing core taxonomies like FINREP (Financial Reporting) and COREP (Common Reporting), which are used in the financial sector. Due to this usage, they are already part of a *standardization* process which supports the standardization of XBRL. But some countries are already using common, two dimensional XBRL as an accepted reporting standard. According to this, some standardization of multidimensional XBRL seems to be likely in the near future, because a broad acceptance of XBRL itself is basically necessary for this step. The growing need and usage of multidimensional data will positively influence XDT. The modeling technique itself is easy to understand.

This aspect is also relevant for *learnability*. If the user has knowledge of multi-dimensions characteristics, the modeling technique is easy to learn. Conversely for some technical details such as naming of arcroles or relationships of taxonomies, a deeper understanding of XBRL seems to be appropriate. If the user has understood non-dimensional XBRL, the intellectual transfer to dimensional XBRL is just a small step. To summarize this aspect with an appropriate introduction, the multidimensional modeling of a problem domain is possible.

Efficiency and the related criteria time consumption and usage behavior are now examined. The time and effort developing a model is strongly dependent on the size and complexity of the specific problem domain. It is not surprising that the larger the model, the larger the necessary database storage is required as result. The development of the XDT model and its validation demands the usage of a taxonomy editor. The editor is doing the translation from the logical layer to the internal layer. The conceptual layer is integrated in the logical layer, so there is no need for different layer descriptions. An advantage of this is that the real word image described is understandable when the user has some technical background with XDT. A visual examination of the model has to be done by using XBRL-Dimensions 1.0. Unfortunately, a software-aided analyzability of model errors does not exist at this time. A visual presentation and a visual maintenance support would reduce the maintenance effort of such a reporting system.

Neutrality of XDT to all subsequent development steps cannot be stated. XDT is not an independent layer like the schemas of the ANSI/SPARC architecture. A specific technology and a specific architecture is developed which has to be implemented. A modification, so that there is a usability of different modelling techniques, can just be realized by changing directly the developed models. Thus, an interchange of developed models is problematic. This would lead to a translation component between the developed model and the implemented architecture. In this context, it has to be stated that this problem basically occurs by doing a model-interchange, because there is no common sense of model semantics.

To summarize the results, multidimensional data can be modelled by using XDT. This is shown by the fulfilled evaluation criteria. Due to the graphical representation of the model elements, data warehouse engineers have an improved understanding of the multidimensional data of a data warehouse, because the model elements have more differentiated semantics. The main advantage of these circumstances is in favor of the necessary mapping between the modelled taxonomies and the data warehouse database. Due to the reason that XDT contains the logical and conceptual layer, there is no differentiation between the XBRL-instances and the XDT-model. This supports database consistency.

6   Conclusions

Multidimensionality per se was not born in the research community, but as a response of tool vendors to the demands of analysts. Thus, there was not a strong mathematical foundation for multidimensionality. This is in clear contrast to the theoretical roots of relational databases. Concepts were not clearly stated, and most efforts were devoted to improve performance and presentation. In recent years, multidimensionality has captured the attention of researchers. Data models have appeared without a clearly defined standard, nor even well accepted nomenclature. This makes it complicated to compare the data of different implementations in an automated way.

Of course it is possible to develop a multidimensional model by using different concepts like ADAPT or multidimensional ERM. XDT is also an appropriate attempt to model multidimensional aspects. XDT can represent everything equally as well as ADPAT which is shown in this paper. Due to this reason it has to be thought about the idea that XBRL can be used to work as a data warehouse for decision support. Reports can be generated directly out of the transactional systems in an enterprise. This makes XBRL interesting for small and midsized companies which do not want to invest in a decision support system. Another interesting aspect is that XDT has no need for a specific conceptual layer, to have a close point of view to the modeled reality. The usage of just one layer instead of a conceptual and logical layer supports a clear and understandable model. This is a positive result of using XDT. Maintenance is also supported, because is can be done directly inside this model. Something like this does not exist in consisting multidimensional modeling approaches. All changes of the physical layer are done within the model. Therefore the maintenance is simplified compared to a decision support system, which extends the operating time of such a system.

To summarize the evaluation, not all the criteria are marked positively in particular interoperability, usage behavior, analyzable, verifiable, and conformance. The main criteria of multidimensionality and model ability are fulfilled. In case of the negative aspects has to be stated that this result also applied to all multidimensional modeling approaches like ADAPT or multidimensional ERM. XDT is, then, an appropriate modeling technique to be used in favor of multidimensional databases for supporting analytical tasks.

The implementation of multidimensionality is reflecting analyst's queries. But it is an initial point for further research activities, too. This paper can be continued by different research lines. It can be related to other areas like data quality, database security, temporal issues, query optimization, and translation to logical/physical level methodologies, or just studying modeling problems at conceptual level. Especially the conceptual level offers research potential. According to the ANSI/SPARC-architecture the initial point is to develop a specific logical level in favor of the XDT similarly to common modeling approaches. This leads to the generation of a two-dimensional model which exhibits the dimensional characteristics of the multi-dimensional model content wise. This also could lead to the approach to adapt the semantic characteristics of the entity relationship model. Basis of this approach is to support an easier data exchange of flat XML data via an already existing XML interface. Considered problems within the paper are the handling with exclude hypercube or typed dimension. During the data extraction from the instance, such differences have to be considered. In a data warehouse neither this kind of dimension, nor the form of the hypercubes exist. However typed dimension in XDT have determined functions. It is thus conceivable to transfer this task into a database. The implicit data in the database could be described in form of the specification of the implicit values of the XDT. The assignment of the individual values can be realized via an OLAP tool which uses XML interfaces. A semantically rich schema is useful to help users on understanding data. Semantic optimization should be considered, especially for the OLAP-operation drilling across. Furthermore, the definition of multidimensional views should also be studied in order to support symmetric usage of factual and dimensional data as well as ad-hoc hierarchies. Finally, the XDT is based on XML pattern files which are basically XML files. Due to this reason there should be no serious effort to import the data. This leads to an analysis of the ETL-process, to deal with XBRL in favor of a transmission and transformation from the data sources into the database. An essential issue is that multidimensional structures should be identified and captured from a non-dimensional schema. The shown problems and ideas require further investigations, especially on the way to gain an alternative approach for a decision support system.

References

Bauer, A.; Günzel, H. (2001): Data-Warehouse-Systeme. Architektur, Entwicklung, Anwendung, 2. Edition. dpunkt Verlag, Heidelberg.

Bulos, D. (June 1996): A New Dimension, in: Database Programming & Design, Vol. 9, No. 6, pp. 33 - 38.

Chamoni, P. (1998): Ausgewählte Verfahren des Data Mining. In: Chamoni, P.; Gluchowski, P. (ed.): Analytische Informationssysteme. Data Warehouse, On-Line Analytical Processing, Data Mining, Springer, Berlin [u. a.], , pp. 355 - 373.

Chamoni, P.; Gluchowski, P. (Ed) (1999):Analytische Informationssysteme. Data Warehouse, On-Line Analytical Processing, Data Mining, 2nd edition. Springer, Berlin [et al.].

Codd, E. F. (June 1970): A Relational Model for Large Shared Data Banks, in: Communications of the ACM, Volume 13, Nr. 6, pp. 377 - 387.

Devlin, B. (1997): Data Warehouse – from Architecture to Implementation. Addison Wesley , Reading (Mass.) [et al.].

Fenn, J.; Linden, A. (2005): Gartner's Hype Cycle Special Report for 2005, Gartner Inc, http://www.gartner.com/resources/130100/130115/gartners_hype_c.pdf, downloaded on 2006-07-19.

Gabriel, R.; Gluchowski, P.(1998): Grafische Notationen für die semantische Modellierung multidimensionaler Datenstrukturen in Management Support Systemen, in: Wirtschaftsinformatik, Nr. 40, pp. 493 - 502.

Gluchowski, P. (1997): Data Warehouse. In: Informatik-Spektrum 20. Jahrgang, Heft 1, pp. 48-49.

Hernández-Ros, I., Wallis H. (2006): XBRL Dimensions 1.0 Candidate Recommendation, dated 2006-04-26, XBRL International, http://www.xbrl.org/Specification/XDT-CR3-2006-04-26.rtf, downloaded on 2006-07-19.

Holthuis, J. (1999): Der Aufbau von Data Warehouse-Systemen - Konzeption, Datenmodellierung, Vorgehen, 2. Auflage, DUV, Wiesbaden.

Inmon, W. H. (2002): Building the Data Warehouse, 3rd edition. Wiley, New York [et al.].

Kimball, R.; Ross, M. (2002): The Data Warehouse Toolkit: The Complete Guide to Dimensional Modeling, 2nd edition, John Wiley & Sons, Inc.

Lehner, W. (2003): Datenbanktechnologie für Data-Warehouse-Systeme. Konzepte und Methoden. dpunkt Verlag, Heidelberg.

Lusti, M. (2002): Data Warehousing und Data Mining. Eine Einführung in entscheidungsorientierte Systeme. 2. Edition. Springer Verlag, Berlin [et al.].

Nußdorfer, R. (1998): Neue Anforderung an die Datenmodellierung. E/R-Modellierung im Jungbrunnen, in: Datenbank Focus, Heft 10, pp. 16-19.

Poe, V.; Klauer, P.; Brobst, S. (1998): Building a data warehouse for decision support, 2nd edition, Upper Saddle River.

Raden, N. (1996): Star Schema 101. White Paper, Archer Decision Sciences Inc., Santa Barbara CA 1996, http://members.aol.com/nraden/str101.htm, downloaded on 2006-08-28.

Schlenker, U. (1998): Datenmodellierung für das Data Warehouse- Vergleich und Bewertung konzeptioneller und logischer Methoden, Juni, http://www.ub.uni-konstanz.de/v13/volltexte/1999/187/pdf/187_1.pdf, downloaded 2006-07-07.

Schinzer, H.-D.; Bange, C. (1999): Werkzeuge zum Aufbau analytischer Informationssysteme, in: Chamoni, P.; Gluchowski, P. (Hrsg.): Analytische Informationssysteme - Data Warehouse, On-Line Analytical Processing, Data Mining, 2nd edition. Springer, Berlin, pp. 45-74.

Process and Technical Design of an Integrated Solution for (Semi-) Automated Basel II-Reporting Using XBRL and Web Services

Peter Gluchowski, Alexander Pastwa

Chemnitz University of Technology,
Ruhr-Universität Bochum,
Germany

peter.gluchowski@wirtschaft.tu-chemnitz.de
apastwa@winf.rub.de

Contents

1   Introduction

Among the various processes deemed critical by a firm, financial reporting is continuously moving up the scale of priorities. The design of a reliable, fast and IT supported system for providing relevant business and financial data for management accounting purposes has always been one of the main fields of study in management information systems. Under the *umbrella* of Management Support Systems (MSS) various technical solutions to providing information for decision makers were presented, based primarily on data warehousing concepts (Gluchowski, Gabriel, Chamoni 1997, pp. 147).

Amongst the various demands induced by regulation concerning reporting, the demands set by the Basel II equity decree have especially influenced the design of IT supported reporting systems within financial institutions. The ability to provide a rating process with the necessary, relevant and consistent business and financial data in a timely fashion represents an important factor of success for securing favourable loans since the Basel II convention became effective.

This paper investigates ways to realize reliable and fast exchange of business and financial data through the use of powerful technologies. In order to improve the reliability of the data exchange process, the question focussed on is how Basel II reporting can be automated or at least semi-automated. Apart from the semi-automated processing of credit requests as a classic field of application, the possibility of offering potential customers a preliminary rating as a standardized service opens up banks.

As recent developments have shown, many innovations in the field of business studies were induced by the arrival of new technologies or technology driven concepts.[1] One important topic is the Extensible Markup Language (XML). The following discussion will show how this standardized meta-language developed by the World Wide Web Consortium can be used for the purposes of an integrated financial reporting system.

The paper is organized as follows: The weaknesses of financial reporting, which still hamper efficient and effective financial reports in many firms, are discussed in the second section. In the following sections the potential of implementing XML in financial reporting systems is examined. A practical and for the purpose of financial reporting useful technical form of XML is the Extensible Business Reporting Language (XBRL) on the one hand and Web services on the other hand. The third section of the paper deals with the way Web Service technologies work and what potential uses arise

---

[1]   E. g. the utilisation of Data Mining in the context of Customer Relationship Management (CRM).

from them. The fourth section deals with the basic content and consequences of the Basel II equity decree. Based on this analysis, the final section gives an example for the conceptual and technical design of an integrated and IT supported solution for (semi-)automated Basel II reporting using both XBRL and Web services.

2   The Reporting Process as an Object of Examination

Financial reporting is an important part of a broader financial and managerial function. It can be described as a process that gathers business and financial data, analyzes it and channels it to other entities downstream. However, the practical implementation of financial reporting is confronted with a variety of challenges, which can make efficient and effective processing and provision of information difficult.[2] One challenge is the medium of information distribution. The other challenge is related to the amount of data accumulated during the reporting process. Figure 1 serves to emphasize these aspects.

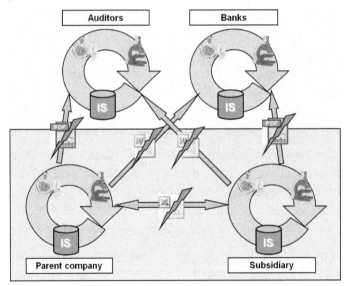

Figure 1: Information exchange processes in a corporate structure.

The starting point depicted here is a simplified corporate structure between a parent and a subsidiary company. The parent company, for example, requests financial data from the subsidiary. The parent will, in turn, pass down plans and analysis results for

---

[2]   Further problematic ares in reporting are presented by Müller et al. (2000), pp. 354 and Göricke, Kirchhof (2006), p. 55.

corporate development. Furthermore, information exchange processes exist between both entities and their share- and stakeholders, in part due to regulatory obligations. In this example, auditors and banks represent two potential stakeholder groups. The relationships between the four depicted enterprises are characterized by the fact that inside each of the organisations labour intensive and IT supported information processing takes place. The results of this processing are usually presented in various types of documents containing relevant information about the business and being shared among internal and external entities of the company.

Generally, the process of financial reporting is characterized by the different data formats in use. They are the output of various information systems (Gluchowski, Pastwa 2006, p. 66). Although many commercial analysis and planning tools support common data formats, it may still be necessary to transform data from one format to another or at least manually adjust data to fit the next step of evaluation (Göricke, Kirchhof 2006, p. 56; Gabriel, Gluchowski, Pastwa 2006, p. 939). But data manipulation is connected to the danger of losing or corrupting data. Potential breaks in information chains caused by incompatibility in media formats or other issues in media interchanges can have deleterious impact on business processes as a consequence (Gabriel, Gluchowski, Pastwa 2006, p. 939). In the worst case such breaks can cause the processing chain to be aborted, or at best slow down financial reporting.[3]

The elimination or reduction of breaks in media interchange can often only be accomplished by modifying the interfaces of the information systems participating in the exchange process. Generally, the implementation and subsequent maintenance of interfaces is costly. Furthermore, the linking of information systems from separate enterprises compromises highly specific requirements concerning the implementation and maintenance of interfaces.

The second obstacle for efficient and effective reporting is the problem of information overload. Management of a firm typically focuses on a few selected balance and index numbers, which, as aggregated data, have enough expressive value to be used for the planning and managing the firm. For example, the analysis of a potential creditor's financial situation as part of the process of granting credit according to the regulations of Basel II does not require all the data from the annual statement of accounts. Consequently a desired characteristic for an efficient and effective reporting process following the stakeholder-management-approach would also be the exclusion of entities from

---

[3]   The problem of using various data formats is especially troublesome when physical storage formats like paper or disks are used. See Hoffmann (2005), p. 34; Nutz, Strauß (2002), p. 448.

access to data which carries no benefit to them. This requirement has the consequence that a requirement profile for user dependent data supply must be defined.

The information overload problem is critical when the identity or meaning of data is not clear during processing. A financial institution, for example, may have contradicting annual statements of accounts from clients as a result of using varying accounting standards. Swift analysis of financial and firm data can be hampered by the omission of information clarifying the relevant data (Kranich, Schmitz 2003, p. 77). In extreme cases, when no agreement is reached concerning the importance and expressive value of the analysed data, an effective and efficient comparison of specific balance sheet items is severely limited.

3   The Technological Basis for an Integrated Solution

In recent papers concerning the possible uses of information and communication technologies for supporting business and financial reporting two concepts are commonly discussed, namely XBRL and Web services (e.g., Gabriel et al. 2006, Garbellotto 2006a; Garbellotto 2006b; Ramin et al. 2006; Gehra, Hess 2004). Both these technologies have become somewhat of a focus for many firms. While the potential uses of XBRL and Web services are mainly discussed separately, approaches compromising both technologies have become prevalent.

Many private initiatives are attempting to make individual dialects of XML standards for particular user communities. Apart from the organisation responsible for the over all design of XBRL, XBRL International and its jurisdictions, many other institutions are concerned with the design and establishment of specific XML dialects (XBRL International 2007). Examples include the Data Mining Group (2007) and RosettaNet (2007).

Web services provide a XML-based foundation for the possible implementation of a firm's internal and external services, in order to generate a complete service oriented process chain (Beimborn, Weitzel 2003, p. 1360). Using Web services in combination with the implementation of a Service-Oriented Architecture (SOA) should enable mostly or even entirely automated information processing in the future.

3.1   Service-Oriented Architecture and Web Services

The concept of a Service-Oriented Architecture is seen by some authors as a new paradigm for the field of application integration within organizations (e.g., Newcomer, Lomow 2005; Erl 2006; and more recently Reinheimer et al. 2007, p. 7). A characteristic of the approach taken by Service-Oriented Architecture is the idea of wrapping functions provided by the different applications running in a firm as individual servic-es and preparing them for multiple uses (Beimborn, Weitzel 2003, p. 1360; Leyking et al. 2006, p. 1037). The services correspond to isolated modules, which, as building blocks for the entire program, can represent various functions (Richter et al. 2005, p. 413). In order to use these services it is necessary to communicate via a defined inter-face. Therefore an approach chosen within the framework of SOA follows the concept of integration at the method and function level.[4]

However, a Service-Oriented Architecture is not a standardized guideline to applica-tion integration. It is an architectural concept, which can take on many different tech-nological forms (Richter et al. 2005, p. 413). Among the various possibilities of im-plementing a SOA, using XML in the form of Web services currently represents the core of ongoing discussion. Alternatively, the COBRA standard has been presented as a possibility for designing a SOA. In order to implement Web services three compo-nents are needed as they form the technological basis (World Wide Web Consortium 2007; Beimborn, Weitzel 2003, pp. 1362).

Firstly, a suitable carrier or packaging protocol is required to enable the exchange of messages between two applications. This is accomplished using the Simple Object Access Protocol (SOAP). SOAP is a standardized format based on XML designed for the communication between two applications. SOAP prescribes the structure of a mes-sage on the one hand, and organizes the function calls on the other. To ensure a web based access to relevant services SOAP employs various transport protocols, for ex-ample *http*, *ftp* and *smtp*.

Secondly, in order to use Web services, access to the service needed must be ensured at all times. Therefore it is necessary to specify which methods and functions are part of a certain Web Service, so the call from the entity requesting information can be processed and answered in form of a results document. This demand shows that the description of a standardized and processable interface is a central condition for an exchange of information between applications. This task is accomplished by the de-scription and definition component, the second building block of a Web Service. For this purpose the W3C developed one of the most established XML standards, the Web services Description Language (WSDL).

---

[4] See Haarländer et al. (2005), p. 351. Many traditional approaches to the integration of applications follow the concept of three software layers: the user perspective, the functional perspective and the data perspective. Therefore integration from the user perspective and from the data perspective can be seen as further forms of application integration.

Third, a standardized directory for finding relevant Web services is required. The Universal Description, Discovery and Integration (UDDI) standard is such a building block. Similar to a branch index, the classification of the Web services registered in a UDDI takes place according to the characteristics of the services offered. In this regard it is possible for any person or group offering a Web Service to have their respective Service registered in the directory free of charge and at the disposal of other users. The directories are divided into three parts, called *White*, *Yellow* and *Green pages*. Similar to the Yellow Pages of a phone book, the Yellow Pages of the Web services concept contain information on which branch of industry a firm is part of. The Green Pages inform users about the technical side of a specific Web Service in a firm. It could be deposited in a WSDL, for example. UDDI can also be used to implement one's own directories, designed specifically for the internal workings of a firm. At the same time the providers of Web services have the possibility of registering their own Services in a public directory, in order to ensure easy access for the demand side.

On the basis of these building blocks and the Web services concept a SOA can be presented as figure 2 shows:

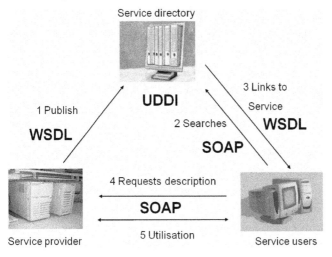

Figure 2: Web Service based SOA, excerpt from: Dostal et al. (2005), p. 28.

The underlying architecture of a Service-oriented application presented here can be considered as a combination of allocated roles, in which the provider of a certain Web Service registers it in a directory and thereby puts it at the disposal of potential users (Dostal et al. 2005, pp. 28). Thus, the first step is to register the service in a directory. With the help of WSDL an interface description of the service can be generated. So when a potential user wants to make use of a Web Service he first has to search for a suitable service and then requests the interface description of the chosen service. For this reason the Directory Service implements a reference in form of an URL on the WSDL document. In a last step the WSDL description is used to create the program parts necessary for the communication between the applications and users. The carrier protocol in this context is SOAP.

3.2 Evaluation of the Performance of Web Services for XBRL-based Financial Reporting

The practical implementation of XBRL and Web services is possible in three technical constellations. First, an integrated solution can be entirely XBRL based. Alternatively, an integrated financial reporting system on the basis of Web services is also possible. The third potential form of an integrated solution is a mixture of both technologies, activating further potentials. Web services especially offer the possibility to automate business processes. Through the implementation of Web services in the form of an SOA and via a Web Service interface the applications already in use throughout a firm may also be integrated (Specht et al. 2006, p. 15). In this regard the integration of older and legacy systems plays an important part, as these historically developed information systems still make up a considerable amount of a firm's application landscape (Hagen, Kappes 2006, p. 38). Many data base systems are still installed on mainframes and serve numerous divisions of companies.[5] Because of their monolithic character linking this category of information system with other applications is technically difficult and expensive. Wrapping functions offered by a legacy system in the form of numerous services enables the cost-effective use of application logic with other linked systems.

The implementation of Web services also offers the advantages of multiple use and re-use, making changes only necessary at one single point in the code, but effective in every instance the service is used. This greatly reduces expenditures for servicing the system and ensures a high degree of flexibility.

Furthermore, using Web services opens up scenarios in which a formulated data query triggers further data queries along a process chain. Thereby different application systems can be linked and the data they hold used in an integrated way. Apart from data queries, more complex process interlinking is also conceivable. An example of such integration is a service which automatically integrates bench marking or a Basel II rat-

---

[5] An example of a monolithic system used in a hospital can be found in Sunyaev et al. (2006, p. 31).

ing into a workflow. An information supply system based on Web services also has the advantage of being able to put relevant firm and financial data at the users' disposal automatically in previously defined intervals. This can be anything from an hourly, a daily and a weekly, to a monthly information supply.

As a supplement to the potential uses of both technologies, a further enhancement of their performance can be achieved through their combined implementation.[6] These so-called XBRL Web services solutions would be characterized by the use of XBRL instance documents as part of a structured financial reporting workflow. The focus of this workflow would be the exchange of standardized firm and financial information, enhanced with specific semantics.

4 Basel II as a Field of Application for an Integrated Reporting Solution

Financial institutions provide an excellent test bed for researching new modes of financial and risk reporting. The requirements for integrated, fast and correct reporting for financial institutions have become more important in recent years, especially due to the guidelines set by the Basel II convention. The regulations concerning equity passed by the Basel committee for bank supervision have the goal of linking the capital a bank must hold in order to give credit with the risk that the bank takes when agreeing to such an investment.[7] According to the Basel II rules the risks a financial institution faces are divided into credit, market and operational risks. While the first two forms of risks cover the danger of a loan not being repaid as well as interest rate and exchange rate fluctuations, the operational risks cover dangers resulting from internal and external influences on a firm's business activities. Hazards, which are the result of the employees' misconduct or of malfunctioning applications can be classed as internal operational risks. External influences compromise all risks which do not belong to the firm's internal workings. According to the guideline „Sound Practices of the Management and Supervision of Operational Risk" it is a bank's or financial institute's responsibility to systematically protect itself from this kind of risk.

The object of the Basel II convention is the rating process, the result of which is a classification by which the probability of a bad loan can be estimated (Maier 2004, p. 407.). When using rating procedures banks may take a variety of internal approaches

---

[6]   Garbellotto presents the advantages arising from the integration of both technologies. See Garbellotto (2006a, pp. 60).

[7]   For the basics of Basel II, see Krumnow (2003, pp. 409).

to draw information from underlying data bases for the rating process. On the other hand banks may employ an external agent for the rating or forgo the rating entirely (Hofmann 2004, p. 1202). Since it may be assumed that bank internal rating approaches lead to a reduction in the underlying equity base, a strong preference of internal rating procedures in comparison with external procedures can be expected (Maier 2004, p. 407).

The basis of the rating process is formed by an analysis of financially relevant key data and balance sheet items describing a firm's situation in regard to assets, finances and income, as well as qualitative factors. Examples of qualitative factors include the security and efficiency of business processes and information concerning the customer structure.[8] Depending on how good or bad a firm's rating is, the financial institution giving credit to the firm must hold more or less equity to cover the loan. This is expressed in a lower credit amount and higher interest rates for firms with a bad rating. Thus banks and financial institutes pass their duties concerning risk protection down to the credit demanding firms. In order to gain a good rating, firms must implement an active, measurable and holistic risk management system.

These increased demands for rated firms set by financial institutions mean that the firm's information systems significantly influence achieving a positive rating. The diverse information systems must on the one hand be capable of delivering the desired data in acceptable quality and in sufficient time. On the other hand there is a strong demand for comprehensible and transparent data.

5   Conceptual and Technical Basis of a Web Services and XBRL Based Reporting Solution

We now introduce preliminary thoughts on how to implement an XBRL and Web services based reporting solution, which meets the demands of the Basel II convention. These considerations are from both conceptual and technical viewpoints. Since reporting is a process, the elaborations below will follow the design approaches of process-oriented information systems.[9] With the demands expressed by Basel II concerning a timely and secure exchange of relevant financial and operational data as a background this section focusses on the formulation of an appropriate process for semi-automated

---

[8]   Bonn and Mosch listed the quantitative and qualitative factors of success in: Bonn, Mosch (2003), pp. 27.

[9]   See Gabriel et al. (2002, pp. 289). The methodical framework is the Architecture of Integrated Information Systems (ARIS). See Scheer (1998, pp. 38; Gadatsch 2001, pp. 93; Seidlmeier 2002, pp. 11).

data exchange. Accordingly, the analysis focusses on the conceptual level of the *Architecture of Integrated Information Systems* (ARIS). The question of how a technical implementation of an integrated Web Service and XBRL based reporting system may be achieved is answered subsequently.

5.1   Process Model for Data Exchange in the Field of Basel II

The following discussion suggests a process model, which describes a semi-automated rating procedure and processing of a credit request respectively at the conceptual level. The formulation of an appropriate process model is an important success factor for the design and implementation of a SOA (Leyking et al. 2006, pp. 1037). Figures 3, 4 and 5 shows an event driven process chain which can be used to introduce the single steps of a rating process.

Depending on a firm's information demand, either the activities *enter parameters for credit request* or *request preliminary rating* form the starting point of the reporting process. In the former case a chief financial officer can enter a value for the credit amount requested and the duration, for example, by using a Web service. After one of these requests has been triggered by the requesting company, the activity *test available inhouse data for timeliness* is executed.

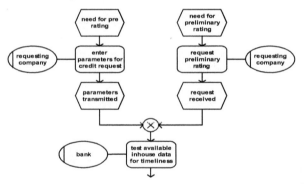

Figure 3: Process model for (semi-) automated processing of a credit or preliminary rating request (Part 1)

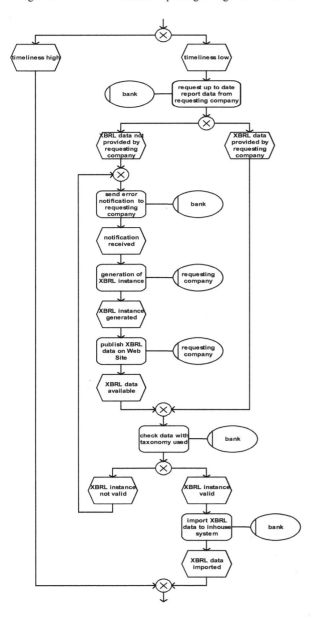

Figure 4: Process model for (semi-) automated processing of a credit or preliminary rating request (Part 2)

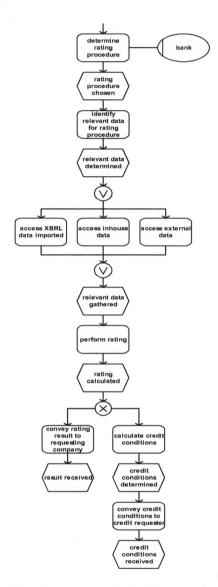

Figure 5: Process model for (semi-) automated processing of a credit or preliminary rating request (Part 3)

Over the course of this activity all the report data of a firm already existing in the information systems of the bank is checked for timeliness by the financial institution. In case the data is up-to-date, (i.e. timeliness is high), it forms the basis of the banks favoured rating procedure. If the timeliness is low, the activity *request up to date report data from the requesting company* needs to be executed. This is done by asking the credit-seeking firm to send a XBRL-instance document containing the relevant and up-to-date report data.

Should the requested report data from the credit demanding firm not be presented in the form of an XBRL document, the extraction of an appropriate XBRL instance is prompted by the bank. This step is represented by the activity *send error notification to requesting company*. After the XBRL document has been generated and published on the Website by the requesting firm, the bank has to check in the next step if the instance follows the taxonomy used by the bank. In case the result is negative, the process returns to the activity *send error notification to requesting company*. A positive result means the XBRL data can be imported to the relevant information systems of the financial institution for further analysis.

The next activities of the process model are performed by the bank. Primarily, the bank must choose the appropriate rating procedure. Examples of such procedures include the IRB approach, CreditMetrics and CreditRisk (Wahrenburg, Niethen 2000, pp. 241). Depending on the procedure chosen, the necessary data for that specific procedure must be determined and provided in the next step. This may include the report data, other bank internal data or data provided by external agencies. The rating procedure is then applied to the chosen data and followed by conveying the rating result to the concerned firm. If the process was triggered by a firm's demand for a credit offer, at this point the credit conditions will be calculated, consisting of interest rate, duration and structure of repayment, and re-sent to the requesting company.

5.2   Referential Architecture of an Integrated Solution

While the preceeding section focussed on theoretical basis concerning the process model of an XBRL and Web services based reporting solution, the following section presents a referential architecture for such a solution. It follows suggestions made in the literature, especially the literature dealing with referential architectures for service orientated applications.[10]

As can be seen in Figure 4, there are five levels in the referential architecture. The lowest level consists of the diverse and heterogenous operating information systems of the credit demanding firm. These hold the business and financial data necessary for the data exchange processes between the firm and the bank. This system category includes

---

[10]   See the suggestions presented by Leyking et al., Hinz, Bernhardt, and Berbner et al. See (Leyking et al. 2006, p. 1038; Hinz, Bernhardt 2006, pp. 172, and Berbner et al. 2005, pp. 272).

Enterprise Resource Planning systems (ERP), for example, as well as other transaction systems. The XBRL instances will be extracted from these systems, which is possible after mapping the items of the taxonomy used with the corresponding data objects in the information systems. In a next step the XBRL instances need to be inserted into an integrated data pool, which is part of the third level. In the figure 6 presented below the steps data mapping, export and import of the XBRL instances is hinted at using an arrow, which connects the firm's information systems, the XBRL taxonomy, the XBRL instances and the integrated data pool. Using XBRL in this context has the advantage that only data which fulfill the requirements set by the semantic and structural conventions of the taxonomies is incorporated into the data pool. Demands for consistent data may be met this way.

The data layer provides a perspective on the data which may be relevant for semi-automated processing of a credit request or a preliminary rating. For these purposes data from the bank's in-house systems and data provided by external agents needs to be merged with the data pool, which collects the reporting firm's financial and operative data supported by XBRL. The in-house systems traditionally contain customer information as well as historical data concerning customer relations. External service providers supply economic data and information on the specific branch a firm operates in, which may or may not be relevant, depending on the rating procedure used. While the latter form of data is stored on the external information systems of potential service providers, the financial institutions are responsible for running the inhouse systems and generating the reporting data in the presented referential architecture.

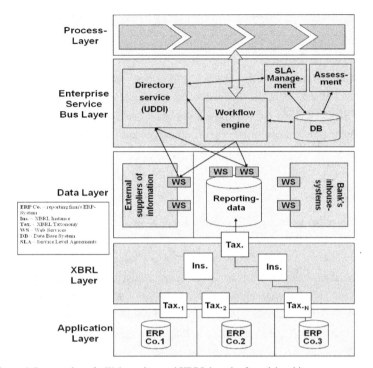

Figure 6: Presentation of a Web services and XBRL based referential architecture

The core component of this referential architecture is the layer containing the enterprise service bus. It consists of the directory service (UDDI) or Web services repository, which is responsible for describing and finding Web services[11], and a workflow engine. Furthermore, a component which supervises the Service Level Agreements (SLA) of the Web services described in the Web services repository needs to be integrated. The SLAs of the Web services used are stored in a database via the SLA management component and evaluated according to specific quality criteria. The assessment component has the task of only accepting those Web services into the directory which reach the set minimum standards for an SLA. It uses exclusion rules to accomplish this (Berbner et al. 2005, p. 268.). As Figure 6 shows by means of the two directed arrows, the call on specific Web services is executed by the workflow component. This is the interface to the level of business processes as the highest level of the referential architecture.

With the formulation of a to-be-supported business process as a starting point, the corresponding avtivities of this process may be implemented as a Web service, described

---

[11] See also section 3.1.

in a UDDI and called upon when the process demands them. By using Web services in the context of the applications for such a solution it is possible to gain read as well as write access to the respective data during runtime. If such services are provided within the specific applications, data from external information systems, data from inhouse systems, as well as data from the report data pool can be directly processed with the help of Web services. Thus the workflow component enables the implementation of (semi-) automatic procedure to support a predefined process with the help of Web services.

6   Conclusions

The goal of this paper was to test the capabilities of XBRL and Web services as XML based technologies for the support of integrated as well as automated financial reporting. The demands of the Basel II convention provide a valuable test bed for such automated financial reporting. For this reason an approach using XBRL and Web services was outlined. This approach eliminates some of the weaknesses of traditional reporting and shows some possible implementations of semi-automated preliminary rating. Both a process model and a referential architecture were presented for such a solution.

An important result of this tentative solution is that both XBRL and Web services technologies have potential uses on their own, as well when they are used in combination. It has become clear that both technologies support the processing aspects of financial reporting. Both Web services and XBRL show the highest number of potential uses when the underlying process and data exchange are structured and standardized. Furthermore and in the context of Service-Oriented Architectures, making business processes more flexible is one of the goals for the implementation of appropriate Web services. XBRL also has potential uses when implementing a flexible ad hoc reporting service, as data from XBRL instances can be accessed online via customized standard applications. Because of the standardized semantics of various taxonomies, a further potential use for XBRL is as an instrument for data quality management, in other words the secure exchange of consistent business and financial data.

In view of the advantages offered by a structured reporting process based on semantically standardized data, it should not take long for first approaches to design reporting processes using XBRL and/or Web services. Besides the requirements resulting from the deficits of currently observable reporting as discussed in section 2, the expanded requirements for stakeholder management have benefitted the dispute surrounding

XBRL and Web services. In this regard demands resulting from regulation must be seen as important drivers including, for example, Basel II and Sarbanes-Oxley.

There are some limitations to our analysis. Questions concerning the aspect of data security were not addressed in this paper. This aspect is crucial to the demands of using Web services in the context of an SOA and is often mentioned as the reason why architectures based on Web services exclusively have so far not been or only partially implemented (Rieks 2006, p. 9.). Since Web services as well as XBRL share the common goal of facilitating a web based data exchange, measures and standards which offer high data security need to be integrated.

Considerations of efficiency were also omitted in this paper, as well as aspects concerning the technical implementation of the proposed referential architecture. A further crucial success factor for such a solution actually becoming reality concerns the adaptability of adequate economic models to suit the organisational design of an integrated reporting solution. In this context the question of how to formulate effective incentives for cooperative work between the financial institution and the reporting firm requires consideration. Approaches for the design of cooperative relationships include Supply Chain Management (SCM)[12] and Open Book Accounting (Hoffjan, Kruse 2006, pp. 94). The technical implementation of an integrated reporting solution generates a further important question: How far can XBRL and/or Web services (for example in the context of an SOA) replace or at least influence the use of traditional information systems like ERP-systems and Data Warehouses (DW) (Herrmann 2006, p. 14). The latter have been established as powerful information systems to support reporting. Further coalescing of SOA, DW and ERP using XML (for example in the form of Web services) is to be expected.

More research is also necessary for all aspects concerned with making the reporting process more flexible. In this regard the design of flexible business processes based on a workflow engine as well as an adequate process description language like the Business Process Execution Language for Web services (BPEL4WS) can be identified as a major field of study for the implementation of Service-Oriented Architectures. Furthermore, we note that the evaluations undertaken over the course of the presented process of preliminary rating and processing of a credit request are exclusively based on quantative data. Qualitative information such as statements concerning the quality of management or the quality of the risk management system used by the firm. These

---

[12] Approaches to the design of SCM strategies can be found in Winkler and Klaas. See Winkler (2006, pp. 47) and Klaas (2005, pp. 9).

can have considerable influence on the ratings result, depending on the banks individual weighting, were not incorporated into the process model. Further demand for research concerning the semi-automatic integration of qualitative information into the reporting process may be derived therefrom.

References

Beimborn, D.; Weitzel, T.(2003): Web Services und Service-oriented IT-Architekturen, Das Wirtschaftsstudium (Wisu), Vol. 32, No. 11, pp. 1360-1364.

Berbner, R.; Heckmann, O.; Mauthe, A., Steinmetz, R. (2005): Eine Dienstgüte unterstützende Webservice-Architektur für flexible Geschäftsprozesse, Wirtschaftsinformatik, Vol. 47, No. 4, pp. 268-277.

Bonn, H. P.; Mosch, T. (2003): Basel II – neue Anforderungen an das Berichtswesen im Mittelstand, HMD – Praxis der Wirtschaftsinformatik, Vol. 40, No. 233, pp. 21-31.

Data Mining Group (2007), http://www.dmg.org, downloaded on 2007-04-04.

Dostal, W.; Jeckle, M.; Melzer, I.; Zengler, B. (2005): Service-orientierte Architekturen mit Web Services: Konzepte – Standards – Praxis, München.

Erl, T. (2006): Service-Oriented Architrecture – Concepts, Technology, and Design, Upper Saddle River, NJ: Pearson Education, Inc..

Gabriel, R.; Gluchowski, P.; Pastwa, A. (2006): Extensible Business Reporting Language (XBRL) für das Rechnungswesen, Das Wirtschaftsstudium (Wisu), Vol. 35, No. 7, pp. 938-944.

Gabriel, R.; Knittel, F.; Taday, H.; Reif-Mosel, A.-K. (2002): Computergestützte Informations- und Kommunikationssysteme in der Unternehmung: Technologien, Anwendungen, Gestaltungskonzepte, Berlin/Heidelberg.

Gadatsch, A. (2001): Management von Geschäftsprozessen: Methoden und Werkzeuge für die IT-Praxis: Eine Einführung für Studenten und Praktiker, Braunschweig/ Wiesbaden.

Garbellotto, G. (2006a): Exposing Enterprise Data: XBRL GL, Web Services, and Google, Part 1, Strategic Finance, Vol. 88, No. 2 (August), pp. 59-61.

Garbellotto, G. (2006b): Exposing Enterprise Data: XBRL GL, Web Services, and Google, Part 2, Strategic Finance, Vol. 88, No. 3 (September), pp. 59-61.

Gehra, B., Hess, T. (2004): XBRL – Ein Kommunikationsstandard für das Financial Reporting, Controlling & Management, Vol. 48, No. 6, pp. 403-405.

Göricke, N., Kirchhof, O. (2006): Optimierung der Prozesse der Konzernberichterstattung, Information Management & Consulting (IM), Vol. 21, No. 3, pp. 54-58.

Gluchowski, P.; Gabriel, R.; Chamoni, P. (1997): Management Support Systeme: Computergestützte Informationssysteme für Führungskräfte und Entscheidungsträger, Berlin/Heidelberg.

Gluchowski, P.; Pastwa, A. (2006): Reporting-Standard vor dem Durchbruch – Details über Grundlagen, Bausteine, Erweiterungen und Potenziale der erhofften "Lingua Franca" des Finanz-Berichtswesens: XBRL, IS Report, No. 1 + 2, pp. 66-69.

Haarländer, N.; Schönherr, M.; Krallmann, H. (2005): Flexibilisierung durch integrierte prozessorientierte IT-Systeme", in Kaluza, B., and T. Blecker, ed., „Erfolgsfaktor Flexibilität: Strategien und Konzepte für wandlungsfähige Unternehmen, Berlin, pp. 341-365.

Hagen, C., Kappes, R. (2006): SOA bringt Legacy-Anwendungen auf Trab, Computerwoche, No. 11, pp. 38-39.

Herrmann, W. (2006): Wie SOA den ERP-Markt verändert, Computerwoche, No. 36, 2006, p. 14.

Hinz, O.; Bernhardt, M. (2006): Interaktive Preisfindung als zwischenbetriebliche Prozessintegration auf Basis von Webservices, Wirtschaftsinformatik, Vol. 48, No. 3, pp. 169-177.

Hoffjan, A.; Kruse, H. (2006): Open book accounting als Instrument im Rahmen von Supply Chains – Begriff und praktische Relevanz, Zeitschrift für Controlling & Management (ZfCM), Vol. 50, No. 2, S. 94-99.

Hoffmann, C. (2005): Finanzdaten mit XBRL austauschen, Computerwoche, No. 15, pp. 34-35.

Hofmann, G. (2004): Basel II, Das Wirtschaftsstudium (Wisu), Vol. 33, No. 10, pp. 1202-1206.

Klaas, T. (2005): Jenseits des Organigramms – Grundsätzliche Überlegungen zur ganzheitlichen Gestaltung der Supply Chain, Logistik Management, Vol. 7, No. 3, pp. 9-20.

Kranich, P., Schmitz, H. (2003): Die Extensible Business Reporting Language – Standard, Taxonomien und Entwicklungsperspektiven, Wirtschaftsinformatik, Vol. 45, No. 1, pp. 77-80.

Krumnow, J. (2003): Basel II und seine Auswirkungen auf die Finanzierungsstruktur und Informationspolitik der Unternehmen, in Küting, K., and C.-P. Weber, (Ed), Vom Financial Accounting zum Business Reporting – Kapitalmarktorientierte Rechnungslegung und integrierte Unternehmenssteuerung, Stuttgart, pp. 409-421.

Leyking, K.; Ziemann, J.; Loos, P. (2006): Geschäftsprozessmodelle und serviceorientierte Architekturen (SOA), Das Wirtschaftsstudium (Wisu), Vol. 35, No. 8-9, pp. 1037-1040.

Maier, M. (2004): Basel II, Rating und IFRS – Reaktionen von Banken und Unternehmen, Controlling & Management (ZfCM), Vol. 48, No. 6, pp. 406-411.

Müller, R.; Klatt, M.; Pfitzmayer, K.-H. (2000): Das Spannungsfeld Konzernreporting, Controller Magazin, Vol. 31, No. 4, pp. 354-360.

Newcomer, E.; Lomow, G. (2005): Understanding SOA with Web services, Upper Saddle River, NJ: Pearson Education, Inc..

Nutz, A.; Strauß, M. (2002): eXtensible Business Reporting Language (XBRL): Konzept und praktischer Einsatz, Wirtschaftsinformatik, Vol. 44, No. 5, pp. 447-457.

Ramin, K.; Kesselmeyer, B.; Ott, S. (2006): XBRL im Internal Financial Reporting von Unternehmensgruppen, Zeitschrift für kapitalmarktorientierte Rechnungslegung (KoR), Vol. 6, No. 3, pp. 179-191.

Reinheimer, S.; Lang, F.; Purucker, J.; Brügmann, H. (2007): 10 Antworten zu SOA, Praxis der Wirtschaftsinformatik (HMD), Vol. 44, No. 253, pp. 7-17.

Richter, J.-P.; Haller, H.; Schrey, P. (2005): Serviceorientierte Architektur, Informatik Spektrum, Vol. 17, pp. 413-416.

Rieks, M. (2006): Service-orientierte Architekturen – Architekturparadigma für die Integration von IT-Systemen, Information Management & Consulting (IM), Vol. 21, No. 1, pp. 6-10.

RosettaNet (2007), http://www.rosettanet.org, downloaded on 2007-04-04.

Scheer, A.-W. (1998): ARIS – Vom Geschäftsprozess zum Anwendungssystem, Berlin et al..

Seidlmeier, H. (2002): Prozessmodellierung mit ARIS: Eine beispielorientierte Einführung für Studium und Praxis, Braunschweig/Wiesbaden.

Specht, T.; Weisbecker, A.; Spath, D. (2006): Integration Engineering-Methode: Realisierung kooperativer Geschäftsprozesse mit Service-orientierter Architekturen, Information Management & Consulting (IM), Vol. 21, No. 1, pp. 11-18.

Sunyaev, A.; Leimeister, J.-M.; Schweiger, A.; Krcmar, H. (2006): Integrationsarchitekturen für das Krankenhaus – Status quo und Zukunftsperspektiven, Information Management & Consulting (IM), Vol. 21, No. 1, pp. 28-35.

Wahrenburg, M.; Niethen, S. (2000): Vergleichende Analyse alternativer Kreditrisikomodelle, Kredit und Kapital, No. 2, pp. 235-257.

Winkler, H. (2006): Entwicklung von Supply Chain Strategien für eine Virtuelle Supply Chain Organistaion (VISCO), Zeitschrift für Planung & Unternehmenssteuerung, Vol. 17, No. 1, pp. 47-72.

World Wide Web Consortium (2007), http://www.w3.org/TR/2004/NOTE-ws-arch-20040211/#meta_concept, downloaded on 2007-04-04.

XBRL International (2007), http://www.xbrl.org, downloaded on 2007-04-04.

Adoption of XML and XBRL Standards

Harald Schmitt

ABZ Informatik GmbH
Germany

harald.schmitt@abz-informatik.com

Contents

1 Introduction

This article is an analysis of adopting technical EDI standards in the field of XBRL-based reporting. The analysis is divided into two areas: current XML standards and future XBRL standards. Before presenting the analysis results we introduce the standards architecture of XBRL and basic functional requirements for implementing automated reporting processes.

Although the application of Webservice technologies is not subject of this paper, webservice frameworks and the evaluated XML and XBRL standards ideally complement one another. Modern service-oriented architectures are well suited to cope with heterogeneity in existing reporting installations. Webservices in service-oriented architectures support arbitrary XML-based data exchange format and as a consequence also XBRL. XBRL can be used in combination with these technologies and it reveals its complete power only in service-oriented architectures. Two fundamental terms of service-oriented processing are introduced which are relevant for reporting:

Composite-Applications unify the benefits of standard software and individual development. The principle of composite-applications is to extend an existing application infrastructure with proofed software components which give relevant functionality – e.g. support for reporting processes. In future ERP and consolidation systems can be deployed by reporting applications as elementary building blocks. They no longer have to be dominating monolithic platform, but rather serve as base functionality for reporting. For this reason companies are more easily able to buy new functionality and to enhance there own software development. Today's focussing on applicationa can be replaced by focussing on processes.

Interaction between reporting services demands an infrastructure. So called Enterprise Service Buses (ESBs) are the first choice in this area. As there is a great variety of heterogeneous information in a reporting system which has to be prepared, a reliable message-based communication has a central meaning.

In the following evaluations of data processing technologies webservice standards are not considered because they can be applied to reporting applications independent of the underlying data processing technology. The focus of the paper is on automation of the data flow and data transition in reporting supply chain.

The outline of the paper is as follows: First we present typical functional requirements for an automated reporting, by example. Subsequently, we evaluate to what extend current XML standards are able to meet these requirements. In addition we explore the applicability of future XBRL standards regarding the given requirements. At the end we summarize the evaluation results.

2   Linking XBRL to XML Standards

Before describing the functional requirements of an automated reporting we point out the interaction of XML and XBRL standards in the overall architecture of the XBRL standards family.

2.1   Architecture of XBRL Standards

Figure 1 shows the architecture of XBRL Standards. The three layers of XBRL standards are essentially build on four XML standards. The core standard XML 1.0 (Bray et al. 2006) provides the syntactical basics for all standards above. XML Schema (Fallside et al. 2004, Thompson et al. 2004, Biron et al. 2004) is the fundamental standard for most XML vocabularies such as XBRL. It facilitates data type definitions which are one of two basic constituent of XBRL taxonomies. The other constituent are linkbases. Linkbases are collections of XLinks (DeRose et al. 2001). The addressing scheme of XLinks are XPointers (Grosso et al. 2003). The XBRL standard only allows shorthand XPointer and element scheme expressions. XPath 2.0 (Clark et al. 1999), a standard for selection of data within XML documents is solely applied by XBRL functions and XBRL formulas.

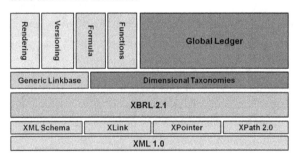

Figure 1: XBRL standards architecture

There are two basic fundamental extensions of the basic XBRL standard XBRL 2.1 (Engel et al. 2006a): Generic Linkbases and Dimensional Taxonomies. The Generic Linkbase (Goodhand 2006) standard serves the purpose to extend existing relations. It is used by the XBRL Formula Specification 1.0 (Engel et al. 2006b) and probably by upcoming standards for versioning of taxonomies (XBRL Versioning Linkbase) and presentation of XBRL reports (XBRL Rendering Linkbase).

Dimensional Taxonomies (Hernández-Ros et al. 2006) base upon XBRL 2.1. XBRL GL is formally an application of XBRL 2.1. If facts of the XBRL GL taxonomy have multidimensional context information, it can be considered as an application of multidimensional taxonomies, too. XBRL Functions (Simmons et al. 2006) is a functions library of common XPath 2.0 functions for the application in the XBRL space. At the moment there are mainly functions to calculate equivalence predicates for facts' contexts and to support the XBRL Formula standard. But future version will contain functions to assist other XBRL related standards and tasks.

2.2 XML Standards and XBRL Processing

Further XML standards that are relevant for XBRL-processing are related to the components of the XBRL architecture beneath. The next section introduces typical technical requirements for reporting automation. On the basis of these requirements two subsequent sections evaluate the utility of current XML standards and future XBRL standards. XBRL-Processing Requirements

Figure 2 localises transitions within an example of a typical enterprise reporting process. In the example a subsidiary's single closing is extracted from an ERP system with XBRL GL. The XBRL GL instance is imported into a central data warehouse (at the parent group). For this step the XBRL GL instance is imported into a relational database which serves as basis for incremental updates to data warehouse's OLAP (on-line analytical processing) cubes. For this purpose currently no XBRL-based standard tools exist and it is not likely thtat XBRL-based implementations will replace performance optimised bulk load toolkits in the short term.

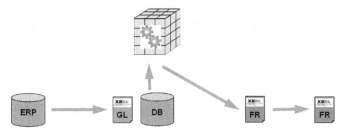

Figure 2: Transitions within a typical enterprise reporting process

Within the OLAP cube financial information for report generation is consolidated and afterwards the relevant aggregated information is exported into an XBRL FR instance which mirrors the group's chart of accounts. Finally this XBRL FR instance is transformed to another XBRL FR instance for external reporting to satisfy for instance a stock exchange's quarterly report requirements.

By means of example in figure 2 five requirement areas for transitions in reporting supply chains are identified:

1. Import/Export
   between non-XBRL formats and XBRL formats

2. XBRL Instance Validation
   XBRL instance validation and plausibility checking

3. XML-Mapping
   transformation description between different XML vocabularies

4. XML-Transformations
   actual transformations between instances from different XML vocabularies

5. XML Queries
   queries which supply XML data as a result

Only those requirements are taken into account which directly influence processing of XML or XBRL. For instance plausibility checking within the data warehouse is not included in this article, because they only refer to relational or multidimensional data.

3   XBRL-Relevant XML Standards

Next, the most relevant standards of the authors' practical experiences with XML-based processing in the reporting supply chain are rated with respect to their adequacy. The following short description does not supersede a proper introduction to these standards to comprehend this rating. It should only provide an orientation for readers who do not have any expertise in this area.

SQL/XML

SQL/XML (ISO/IEC 2006) is an extension to SQL (ISO/IEC 2003) which belongs to the ANSI/ISO SQL 2003 standard. SQL/XML offers storage of XML documents in SQL databases, XPath and XQuery queries for these documents and XML result serialisation. SQL/XML can be used to implement storage and processing of XBRL, regardless what kind of XBRL it is; XBRL 2.1, dimensional taxonomies of XBRL GL.

XML for Analysis

XML for Analysis (Simba Technologies Inc. 2007) is a standard suited for client applications which enables queries on multidimensional data sources. The query and result communication layer is realized with the standard web technologies HTTP, SOAP and

XML. For expressing queries, the multidimensional query language MDX is applied. Thus it is feasible to apply XML for Analysis as a query language to create XBRL 2.1 and it is particularly suitable for dimensional taxonomies.

XPath 1.0

XPath is a query language to select data in an XML document. XPath expressions permit the navigation across the entire XML data model and to filter nodes in the navigation steps. XPath 1.0 (Clark et al. 1999) is used by the XSLT 1.0 standard.

XSLT 1.0

XSLT 1.0 (Clark 1999) is a transformation language specified to transform XML documents into the output formats text, HTML and XML. XSLT processors read XSLT stylesheet documents and transform one or more XML documents according to these stylesheet rules to the desired output format.

XPath 2.0

XPath 2.0 (Berglund et al. 2007) supports all simple data types defined by XML Schema and delivers in contrast to XPath 1.0 ordered node lists, so-called sequences. XPath 2.0 is used by XSLT 2.0 und XQuery 1.0. XPath 2.0 is the default language binding for the implementation of the functions library in the XBRL Functions standard.

XSLT 2.0

XSLT 2.0 (Kay 2007) extends XSLT 1.0's functionality in some respects. It allows the import of type definitions from XML schemas and definition of functions in stylesheets which can be used in XPath expressions. All stylesheet rules can yield sequences as a result. Moreover, there is a *group-by* operation to group data and create nested XML data. Its expressive power turns XSLT 2.0 to an excellent candidate language for the implementation of XBRL Formulas. XSLT 2.0 stylesheets allow the definition of XPath functions. Such a feature can be used to publish extended formulas independent from underlying system platforms.

XQuery 1.0

XQuery (Boag et al. 2007) has the same expressive power as XSLT 2.0. Thus it is in equal measure a superb candidate for the implementation of XBRL formulas. XQuery queries can be converted into a XSLT stylesheets and vice versa. While XSLT is often leveraged for transformation, XQuery is mostly applied (and optimised) for querying XML document collections.

3.1 Rating XML Standards

The figure below visualises the adequacy of the considered standards in regard to the requirements described in section three. The rating are in the range from "−−−" up to "+++". An empty cell represents, that a standard is not applicable for the assigned requirement.

applicability of XML standards	SQL/XML	XML for Analysis	XPath 1.0	XSLT 1.0	XPath 2.0	XSLT 2.0	XQuery 1.0
import / export	⊕⊕	⊕⊖		⊖		⊕	⊕
validity checking	⊕⊕	⊖	⊖	⊕⊖	⊕	⊕⊕	⊕⊕
mapping	⊕⊕			⊕⊖		⊕⊕	⊕
transformation	⊕⊕			⊕⊖		⊕	⊕⊕
querying	⊕⊕			⊕⊖		⊕⊕	⊕⊕

Figure 3: Adequacy of considered standards

3.1.1 Import/Export

SQL/XML is suitable both for import and for export of XML data in conjunction with relational databases. The XML documents are stored as so called *large objects* in the database. SQL/XML does not give possibilities to map imported XML documents to relational table structures. In combination with XQuery any XML export formats and as a consequence also XBRL can be created so that a subsequent transformation (from XBRL to XML) can be omitted.

XML for Analysis only permits generation of an XML document which contains multidimensional query results. This XML format has to be transformed to conform to XBRL. XML for Analysis cannot be used for data import. XPath 1.0 and XPath 2.0 are not applicable both for XBRL import and for XBRL export. But these standards can assist import and export languages. XSLT only offers access to databases via extensions. XSLT itself does not give this possibility. Nevertheless it is well suited to generate DMLs (Data Manipulation Languages) like SQL. If extensions are integrated into XSLT, it can transform query results in any XML format. XSLT 2.0 is much better suited for XBRL export than XSLT 1.0 because grouping of data is supported.

Due to the same expressive power as XSLT 2.0 XQuery 1.0 receives the same rating. When it is used in the context of databases it gains a better evaluation, because many XQuery components are available as connectivity software. At document-based processing XSLT 2.0 performs better because XSLT's concept of transformation rules does not exist in XQuery.

3.1.2 Plausibility Checking (Validity Checking)

If SQL/XML permits XQuery queries, it is rated in the same way as XQuery. Otherwise it is not qualified for plausibility checking. *XML for Analysis* is not suited for checking XBRL, but implementation of plausibility checking in the field of multidimensional taxonomies is very complex. Therefore *XML for Analysis* is a proper support technology. XPath appertains for constructing validation expression. XPath 1.0's insufficient typing results in an inferior rating than XPath 2.0.

Validity and plausibility checking can hold a significant complexity. Moreover storing of calculations and reuse of intermediary results can improve efficiency. Therefore XSLT 2.0 and XQuery 1.0 perform better then XPath 2.0. XSLT 1.0 is significantly worse suited than XSLT 2.0, because it bases upon XPath 1.0's insufficient typing.

3.1.3 Mapping

If SQL/XML permits XQuery queries, it is rated in the same way as *XQuery*. Otherwise it is not qualified for describing mappings. *XSLT 1.0* is less suited for mapping purposes than *XSLT 2.0* because of its week typing and its small amount of build-in functions. *XSLT 2.0* gains its good rating, because of its XML-based syntax that eases the storage and retrieval of mapping descriptions. Because of this reason *XQuery* is not so highly rated as other alternatives. Its syntax is not XML-based, but there exists an XML-based syntax called XQueryX (Melton et al. 2007).

3.1.4 Transformation

If SQL/XML permits XQuery queries, it is rated in the same way as *XQuery*. Otherwise it is not qualified for performing transformations. *XSLT 1.0* processors with its week typing qualifies a lot worse for transformation than *XSLT 2.0* processors. For a large amount of data the execution of transformation is most suitably performed by an XML database. Thus, *XQuery 1.0* has a better rating than *XSLT 2.0*.

3.1.5 Querying

If SQL/XML permits *XQuery* queries, it is rated in the same way as *XQuery*. Otherwise it is not qualified for querying. *XSLT 1.0* is found alright for simple queries. Due to limitations set out in the previously described requirements it is devalued for complex queries in comparison to *XSLT 2.0* or *XQuery 1.0*. Queries that consist of groupings are easier to construct in *XSLT 2.0* than in *XQuery 1.0*. But *XQuery 1.0* implementations are in regard of huge data amount in general better optimized. Such query engines are built into state-of-the-art databases.

3.2   Conclusion

The evaluation results of table 1 clarify that solely *XSLT 2.0* and *XQuery 1.0* can be considered as proper tools for universal XBRL processing. However, neither ideally meets the requirements. This is not surprising, considering the complexity and the high degree of specialization of the XBRL data model. Having in mind that a much larger and more powerful community was involved in the specification of *XSLT 2.0* and *XQuery*, it seems that the development of more sophisticated XBRL processing standard cannot be achieved from scratch. We believe that such XBRL-based reporting standards need to be implemented as applications of XSLT 2.0 or XQuery. Mappings and transformations are the areas where improvements are most desired. In the next section we explore how upcoming XBRL standards perform and whether they have the ability to fill the gap.

4   Future XBRL Standards

Some of the XBRL standards that are in development are relevant for automating the business reporting supply chain. XBRL Formulas (Engel et al. 2006b) and XBRL generic linkbases (Goodhand 2006) are identified as one of those. Other standards are not considered for the main purposes of company reporting, but can assist in some areas. An XBRL rendering solution will take over the last step for publishing the information in human-readable format. And versioning of XBRL taxonomies can be viewed separate from the reporting process.

XBRL Generic Linkbases is a very simple but powerful standard. It takes the definition of relations for presentation, calculation, reference, label and definition linkbases from the *XBRL 2.1* standard and generalises them. In *XBRL 2.1* there are three kinds of relations:

- concept to concept,

- concept to a local resource in the linkbase,

- fact to a local resource in the instance.

The new standard gives the possibility to relate well-formed XML fragments to other well-formed XML fragments. Relations are expressed using arcs. Both sides of an arc point to XML elements outside the actual linkbase or resources within the linkbase. This generic approach qualifies XBRL Generic Linkbases to be used for many purposes in the automation of the reporting supply chain.

The *XBRL Formula* specification uses *XBRL Generic Linkbases* to express formulas. It can take an XBRL instance or XML fragment as an input and outputs facts according to a taxonomy or validation results. In practice XBRL Formulas can be used to specify validation and transformation rules for XBRL instances according to taxonomies. Regulators can publish complex validation rules in a standardized way for submission validation and data producers can use these rules to avoid errors in the submission process. Also collections of business ratios can be published in a normalised way.

The figure below visualises the adequacy of the evaluated standards in regard to the requirements set out in section three. The rating are in a range from "———" up to "+++". An empty cell represents, that a standard is not applicable for the assigned requirement.

applicability of XBRL standards	Formulas	Generic Linkbases
import / export	⊕⊖	
validity checking	⊕⊕⊕	
mapping	⊕	⊕⊖
transformation	⊕⊕	
querying	⊕	

Figure 4: Adequacy of evaluated standards

4.1 Import/Export

Formulas can be used to import data from an XML format. Since it uses *XBRL Generic Linkbases* to identify to input values for formulas any XML data could be the source of formula processing. For export purposes *XBRL Formulas* cannot be applied because a formula result is always connected with a XBRL taxonomy. *XBRL Generic Linkbases* can not be properly applied for import or export purpose if there will be no other linking mechanism used then the *XPointer* (Grosso et al. 2003) subset.

4.2 Plausibility Checking (Validity Checking)

XBRL Formulas are very well suited for plausibility checking. In fact the use cases that were determined before the specification was written identified plausibility checks as one of the main purposes. Additionally, rules that where set out by taxonomy developers can be reused in a standard way. *XBRL Generic Linkbases* cannot be used for plausibility checking.

4.3 Mapping

Mappings defined with *XBRL Formulas* can be very complex and hard to analyse for a drill-down. *XBRL Generic Linkbase* can be used to express very simple mappings.

There it offers a very easy way to describe a path which can be exactly evaluated for a drill-down. The utilisation of additional *XPointer* (Grosso et al. 2003) schemas could extend the application area of mappings significantly.

4.4   Transformation

For transformation *XBRL Formulas* is well suited. The final version of the specification will show if *XBRL Formulas* have enough expression power for all transformation purposes in the XBRL space. In the current working draft an important aspect – tuple creation – is not considered. *XBRL Generic Linkbases* cannot be used for transformation purposes.

4.5   Querying

XBRL Formula can only take XML or XBRL as input. For database or data warehouse queries it cannot be used. *XBRL Generic Linkbases* are not applicable for querying.

4.6   Conclusion

In comparison to current XML standards evalutated in section 3. the XBRL Formula standard performs slightly better for evaluation and transformation tasks than the best suited XML standards XSLT 2.0 and XQuery 1.0. However, the effort of learning a new language which can be applied in a very limited scope of applications is not very promising.

5   Conclusions

It seems that current XBRL standardization efforts towards improved transitions along the reporting supply chain has met a clear market need. Although considerable effort has been spent for providing improvements via the XBRL formula standard, the outcome for improving the efficiency of supply chain automation is quite limited. We are confident that better improvements will result by proper extensions of current XML processing standards and the adoption of existing XML processors. In the past the authors developed an open source XBRL processor (OpenXBRL 2007) based on *XSLT 2.0* to ease implementations of XBRL-enabled reporting without loosing the expressive power of current XML processors.

Besides the exploitation of current XML technologies the application of XBRL's semantic Web features (provided by linkbases) still receives little attention. In order to encourage a broader use of custom linkbases, we note that currently additional XBRL standards based on the Generic Linkbase (e. g. versioning linkbase and rendering link-base) are under way.

To tap the full potential of XBRL (e. g. to build highly interactive and intelligent applications) current XBRL applications should concentrate on the excessive use of existing and custom linkbases. Our future research activities deals with novel full-text retrieval methods considering the semantics of XBRL particularly with regard to XBRL linkbases.

References

Berglund, A.; Boag, S.; Chamberlin, D. Fernández, M. (2007): XML Path Language (XPath) 2.0, http://www.w3.org/TR/xpath20/, downloaded in April 2007.

Biron, P.; Malhotra, A. (2004): Datatypes Second Edition, http://www.w3.org/TR /xmlschema-2/, downloaded in April 2007.

Boag, S.; Chamberlin, M. (2007): XQuery 1.0: An XML Query Language, http://www.w3.org/TR/xquery/, downloaded in April 2007.

Bray, T. Paoli, J.; Sperberg-McQueen, C. (2006): Extensible Markup Language (XML) 1.0 (Second Edition), http://www.w3.org/TR/REC-xml, downloaded in April 2007.

Clark, J. (1999): XSL Transformations (XSLT) Version 1.0, http://www.w3.org/TR /xslt, downloaded in April 2007.

Clark, J.; DeRose, S. (1999): XML Path Language (XPath) 1.0 Specification; http://www.w3.org/TR/xpath, downloaded in April 2007.

DeRose, S.; Maler, E.; Orchard, D. (2001): XML Linking Language (XLink) Version 1.0, http://www.w3.org/TR/xlink, downloaded in April 2007.

Engel, P.; Hamscher, W.; Shuetrim, G.; vun Kannon, D.; Wallis, H. (2006a) Extensible Business Reporting Language 2.1 – Recommendation with corrected Errata dated 2006-12-18, http://www.xbrl.org/Specification/XBRL-RECOMMENDATION-2003-12-31+Corrected-Errata-2006-12-18.rtf, downloaded in April 2007.

Engel, P.; Shuetrim, G.; vun Kannon, D. (2006b): XBRL Functions 1.0, http://www.xbrl.org/Specification/XF-PWD-2006-12-07.rtf, downloaded in April 2007.

Fallside, D.; Walmsley, P. (2004): XML Schema Part 0: Primer Second Edition, http://www.w3.org/TR/xmlschema-0/, downloaded in April 2007.

Goodhand, M. (2006): Generic Links in XBRL, International Working Draft.

Grosso, P.; Maler, E.; Marsh, J.; Walsh, N. (2003): XML Pointer Language (XPointer Framework) 1.0, http://www.w3.org/TR/xptr-framework/, downloaded in April 2007.

Hernández-Ros, I.; Wallis, H. (2006): XBRL Dimensions 1.0, http://www.xbrl.org /Specification/XDT-REC-2006-09-18.rtf, downloaded in April 2007.

ISO /IEC 9075:2003 (2003): Information technology – Database Language SQL, http://webstore.ansi.org/ansidocstore/product.asp?sku=ISO%2FIEC+9075%2D1%3A2 003, downloaded in April 2007.

ISO/IEC 9075-14:2006 (2006): Information technology - Database languages - SQL - Part 14: XML-Related Specifications (SQL/XML), http://webstore.ansi.org /ansidocstore/product.asp?sku=ISO%2FIEC+9075%2D14%3A2006, downloaded in April 2007.

Kay, M. (2007): XSL Transformations (XSLT) Version 2.0, http://www.w3.org/TR /xslt20/, downloaded April 2007.

Melton, J.; Muralidhar, S. (2007): XML Syntax for XQuery 1.0, http://www.w3.org /TR/xqueryx/, downloaded in April 2007.

Simba Technologies Inc. (2007): XML for Analysis, http://www.xmla.org, down-loaded in April 2007.

Simmons, C.; Hernández-Ros, I. (2006): XBRL Functions 1.0, http://www.xbrl.org /Specification/XF-PWD-2006-12-07.rtf, downloaded in April 2007.

Thompson, H.; Beech, D.; Maloney M.; Mendelsohn, N. (2004): XML Schema Part 1: Structures Second Edition, http://www.w3.org/TR/xmlschema-1/, downloaded in April 2007.

XBRLopen.org (2007): ABRA – The Adaptive Business Reporting Automat, http://www .xbrlopen .org/abra/, downloaded in April 2007.

Standardized Company Reporting with XBRL

Thomas Klement

ABZ Informatik GmbH
Germany

thomas.klement@abz-informatik.com

Contents

1   Introduction

Today the eXtensible Business Reporting Language (XBRL) is accepted as the standardized international exchange format in external business reporting. This objective does not, however, realise the full potential of XBRL. The XBRL standard was established with the vision to improve the whole information supply chain within enterprise reporting. XBRL may provide significant benefits for collection of information from heterogeneous data sources and subsequent preparation of enhanced information. Implementation of enterprise reporting processes on the basis of a standardized data format offers possibilities to improve quality of reported data, to speed up creation processes and to eliminate sources of errors.

This paper deals with two important XBRL taxonomy types, *XBRL Global Ledger* (XBRL GL) (Fedor et al. 2006) and *XBRL Financial Reporting* (XBRL FR), compares them with each other and assesses their combined functionality as a foundation for a truly integrated supply chain. Both classes of taxonomies are used in internal company reporting. While FR taxonomies are explicitly designed for external reporting the GL taxonomy could be used for some types of external reporting, such as transaction level data for analytical or compliance purposes. Both taxonomy application areas overlap and yet the design is quite different. This article is an analysis of adopting of combined XBRL-GL and FR based reporting. In doing so professional aspects of internal reporting are mostly omitted. They are considered for motivation and illustration only.

The remainder of the paper proceeds as follows: First the paper presents the results of a complexity evaluation for the adoption of different XBRL taxonomy types. Since XBRL is a powerful but complex standard, the implementation of XBRL-enabled reporting processes often causes high expenses. The complexity evaluation section provides a survey of the complexity of XBRL adoption for typical reporting tasks. Subsequently, an exemplary scenario shows how a company's XBRL-enabled reporting process may look like. Finally having the XBRL-enabled enterprise reporting scenario in mind, future prospects for the accounting area are presented. Accounting applications discover data of reports in the opposite direction. Thus new challenges arise in taking advantage on a standardized underlying data model.

2   Heterogeneous Reporting Systems

2.1   Introduction

The internal and external business reporting processes of enterprises are both affected
by complex and often changing professional requirements and by heterogeneous technical infrastructures. Because of the high degree of customisation, it is difficult to classify the components of today's reporting software. Normally in reporting processes
information flows from various document formats (Excel, Webforms, etc...), relational *data warehouses* into a reporting system. The most important information in business reports are typically extracted out of ERP systems or consolidation software. As a
rule these systems have some components for generating various reporting formats
(e.g. annual reports) in place. To shorten the creation process time and to accomplish
individual recipients' requirements, publishing solutions are often integrated into the
reporting process, which transform consistent reporting data into various output formats.

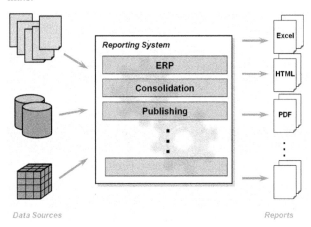

Figure 1: Business reporting processes

Off-the-shelf reporting software often lack extensibility and flexibility to couple all
required components of a reporting system in a homogeneous way. In the past the
standardization of reporting processes in enterprises was fallen by the wayside because
of a continuously rising complexity of financial reporting standards in external reporting as well as a demanded flexibility for corporate management in internal reporting.
This led to adoption of proprietary internal enterprise standards in order to integrate all
systems involved in the reporting process. Many companies run multiple independent

reporting systems, not synchronised with each other for different reporting purposes (e. g. monthly and yearly reporting). This causes enormous consistency problems.

XBRL can be used an interface to bridge the gap between different storage formats and software components in the reporting process. Therefore, two kinds of XBRL taxonomies can be applied: *XBRL Global Ledger* (GL) and *XBRL Financial Reporting* (FR) taxonomies. The decision, what kind of taxonomy to apply, can not be done by simply considering the type of data source or the kind of component in the reporting system. The decision heavily depends on local reporting requirements. Sometimes both kinds of taxonomies GL and FR need to be adopted. The third section provides more details about the characteristics of the underlying data model of GL and FR taxonomies, which is needed to make the right decision what XBRL standard has to be applied.

2.2 Service-Oriented Reporting Architectures

Modern service-oriented architectures are well suited to cope with heterogeneity in existing reporting installations. Webservices in service-oriented architectures support arbitrary XML-based data exchange format and as a consequence also XBRL. XBRL can be used in combination with these technologies and it reveals its complete power only in service-oriented architectures. Two fundamental terms of service-oriented processing are introduced which are relevant for reporting:

Composite-Applications unite benefits of standard software and individual development. The principle of composite-applications is to extend an existing application infrastructure with proofed software components which give relevant functionality – e.g. support for reporting processes. In future ERP and consolidation systems can be deployed by reporting applications as elementary building blocks. They no longer have to be dominating monolithic platform, but rather serve as base functionality of reporting. For this reason companies are more easily able to buy new functionalities and to enhance there own software development. Today's application focussing can be redeemed by a process focussing.

Interaction between reporting services demands an infrastructure. So called *Enterprise Service Buses* (ESBs) are the first choice in this area. As there is a great variety of heterogeneous information in a reporting system which has to be prepared, a reliable message-based communication has a central meaning.

2.3   Interactive Data

In conjunction with XBRL-based applications the term interactive data is widely-used.
In fact the high degree of metadata in XBRL documents can support an improved interaction of reporting applications. The semantic information contained in an XBRL
taxonomy (calculation rules, legal reference, multilingual labels) do only improve interaction when the relation between XBRL-(meta) data and the presentation view is not
lost.

For instance legal references can be used to search all concepts according to a single
law. Typically, search engines are not able to link facts in a company report and legal
references contained in the reference linkbase of an XBRL taxonomy, because they are
not aware of *XLinks* (XLINK) which are used in XBRL to express relations.

3   The XBRL-Data Model

3.1   Introduction

The *XBRL 2.1* standard is a technical framework to define taxonomies for any report
format. It describes XBRL's data model. This data model inherits features from three
application areas of data management. As an XML-based standard XBRL inherits features from XML. More precise XBRL rules embedded in the XBRL Specification re-
stricts the underlying XML data types. Moreover XBRL utilises features from data
warehousing what is reflected in the data model of an XBRL instance: XBRL instances contain facts with multidimensional contexts. Furthermore the semantic web
area affected the XBRL standard. Analogous to in XML-based semantic web standards
like RDF (Herman et al. 2007), XBRL taxonomies describe complex relationships between resources. The relationships span a so-called network of relationships (which is
in terms of semantic web an ontology). In XBRL type definitions of an XML schema
are linked to a couple of different resource types. Thus, the scope of XBRL taxonomies less generic than typical ontologies built with current semantic web standards.

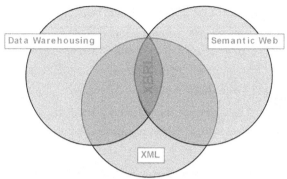

Figure 2: XBRL data model

Newer XBRL standards utilise or extend the basic data model of XBRL. *XBRL GL* is an application of the base standard *XBRL 2.1*. The GL (Global Ledger) taxonomy is a specific instantiation of the set of taxonomies that can be defined with XBRL e.1. In contrast, the dimensional taxonomies (Hernández-Ros et al. 2006) introduce new types of relationships to describe the multi-dimensional characteristics of XBRL facts more precisely that the base standard. In almost the same manner as *XBRL 2.1* the dimensional taxonomies are a framework for the definition of XBRL taxonomies and not an application of XBRL such as *XBRL GL*. For the sake of simplicity dimensional taxonomies are not a subject of this paper. Simplified dimensional taxonomies can considered as more precisely defined *XBRL FR* taxonomies. Newerthless they play a crucial role in XBRL adoptions. Having the XBRL standards *XBRL 2.1*, *XBRL GL* and *XBRL Dimensional Taxonomies* in mind, within the company reporting information supply chain there may exist different kinds of XBRL data models. Furthermore extensibility plays an important role in XBRL applications. Common externally standardized XBRL taxonomies, may be extended for use in certain industries or may be extended by a company individually as well.

3.2   XBRL Data Model Description

XBRL differs from most data exchange vocabularies in XML thereby that it defines a meta language. This meta language is used to define exchange formats in form of taxonomies. All taxonomy data types are determined by the W3C Standard *XML Schema* (Biron et al. 2004, Thompson et al. 2004). Typing of a fact at the metadata layer is called concept. Concepts can be arranged together in tuples. For instance a tuple *address* can consist of the concepts *street*, *zip code* and *city*.

The specification of metadata exceeds the common degree in XML languages. XBRL models not only typing, it also determines semantics for concepts. A concept's semantic specification results from definitions of relations that are valid between the concept and other information. Thus, the professional meaning of a taxonomy defined by XBRL is more precisely and extensively described then in most XML languages. It is possible to use all relations in order to receive information about the meaning of a concept or make assumptions about a concept's semantic.

XBRL taxonomies' data model with their concepts and relations is similar to semantic web-based data models to represent knowledge. From this perspective the concepts and relations span a knowledge network.

Figure 3 indicates the correlation between data contained in XBRL instances and metadata that are part of the taxonomy definition.

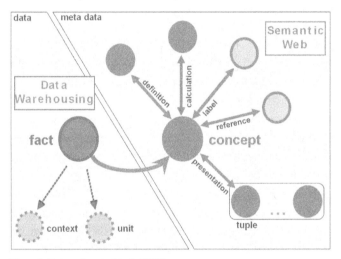

Figure 3: Data and meta data in XBRL

Data in a business report consist of a collection of facts which have an assigned context (e.g. key date and organisational unit) as well as a defined unit (e.g. Euro, kilogramme).

A concept's properties are derived from relations on the metadata level. Thereby five kinds of relations can be distinguished:

- *Presentation relations* (presentation links) establish a hierarchy which give a tree-like order to taxonomy's concepts.

- *Calculation relations* (calculation links) identify simple calculation rules, to check for fact's consistence according to other facts.

- *Label relations* (label links) are used to give multilingual descriptions to a concept.

- *Reference relations* (reference links) locate additional information to describe a concept in more detail (e.g. references to legal directives, laws, etc).

- *Definition relations* (definition link) specify additional relations among concepts like equivalences.

In XBRL relations are stored in so-called *linkbase documents*.

XBRL taxonomies consist of XML Schemas (Fallside 2004), which define concepts and linkbase documents which contain relations and additional information.

3.3   XBRL Taxonomies within the Information Supply Chain

If the vision of XBRL was turned into reality — a homogeneously implemented reporting supply chain with XBRL as basically one single data exchange format — figure 4 could depict an XBRL-enabled enterprise reporting process.

Within the reporting information supply chain different XBRL data model variations are utilised. These variations restrict *XBRL 2.1*'s framework for different application purposes and they are compatible with *XBRL 2.1*. The following figure reflects exemplarily what variations could be used within a group's reporting process. They are described in more detail below.

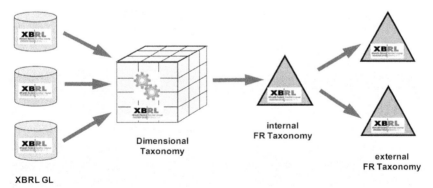

Figure 4: XBRL GL and XBRL FR

In the information supply chain shown in figure 4 *XBRL GL* data are exported from data sources (e.g. subsidiaries' ERP systems). The information is collected in a central data warehouse and for this reason transformed to instances according to a multidimensional taxonomy (Hernández-Ros et al. 2006). Next the information contained in the data warehouse is filtered and moved into an *XBRL FR* instance which could conform to a corporate group's chart of accounts. Finally this chart of accounts is mapped to different reporting standards (e.g. IFRS or US GAAP).

The *XBRL GL* taxonomy describes in broadest sense financial transactions. It features characteristics like typical data exchange formats where common complex data structures are described.

The application areas of *XBRL GL* and *XBRL FR* taxonomies overlap. Both kinds of taxonomies differ in their characteristics and their application. Figure 5 illustrates areas where either of them is mostly used.

The syntactical transformation from *XBRL GL* to *XBRL FR* reports can be implemented with typical XML-based transformation languages easily. However, a semantically valid transition can be more difficult. In the paper *Adoption of XML and XBRL Standards* we investigate the applicability of current XML standards to implement common syntactical transformations.

Figure 5: Overlap of XBRL GL and XBRL FR

In many application scenarios *XBRL GL* extends an XBRL-enabled financial reporting supply chain down to data sources. The data sources of the reporting supply chain often cover deep structurerd information that can not be modelled with *XBRL FR* taxonomies properly. Thus, without *XBRL GL* the exploitation of meaningful information for the reporting process would be less. With establishment of *XBRL GL* an intention is associated to automate the whole reporting process from data sources to a final business report. Companies with heterogeneous ERP or consolidation systems can benefit from *XBRL GL* as a standardized interface. Standardized Interfaces offer cost savings and reduce dependencies on software providers. Data which are available in XBRL GL format can be incorporated into external reporting that results in an added value.

The following sections provide an overwiev about what kind of information is modelled within *XBRL FR* taxonomies and what kind of information is contained in the XBRL GL taxonomy. The overview enables the reader to understand the differences between both XBRL standards. Finally, their basic differences are outlined the last section of the section.

3.4   Financial Reporting Taxonomies

XBRL FR taxonomies serve as a description and for automatic validation of reports which contain information on companies. They are XBRL taxonomies, which are used mainly in external reporting. They contain financial and non-financial information, whereas the financial information plays a more important role.

As an example for XBRL FR taxonomies figure 6 shows a balance sheet according to IFRS. The *IFRS Sample Company* publishes its financial report for the 2003 year. This Balance Sheet was generated from an XBRL instance as a Web page coded in HTML.

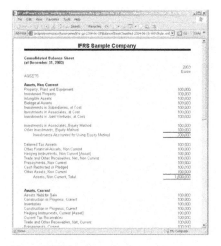

Figure 6: IFRS balance sheet

Figure 7: Instance document

The numbers in the right column are the balance sheet facts. Facts are defined as concepts in a taxonomy. A concept is an XML type definition. Furthermore a concept might be related to other information via relations as shown in figure 3. The context of the facts consists of company name *IFRS Sample Company* and an effective date. The currency unit of these financial facts is Euros. The fact values, its context and unit information are contained in XBRL instance documents. All other Balance Sheet information opens up from an IFRS taxonomy, which is connected to the XBRL instance document. By providing a rich set of metadata within taxonomies, redundant data in XBRL instances is avoided. Moreover, the concept definitions of a taxonomy assure an unambiguous definition of the facts. It does not matter in which document or at which position a fact occurs. Its semantic is well-defined due to its context and its assigned taxonomy.

The Balance Sheet view in figure 6 is derived from IFRS taxonomy's linkbases. With this example three kinds of relations can be clarified: On the left side presentation relations specify Balance Sheet facts' order and structure. English labels are connected to Balance Sheet items via label relations to make Balance Sheets readable. The aggregated amounts (in the example underlined) can be checked for correctness via calculation relations. Figure 7 shows the XBRL document that was used as basis for the HTML view in a XML Editor.

All XBRL instances must point to one or more XBRL taxonomies (schemas). By connecting a schema the instance both is typed and assigned to the underlying taxonomy. In this example a schema (ifrs-gp-2004-06-15.xsd) for the IFRS reporting standard and a schema (iso4217-2003-05-16.xsd) for currency codes are referenced. Below there are declarations for contexts and units. Only one context is defined for the instant *2003-12-31*. For all facts a monetary unit *iso4217:EUR* is set. Subsequently facts as elements with prefix *ifrs-gp* are listed. Every fact has a context and a unit assignment in its attributes *contextRef* and *unitRef*. Furthermore, every fact has a value. The example only shows numeric facts although more types exist in XBRL, e.g. text and date. The XBRL standard provides users with more than 30 data types. Additional data types can be derived from these basic types by restrictions. In this example, the precision of the sample facts are set out by a *decimals* attribute (0 corresponds to no decimal places).

3.5   The GL Taxonomy

XBRL GL is designed in a way that preconditions for integration of transactions, accounting records, etc. into the highly aggregated XBRL report facts are met. In XBRL GL an entry, e.g. a journal record, can be linked to a taxonomies' concept. Moreover an entry can be mapped to multiple concepts from different *XBRL FR* taxonomies (for example in Multi-GAAP reporting). However, in *XBRL GL* no complex functions can be defined to map to *XBRL FR* taxonomies or formulas to calculate financial ratios.

The Global Ledger taxonomy represents journal entries, historical entries and chart of accounts and other facts. It can be used generically. It is not limited to a certain chart of accounts.

The most important *XBRL GL* features are:

- *XBRL GL* is not dependent on a certain reporting standard. In XBRL GL both Anglo-American and continental European accounting systems are accommodated.

- The *XBRL GL* taxonomy is extensible in a modular way and adjustable to individual requirements.

- *XBRL GL* ensures independence from software systems. Accounting software developers can implement import and export interfaces which convert from and to the *XBRL GL* format. *XBRL GL* is a neutral format, which provides a data model and which eases integration with various software solutions (e.g. SAP, Oracle, etc.).

- *XBRL GL* can represent both detail and aggregated information. *XBRL FR* taxonomies are better suited, however, for highly aggregated information and information which should be exchanged with a defined semantic amongst different parties,. To represent transactions and exchange of information from individual ERP systems without a semantic model in XBRL, application of *XBRL GL* is more adequate.

The overall structure of an *XBRL GL* instance document is shown in the next figure:

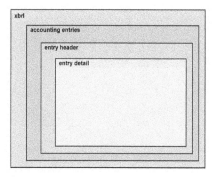

Figure 8: XBRL GL document structure

In general the structure of *XBRL GL* instances represents collections of grouped data by some grouping criterion. The GL taxonomy is extensible and thus the grouping criterion can vary in an application dependent manner. There are three basic levels of an XBRL GL instance: accounting entries, entry header and entry detail.

- The element *accountingEntries* is a child of the root element of the XBRL instance (xbrl). It's content model contains common information about the kind of entries (e. g. trial balance), their language, date of creation etc.

- The element entryHeader groups sets of *entryDetail* elements. Its content model includes information like the origin of the entries, its posting date and the creator.

- An entryDetail element consists of detailed information depending of an application area. A typical concent of *entryDetails* are transactions and journal entries. An *entryDetail* can mapped to one or many conepts of XBRL taxonomies. The meaning of such a mapping for intance could be the aggregation of accounts.

Figure 9 shows how account balances could be represented in an *XBRL GL* instance:

	2006-05-01
Accounting Entries	
Document Information	
Document Type	trialbalance
Audit Number	001
Language	iso639:en
Creation Date	2006-05-05
Creator	XBRL GL Working Group
Document Comment	An GL to IFRS trial balance instance document
Period Covered Start	2005-01-01
Period Covered End	2005-12-31
Source Application	Notepad
Default Currency	iso4217:EUR
Entity Information section	
Identifiers	
Organization Identifier	SampleCompany
Organization Description	Sample Company For Madrid
Entry Information	
Entry Qualifier	balance-brought-forward
Entry Detail	
Line Number	1
Account Identifier	
Main Account Number	600
Main Account Description	Finished Goods
Purpose of Account	iasb
Account type	account
Monetary Amount	2.500.000
Debit/Credit Identifier	D
Posting Date	2005-12-31
XBRL Information	
XBRL Allocation	ending_balance
Summary Reporting Element	ifrs-gp:Inventories
Entry Detail	
Line Number	2
Account Identifier	
Main Account Number	310

Figure 9: Account balances

The XBRL GL instance is a trial balance of *Sample Company*. The entry details account balances of the trial balance. The *XBRL GL* instance can be used to aggregate account balances to concepts of an IFRS taxonomy. The mapping to an XBRL concept is indicated by the XBRL information section in an *XBRL GL* instance. The example in figure 10 shows how entries in a GL instance are aggregated to facts in an *XBRL FR* instance.

XBRL GL Data (Trial Balance)

Account	Amount	d/c	Account #
Finished Goods	2 500 000 €	debit	600
Raw Materials	2 500 000 €	debit	310
Work in Progress	2 500 000 €	debit	650
Goods in Transit	1 000 000 €	debit	300
Allowance for Inventories	2 500 000 €	credit	699

XBRL FR Data (Balance Sheet)

Balance Sheet Item	Amount	d/c
Inventories	6 000 000 €	debit

Figure 10: Entries in XBRL GL instance

The value of the concept *Inventories* is the total of the accounts 600,310,650,300,699. Since 699 is a credit account, the amount is subtracted from the debit accounts.

3.6   Comparison of XBRL GL versus XBRL FR

Given that *XBRL GL* and *XBRL FR* application areas overlap, in this section we compare the characteristics, typical applications and their extensibility. Figure 11 below summarises the most important features of XBRL GL and XBRL FR and sets them in contrast to each other.

Comparison of GL versus FR	XBRL GL	XBRL FR
Characteristics	- low complexity - grouped data - flat structure - grouped mass data - predefined taxonomy	- high complexity - atomic data - complex links - multidimensional grouping - high number of taxonomies
Typical Applications	- trial balance - bookings - account balance	- annual financial statement - quarterly statement - regulatorz filing
Extensibility	- types - modules/palletes	- types - taxonomies

Figure 11: XBRL GL and XBRL FR comparision

XBRL GL's and *XBRL FR*'s qualification for a certain application is best differentiated by their diverse characteristics in data management. While *XBRL GL*'s data model is simply structured and shows a low level of complexity, *XBRL FR*'s model contains multidimensional fact descriptions and various metadata relations and bears a high degree of complexity. For *XBRL FR* this is achieved by combining atomic data (facts) with complex links (relations) and grouping by multiple predefined dimensions. Atomic data means that each fact in *XBRL FR* is related to a unique context. Thus moving an *XBRL FR* fact to another XBRL instance usually does not affect semantics. In contrast, moving entry details of *XBRL GL* instances to other instances usually would cause problems regarding semantics. These problems arise primarily from the grouping criterion of entry headers and the global accounting entries information is significant regarding its meaning.

GL data typically are transported as grouped mass data. An entries list (e.g. accounting entries) is arranged by grouping information into a certain context. *XBRL GL* instances can be processed in applications by standard XML tools even without most typical features of an XBRL processor.

Common applications of *XBRL GL* are date exchange of accounting entries, account balances and vouchers. On the other hand *XBRL FR* is suitable for exchange of highly aggregated data like annual statements or trial balances.

4 Complexity of Current XBRL Standards

In enterprise reporting there are no clearly defined boundaries for the application of the XBRL standard. After discussing features and adequacy of XBRL standards in the following section gives on overview over the complexity of current XBRL standards which could be used within the reporting supply chain processing. For this reason the standards *XBRL FR*, *XBRL GL* and *XBRL Dimensions 1.0* are explored. The complexity rating does not make a judgement about the standard's concrete benefits within company reporting. It only serves the purpose to show how complexity can change by applying an XBRL data model.

complexity applying XBRL standards	XBRL FR	dimensional taxonomies	XBRL GL
import / export	⊕	⊕⊖	⊕⊕
validity checking	⊕⊕	⊖⊖	⊕⊖
mapping	⊕⊕	⊖	⊕⊕⊕
transformation	⊕	⊕	⊖
querying	⊕	⊕⊕	⊕⊕⊕

Figure 12: Adequacy of analysed standards

The rating scale shown in figure 12 again is from "——" (very high complexity) to "+++" (very low complexity). Because at the moment no multidimensional extended *XBRL GL* taxonomies occur in practical use only multidimensional XBRL FR taxonomies are taken into consideration for the middle column.

4.1 Import/Export

The import and export of *XBRL GL* data shows is easiest possibility since it is about very simple (hierarchal) structured data. Processing of *XBRL FR* data is slightly more complex due to checking of equivalence predicates for context and unit information demands a collection of functions. The evaluation of equivalence predicates is required for detection of duplicates when reported data is collected in a central database or repository. Multidimensional taxonomies often require a conversion of star or snowflake schema into the XBRL dimensions format. In doing so special XBRL characteristics must be taken into account. The XBRL dimensions can cause implementation problems in relational databases, for instance representations of so called *typed dimensions* or references to a dimension's member.

4.2   Plausibility Checking (Validity Checking)

XBRL FR is a proper standard for validation of financial information. The extra information at the metadata level (e.g. calculation instructions) provides a set of plausibility rules. The metadata's expression power is indeed limited, but extensible. In the *XBRL GL* taxonomy relatively little information is at the metadata level as compared to *XBRL FR* taxonomies. Multidimensional facts with their definite dimension assignment are in theory well suited for validation, but currently proper tools to describe plausibility rules for multidimensional facts in a simple way are missing. Moreover those checks require considerable processing power which will probably require well optimized OLAP applications on top of the classic multidimensional data warehousing data models.

4.3   Mapping

The description of mappings to *XBRL GL* data is easy to accomplish because of its relatively simple data structure. The mappings in conjunction with *XBRL FR* taxonomies turn out to be slightly more complex. In contrast to mappings of XBRL GL taxonomies for *XBRL FR* mappings the references between context, unit and fact information have to be considered more carefully. Mapping rules for multidimensional taxonomies could turn out to be significantly more elaborate for reasons related to the dimensional context of facts. A considerable (manual) effort has to be spent for the creation of dimension mappings. Furthermore, dimensional taxonomies restrict a facts value space of hypercubes spanned by its dimensions. This restriction has to be validated statically during the creation process of the mapping or (if this is not possible) dynamically at run time of fact conversion..

4.4   Transformation

Transformations to the *XBRL GL* format are very complex by reason of its deep structured data format. The creation of deep structures requires heavy use of *GroupBy* operations. On the other hand transformations from *XBRL GL* to other formats are simple because XML languages provide excellent traversal mechanisms to navigate deepl nested structures.

Transformations into *XBRL FR* taxonomies and multidimensional taxonomies are simpler than to *XBRL GL* because the results of *groupBy* and aggregation operations are reflected by *XBRL FR*'s context structure. Thus, there is no need to restructure intermediate query result. *XBRL FR* can be easily transformed into various target formats thanks to their multidimensional context properties that serve most query criterions without complex modifications.

4.5   Querying

XBRL GL data can easily be processed by XML query languages due to their stable structure. Efforts for querying *XBRL FR* data are, however, significantly more difficult because of the requirement to join context and unit properties via XBRL's contextRef and unicRef attributes. Conversely, filtering and selection of data is facilitated by accessing context and unit properties. In reporting the *groupBy* operation is frequently used. This particular operation can be best applied to multidimensional XBRL data

5   Usage of XBRL Standards

If XBRL as data exchange format is adopted in the whole information supply chain process it will be most unlikely that all information in the data flow from data sources up to the final publishing process would be implemented solely in XBRL. The following figure 13 shows a simple example of a reporting process.

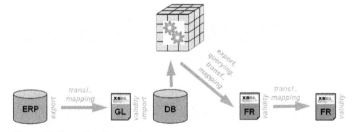

Figure 13: Example of a reporting process

In this example data from a subsidiary's single closing is extracted from an ERP system with *XBRL GL*. The *XBRL GL* instance is imported into a central data warehouse at the parent group. For this step the *XBRL GL* instance is imported into a relational database which serves as basis for incremental updates to data warehouse's OLAP (Online Analytical Processing) cubes. Currently no XBRL-based standard tools exist for this purpose. For data import into relational databases highly optimized bulk load toolkits exist to avoid large quantities of transactions. It is not likely that XBRL-based implementations will replace performance optimised bulk load toolkits in the short term.

Within the OLAP cube, financial information for report generation purposes is consolidated. Subsequently the relevant aggregated information is exported into an XBRL FR instance which mirrors the group's chart of accounts. Finally this *XBRL FR* instance is transformed to another *XBRL FR* instance for external reporting to satisfy for instance a stock exchange's quarterly report requirements.

In this example there exist three transitions between non-XBRL and XBRL formats:

1. ERP data export to *XBRL GL*

2. *XBRL GL* import into a relational database (a typical Extract-Transform-Load application)

3. OLAP cube data export to an *XBRL FR* instance

The fact that XBRL is an XML format eases the implementation of these transitions. In the following we cite examples of non-XBRL standards that facilitate transition steps:

For the data export from relational databases (1.) respectively OLAP cubes (2.) there are standards which serialise query results in XML, e.g. SQL/XML or XML for Analysis.

SQL/XML (ISO/IEC 2006) is an extension to SQL (ISO/IEC 2003), which belongs to the ANSI/ISO SQL 2003 standard. SQL/XML offers an automated transformation from SQL query results into XML output documents (XML result serialisation). XML for Analysis (Simba Technologies Inc. 2007) is a standard suited for client applications which enables queries on multidimensional data sources. For expressing queries in XML for Analysis, the multidimensional query language MDX is applied. The results are serialized in a given XML format of the *XML for Analysis* standard. The opposite way round to import XBRL into OLAP cubes no standardized XML formats are in place.

Utilisation of these standards facilitates creation of XBRL formats; because transformations to XBRL can be solely accomplished using XML-based transformation Standards and no type mappings (e.g. JDBC to XML schema) between basic types is necessary.

6   Conclusions

If XBRL becomes accepted in future enterprise reporting scenarios, the inversion of the data flow in the reporting process will cause new challenges. For example, auditing applications may well require reverse traversal of the information supply chain. Figure 14 points out how the process of XBRL and XML-facilitated auditing applications could work. If all information accrued in the reporting process is collected in a central XBRL repository the mapping description (red documents) combined with the *XBRL FR* and *XBRL GL* documents would expose information about the origin of facts in a financial statement. If the transformation functions and the results of intermediate results in the enterprise reporting process of figure 14 are stored in a central repository, there is a great chance that an auditing application would require less effort to archive and access all relevant information and can provide more intelligent auditing methods as well.

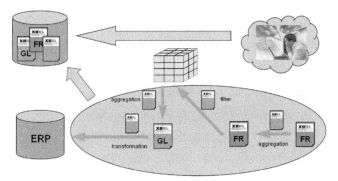

Figure 14: Transformation functions and the results of intermediate enterprise reporting process

The severest problem at the so called *drill-down* or *drill-around* is likely to be data access over system boundaries. A central XBRL repository for storing reporting facts and data mappings promises significant advancement. However, some problems of bidirectional mappings persist and need to be solved. A common problem is that for aggregation functions there is no inverse drill-down function back to the original facts available. Just like aggregation functions many other transitions along the reporting supply chain are described by functions that cannot be inverted. This is stressed by another example about a group consolidation process shown in figure 15. The involved complexity in consolidation leads one to suspect that a *drill-down* to subsidiary's individual report and the discovery all relevant documentation materials to understand the purpose of bookings and reclassifications is hard to realise.

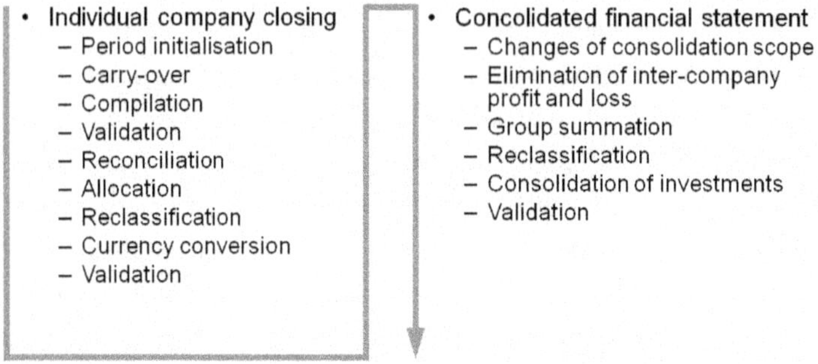

• Individual company closing	• Concolidated financial statement
– Period initialisation	– Changes of consolidation scope
– Carry-over	– Elimination of inter-company
– Compilation	profit and loss
– Validation	– Group summation
– Reconciliation	– Reclassification
– Allocation	– Consolidation of investments
– Reclassification	– Validation
– Currency conversion	
– Validation	

Figure 15: Group consolidation process

An important prerequisite to improve *drill-downs* are mapping descriptions which support efficient analysis queries. For that purpose suitable XBRL standards not yet exist. Combined with the versatile and extensible meta information which XBRL provides serious improvements seem to be possible.

References

Biron, P.; Malhotra, A. (2004): Datatypes Second Edition, http://www.w3.org/TR /xmlschema-2/, downloaded in April 2007

Fallside, D.; Walmsley, P. (2004): XML Schema Part 0: Primer Second Edition, http://www.w3.org/TR/xmlschema-0/, Downloaded in April 2007

Fedor, J.; Wallis, H.; Cohen, E.; Nobuyuki, S. (2006): XBRL Global Ledger 2006 Taxonomy, http://www.xbrl.org/int/gl/2006-10-25/gl-2006-10-25.htm, downloaded in Aptil 2007.

Herman, I.; Swick, R. Brickley, D. (2007) Ressource Description Framework, http://www.w3.org/RDF/, downloaded in April 2007.

Hernández-Ros, I.; Wallis, H. (2006): XBRL Dimensions 1.0, http://www.xbrl.org /Specification/XDT-REC-2006-09-18.rtf, downloaded in April 2007.

ISO /IEC 9075:2003 (2003): Infomration technology – Database Language SQL, http://webstore.ansi.org/ansidocstore/product.asp?sku=ISO%2FIEC+9075%2D1%3A2 003, downloaded in April 2007.

ISO/IEC 9075-14:2006 (2006): Information technology - Database languages - SQL - Part 14: XML-Related Specifications (SQL/XML), http://webstore.ansi.org /ansidocstore/product.asp?sku=ISO%2FIEC+9075%2D14%3A2006, downloaded in April 2007.

Simba Technologies Inc. (2007): XML for Analysis, http://www.xmla.org, downloaded in April 2007.

Thompson, H.; Beech, D.; Maloney M.; Mendelsohn, N. (2004): XML Schema Part 1: Structures Second Edition, http://www.w3.org/TR/xmlschema-1/, downloaded April 2007.

GPSR Compliance
The European Union's (EU) General Product Safety Regulation (GPSR) is a set
of rules that requires consumer products to be safe and our obligations to
ensure this.

If you have any concerns about our products, you can contact us on

ProductSafety@springernature.com

In case Publisher is established outside the EU, the EU authorized
representative is:

Springer Nature Customer Service Center GmbH
Europaplatz 3
69115 Heidelberg, Germany